# AN ENGLISHMAN'S HOME

Held captive by guerrillas in the mountains of Central American danger zone the Darién Gap, Tom Hart Dyke kept his sanity by dreaming of building a garden filled with plants from every corner of the globe. He would recreate a map of the world, with indigenous plants growing in their native countries — nature's most wonderful flora to delight all who saw it. Safely back home in Kent, Tom realised that if he built his dream, he could finally lay his demons to rest, and revive the failing fortunes of his family home, Lullingstone Castle. *An Englishman's Home* charts the highs and lows of Tom's quest to build a world garden, and highlights the determination that helped him to turn Lullingstone into a major tourist attraction.

*Books by Tom Hart Dyke*
*Published by The House of Ulverscroft:*

THE CLOUD GARDEN (with Paul Winder)

TOM HART DYKE

# AN ENGLISHMAN'S HOME

*Complete and Unabridged*

# CHARNWOOD
Leicester

First published in Great Britain in 2007 by
Bantam Press
a division of Transworld Publishers
London

First Charnwood Edition
published 2008
by arrangement with
Transworld Publishers
a division of The Random House Group Ltd
London

British Library CIP Data

Hart Dyke, Tom
    An Englishman's home: the adventures of an
eccentric gardener.—Large print ed.—
Charnwood library series
1. Hart Dyke, Tom 2. Lullingstone Castle
Gardens 3. Gardens—England—Kent 4. Gardens
—England—Kent—Design 5. Large type books
I. Title
712.7′092

ISBN 978–1–84782–381–6

Published by
F. A. Thorpe (Publishing)
Anstey, Leicestershire

Set by Words & Graphics Ltd.
Anstey, Leicestershire
Printed and bound in Great Britain by
T. J. International Ltd., Padstow, Cornwall

This book is printed on acid-free paper

# Contents

# Acknowledgements

I would like to thank Tristan Davies for his skill and good humour in helping me to set down the story of the World Garden. Thanks are also due to my agent, Mark Lucas, and everyone at Transworld, particularly the superlative Doug Young, Emma Musgrave and Sam Jones.

Special thanks are due to all those who have helped to create the World Garden — you know who you are and to list you all would require another book! A more profound credit, however, must be assigned to horticultural marketing wizard Tony Russell, creatively minded designer Adam Bailey, all the guys at Star Plant, adorable Louisa, PR extraordinaire and dearest friend Vikki Rimmer, Jim, Sylvia and Mr Adrian for their tireless endeavours in creating the World Garden and keeping it afloat.

In commissioning the two TV series, the BBC have helped immensely with the World Garden project. From KEO Films (the independent film company making the programmes for the BBC), I'd particularly like to thank Zam Baring and Ben Roy, and Anthony Palmer who worked for KEO Films on this project as director extraordinaire, for their patience over the past couple of years.

Finally, a hearty thanks to Mum, Dad and my sister Anya for their unfailing support and patience. The World Garden and even this book could not have come into being without their help. I am particularly grateful to my grandmother, Crac, who first introduced me to gardening and continues to be an inspiration.

# Picture Acknowledgements

All photographs have been kindly supplied by the author and his family apart from the following:

*Colour section 1*
Gatehouse: Vikki Rimmer
Anonymous pen and wash drawing of Lullingstone Castle, c.1670: © Yale Center for British Art, Paul Mellon Collection/The Bridgeman Art Library; triptych: photo © Howard Wrighton; Lady Zoë Hart Dyke inspecting silk camisole: photo by M. McNeill/Fox Photos/Hulton Archive/ Getty Images.
Colour views of Lullingstone: Vikki Rimmer.
Tom and Gum Nut Steve: Louisa Cowling; Tom, James Spring, Paul Winder: Brian Winder.

*Colour section 2*
Moon Gate: Vikki Rimmer.
Portrait of John Tradescant the Elder attributed to Cornelius de Neve: © Ashmolean Museum, University of Oxford/The Bridgeman Art Library: portrait of John Tradescant the Younger as a gardener attributed to Thomas de Critz: © Ashmolean Museum, University of Oxford/The Bridgeman Art Library; portrait of Sir Joseph Banks by Benjamin West, 1773: © Lincolnshire County Council, Usher Gallery, Lincoln/The Bridgeman

Art Library; watercolour of *Phormium tenax*, New Zealand flax, by Fred Polydore Nodder from an original outline drawing by Sydney Parkinson made during Captain James Cook's first voyage across the Pacific, 1768–71: Natural History Museum Picture Library, London; crayon portrait of David Douglas attributed to Sir Daniel McNee: © copyright the Board of Trustees of the Royal Botanic Gardens, Kew; Sugar Pine specimen collected by David Douglas: © copyright the Board of Trustees of the Royal Botanic Gardens, Kew; George Forrest in his camp in Yunnan during his fourth expedition, 1917–20: © copyright the Board of Trustees of the Royal Botanic Gardens, Kew; illustration of *Primula forrestii* by Matilda Smith from 'Curtis's Botanical Magazine', 1910: © copyright the Board of Trustees of the Royal Botanic Gardens, Kew.

Walled garden before planting, except for Granny's herb garden: all Vikki Rimmer.

Clearing the walled garden: all Vikki Rimmer.

Reg; Sylvia Halls and Jim Buttress; Tom and Tony Russell: all Vikki Rimmer; Laurence Dell: Louisa Cowling; Vikki Rimmer: Jason Dodd Photography.

*Colour section 3*

Gatehouse: Vikki Rimmer.

Greenhouse; Tom, Dad and the Wollemi Pine: Vikki Rimmer; inset aerial shot: Ant Palmer.

Tom and four specimens: all Vikki Rimmer.

World Garden 2006: all Vikki Rimmer.

Tom and the family; Tom and his grandmother: both Vikki Rimmer.

# 1

## Jungle Fever

*I was a hostage once more, stumbling through the tangled forest of the Darién. Only now I was alone — there was no Paul — and this time it was clear from the look on the guerrillas' faces that I would not be leaving Colombia alive. Having led me deep into the jungle, they ordered me to kneel against a tree, my hands on my head. I closed my eyes and with a thumping heart I waited to hear the crack of the rifle and feel the burn of the bullet as it drilled into the back of my head . . .*

It was at this point that I usually woke up, drenched in a clammy, cold sweat. Tonight was no different.

It was the autumn of 2002 and I had been home for nearly two years. The nine months I had spent as a prisoner had left an indelible mark on me, and the nightmares had not gone away. In the panic they brought on, it was sometimes hard to remember that my release and the joy of being reunited with my family hadn't just been make-believe.

In reality, of course, I was tucked up in bed in a castle in rural Kent and was as safe as houses. My captors had been a ragbag of illiterate, AK-47-wielding crazies who probably couldn't have found their way to Bogotá, let alone to

Blackfriars to catch the train to Lullingstone had they decided to come after me for my ransom. And even if they had been lurking in the grounds, my bedroom was in a fortified Tudor gatehouse. With running repairs it had survived, more or less intact, the English Civil War, the Luftwaffe and some lively weekend visits by my chainsaw-wielding gardening mates from horti-cultural college. Its massive brick-built bulk and battlements still looked as impregnable as they had when they went up in 1497; and Whispering Death, Trouble Ahead, Loose Teenager and the rest — Paul and I gave all our captors nicknames — would have had quite a job getting in.

Nevertheless, on this particular night I still didn't feel safe enough to close my eyes again. The nightmare had been so graphic my body was once again convinced it was back in the Darién, consumed by the fever and fear of being a hostage in the jungle. I knew I was in for another sleepless night; and to break the spell I got up, turned on the light and looked for something to occupy me on the long climb to sunrise, when everything would feel normal and I could get back out into the garden.

At anxious times like this I would often flick through a magazine. Not a *Nuts* or a *loaded*, you understand. I tend to need something stronger and more hardcore; and for me the chlorophyll-fuelled *Hillier Manual of Trees and Shrubs* always hits the spot. With its explicit, horticultur-ally endowed text, mostly concerned with hardy, woody plants, it's an indispensable guide that's been updated regularly since 1971, five years

2

before I was born. I realize it isn't a top read for many twentysomething males, but along with the quirkily seductive Chiltern Seed Catalogue that I devour for two or three weeks when it arrives in late autumn, and various plant lists from nurseries, garden centres and horticultural societies around the world, I've read it passionately for as long as I can remember.

To be honest, seed and plant catalogues are my Shakespeare and my Dan Brown. They make me light-headed with awe sometimes and transport me to the place I am happiest: the garden. So it was unusual on this particular night that for once my eyes were drawn instead to the mess on my desk and to what I'd been doing earlier in the day. There, next to the PC, was the diary of the nine months I spent as a hostage. I'd been poring over its grubby pages, trying to make sense of those crazy days for a book I was writing about my Darién disaster; and I decided, wisely, to shun the *Hillier* for once and have another look.

The pages of the diary still held the damp, fetid smell of jungle. Not that I needed much reminding, but the whiff of rotting vegetation brought everything back so vividly I could almost taste the mulch.

The actual words on the page were hard to read. When Paul and I were captured, I had only one empty exercise book in my rucksack, and not knowing how long we might be held I had made my writing microscopically small. Using our only pen, a red biro, I wrote in secret when the guerrillas weren't watching us.

I carried the diary back to bed and flicked through its pages to the entries for July 2000 and the dreadful seven weeks we spent at the camp Paul and I called 'Lost City'. As I read I was immediately back in the darkness of our grotty wooden hut there, fearing for my life.

*Paul's leg is rotting. The worms have got in and one died. The guerrillas have turned to quackery in a bid to save his limb. They found a tube of his Deep Heat and the silly buggers, believing it to be some miracle cure, rubbed it into the open, gaping sore while he screamed in excruciating agony. 'They only want to kill me and cause me pain,' he shrieked. There was nothing I could do: there is nothing I can do. I feel helpless, hopeless. His leg has swollen to twice its normal size and is infested with maggots. The humid jungle air is a ripe breeding ground for infection and infestation. We have said nothing about it, but I feel certain at some point they will have to amputate. Either that or they will shoot him, like a horse gone lame. I am doing all I can to keep his spirits up, but he is withdrawing further into himself, unable to move, even to wash himself. His side of the hut stinks.*

*The frustration of our captors grows daily. It spreads through the camp like disease. The guerrillas whip themselves into frenzy, believing the money will come tomorrow, always tomorrow. They talk about it obsessively. 'If it doesn't come, we will kill them,' they say. They cock their guns and point them at us, mimicking blowing us away. I have heard talk of*

4

decapitation, of being buried. I'm terrified. When they finally realise no money is coming, what will they do then? Do I really want to know?

Paul is confined to his bed, partitioned off on the other side of the sweltering hut. I try to occupy myself: keep sane and fend off thoughts of what is going to happen. I dream about my ideal garden. Each day it gets more vivid in my mind. I will fill it with every plant I have ever loved. I want the biggest stock of horticulturally endowed plants the world has ever seen: plants with big leaves, pungent smells, colourful flowers, plants that the public will come and see in all their glory. If I'm going to die tomorrow, I'd better get cracking . . .

I smiled. Across the page was the red biro sketch in which I had noted some of the species I wanted to include in my wowzer of a dream garden, and I'd designated where they should be planted. There would be four main beds, each devoted to a particular continent. I wanted the world to flock to this garden and gaze in awe. I hoped that people who saw it might feel a hint of the passion that has excited me ever since, aged three, I planted my first carrot seeds here at Lullingstone with Granny and became a self-confessed plant nut.

Paul and I were captured on 16 March 2000 and it was on 16 June that we were told we would be executed. Paul prayed that night but I couldn't. Instead I thought about plants. From that moment on, the garden was *all* I thought of. Every minute of every day and during the darkest hours of the night too. Without my imaginary garden to escape to, I would have gone properly insane, as opposed to merely a bit unhinged — which many friends, my dad included, thought I was already.

As dawn began to break on this sleepless night, I realized how clinging to the vision of my garden of dreams had helped save my life. If I could only build it for real now, perhaps I could do something to help save the house and estate that my parents were, with diminishing success and increasing exhaustion, struggling each year to hang on to.

Under a variety of surnames, our family has been on this bit of land since 1361. But in the autumn of 2002 our continued presence was looking shakier than ever. Money was already tight when I set off on my travels; but in the two years since my belated return I could see that Mum and Dad were really up against it. The number of visitors, mostly elderly, who paid to see round the house and grounds had hit rock bottom — there had been just over 2,000 of them, I think, that summer — and there was nothing left to sell. All the land and property that could easily be flogged off or leased out already had been; and with our income drying up faster than the morning dew on Dad's lawn, my parents were in dire straits. Their hopeless son and heir, meanwhile, was earning the princely sum of £10 an hour as a jobbing tree surgeon. And you can't repair many rotting eighteenth-century window frames with that.

The money I was expecting for writing about

my unexpected stay in the Darién might fund a second-hand car and new sofa for me, but it wouldn't go far towards creating the major new visitor attraction that the estate needed. Besides which, I still didn't have a really clear idea of how I could make my dream garden sufficiently different and retina-blasting to divert visitors away from their Sunday shopping pilgrimages to Bluewater or wherever.

I put the diary down and started to feel pretty glum. Turning on my side and facing the wall, I looked at the National Geographic map of the world that was hanging there.

'Hm. Interesting planet,' I thought. 'Perhaps I should just go off and see some more of it.'

My eyes moved back and forth between the map on the wall and the red biro sketch in my diary. Until that night I had never believed in 'Eureka!' moments. But suddenly I found myself sitting bolt upright, staring at each continent on the wall in turn. Glancing back at my diary, the clunky rectangular European bed I had drawn suddenly morphed in my mind's eye into a curvy and contoured version of the UK, Ireland and mainland Europe, reflecting their *actual* shapes.

*Wow!* This was interesting . . .

I started to stare at the other continents too, and each of my boring rectangles now began to redraw itself into a familiar, continent-shaped land mass that actually meant something.

I leapt out of bed, grabbed a fistful of A4 and started to draw. *Yes!* I could build my dream garden in the shape of the flaming world! I'd fill its map-like continents with their native plants and create *a world map of plants that looked like a map*! That would be worth a detour and £5.50 of anyone's money! Once built, I could be there every day, skipping between the Americas and Africa and Australasia, telling visitors about the plants and where they came from and how to grow them. I could even sell them the seeds and plants from my very own nursery!

I was on a definite high now, experiencing the sort of concentrated horticultural tunnel vision I usually get only when plant-hunting in the wild. I knew *exactly* what I wanted. I would have the whole world in one acre. With raised beds and mountain ranges, I would contour my continents so visitors could climb Mount Everest, clamber over Ayers Rock and sip water from the Niagara Falls, swooning at the wondrous species from those regions displayed in their natural mini-habitats.

I would have mountains, rivers and deserts. Sod it — I could even put in the Darién Gap between North and South America and ask dear old Paul to sit there, playing cards and smoking fags in the knackered jeans and wellies he had worn for nine months!

I was so excited I had to get up and walk around. I went over to the window and looked across the lawn to my parents' house, its majestic silhouette now slowly emerging in the dawn. No light showed in any of the windows yet, but the gorgeous old house became clearer and clearer as day descended. Lit by a reddening sky, it was an enchanting sight and I wanted my family to be able to stay here.

Across the grass, which was frosted with cold, the mist hung low around the nether regions of St Botolph's, making the tiny flint church look like a stone galleon on a foggy sea. But there behind the church, beyond my ancestors in the little graveyard, lay the site of our salvation: the walled garden, future home of . . . Tom Hart Dyke's World Garden of Plants at Lullingstone!

The euphoria on Planet Tom lasted several nanoseconds before I landed back on Planet Earth and remembered I didn't have the first penny to make any of this happen for real. But I didn't stay low for long.

'Don't be so negative, Tom!' I told myself, remembering the motto my best mate Tom Stobbart, the Big Friendly Giant, and I had coined before setting off on our travels.

'Tom' — it was handy that we were both called Tom — 'Tom, if you want to do it . . . just do it!'

And why not? If I put my mind to it, why couldn't I raise the money to get my garden built? I did have some income from tree surgery after all; and taking a leaf from Granny's book, I would eventually be able to earn a little more by selling my plants to visitors in the summer. It might take a while — might take years — but it had to be possible. It had to be worth the effort. I'd just . . . do it!

I went back to my desk and the ideas seemed to gush out in a flood. The size of each continent and country would be dictated by the richness of its flora. Iran, with its mountains of Imperial Fritillaries and Persian Ironwoods, would dwarf

Iraq. China would be far larger than Russia. The Canaries would be prodigious. People would walk into my garden through the circular Moon Gate in the east wall and be blown away.

The world's oceans would become pathways along which you could follow the adventures of the intrepid plant-hunters. Visitors would arrive at Britain first, which was where the early plant-hunters came from, and I'd tell them the stories of passionate plant nuts like George Forrest, who in the first three decades of the twentieth century risked life and limb in China to bring back everything from primulas and camellias to gentians and rhododendrons. With his reckless disregard for personal safety, he was one of my all-time heroes and I wanted people to know about him. And men like David Douglas in the 1820s, and before him the great eighteenth-century plant-hunters Francis Masson and Joseph Banks. All of them nutters in their own way and all of them brilliant.

It was these adventurers whose horticultural derring-do had inspired my own more modest travels; and it was their discoveries that had transformed British gardens into the riot of non-native species that they are today. I wanted visitors to understand how our gardens only look the way they do thanks to the bravery and obsession of men like Forrest and Banks. I wanted them to understand the connection between what the great Victorian and Edwardian plant-hunters achieved and all that pretty stuff that now flies off the shelves at Homebase every weekend. Most of all, I wanted them to know where the plants we love and take for granted originally came from.

Then, in the borders inside the walls of the garden, I would plant the best-known cultivars and hybrids created by man, plant descendants of the true species in my continents, so visitors could compare them with their ancestors. The whole thing would be a world first: an interactive world map of plants. A garden to put Lullingstone back on the map. A garden that was, in short, the absolute Dog's Bollocks.

I didn't sleep for thirty-seven hours.

# 2

## Look, No Orchids

Despite the lack of sleep, after my 'Eureka!' moment I was buzzing. It was as if I'd been treading water for the two years since my release, and my feet had suddenly hit something solid and I could at last scamper up the bank and get on with the rest of my life.

In that first burst of excitement I worked through till it was fully light, sketching and writing like crazy. My bed was strewn with seed catalogues and plant lists, the desk too. Trying to make a proper plant list for a lush World Garden that had a chance of surviving in chilly north-west Kent, and then working out where I might find some of the 10,000 or so species I wanted to see growing in it, was going to take time. A lot of time. Given the limited number of plants and seeds in my own collection, it was also going to be expensive. But I felt turbo-charged inside and was well up for the challenge.

Some of the species I wanted would be no trouble to find, and best of all they would be entirely free. *Acacia riceana*, for example, my favourite plant from Tasmania: I'd seen it in the wild and collected the seed myself. The Prickly Moses, as it's known, is a genuine five-star weirdo and looks like something out of a sci-fi film, not having anything you would normally recognize as leaves. It doesn't even have thorns, in fact, just prickly foliage — a response to the freezing winds that blast parts of southwest Tasmania — and I felt sure visitors would love it as much as I do.

But where was I going to get my hands on a *Pseudopanax ferox*? The Toothed Lancewood — or, more accurately, the Upside Down Dead Stick Tree — comes from New Zealand's South Island and is an absolute maniac. With its long, black, narrow leaves that point downwards like daggers, it looks as if it's been growing upside down and then suddenly popped its clogs. I knew that anyone who saw one growing in our bit of south-east England would be gobsmacked.

'What the **** is that?' they'd cry.

'Why's this guy got a plastic plant in his garden?'

It's just very, very waxy and, quite simply, extraordinary. I had to find one somewhere.

The sedentary plant-hunting continued over the next days and weeks. If I didn't have my nose buried in a seed catalogue, I scoured plant lists over the internet — a brilliant resource for plant anoraks like me — checking the availability (and price) of species against the likelihood of my ever being able to get them to germinate and survive in the Lullingstone frost bowl. Given our local climate, this was going to be horticulture on the edge — a bit of an ego trip for me as a gardener — and there had to be some limits to my crazy optimism. Thus I found that I was ignoring the group of plants that had been easily the most

13

influential in my life so far: the mighty Orchidaceae family.

With the exception of one or two of the hardier beauties, like the *Dactylorhiza* hybrids, which are cousins of our native Common Spotted Orchid, *Bletilla striata*, the Hyacinth Orchid, and *Cypripedium reginae*, the North American Slipper Orchid, I knew Lullingstone's World Garden was going to be a more or less orchid-free zone. This was ironic.

First, if hardy woody plants are constant objects of desire in my ongoing love affair with horticulture, orchids must be my foxy long-term mistress. They make me do dumb things — they have nearly cost me my life, after all — and I know I will never be able to end the affair.

I find orchids mouth-wateringly beautiful and beguiling, and just thinking about some species literally brings me out in goosebumps. Although other plants can do that too, orchids are different. I've been smitten since I was a child and used to spend my days growing them up in my bedroom in the old servants' quarters or outdoors counting them — on one occasion in the school holidays, on Lullingstone Park golf course, I counted all the way up to 63,424. Or thereabouts.

It was never their profusion, however, that hypnotized me, fascinating though that was. I was mesmerized, and still am, by the delicacy and unbelievable variety of shapes, colours and smells that orchids offer. The Lizard Orchid pongs of dead goat hair, for heaven's sake! I'm also fascinated by their ability to adapt to every single continent bar the frozen wastelands of Antarctica. And I'm blown away by their tricksiness. Take the mimicry of the Bee Orchid: a flower that looks like a bee and can make itself smell like a randy female to ensure pollination by giving off fake pheromones. What on earth is that about?

The fact that I knew that these delicate delights could never be central to my new, open-to-the-elements gardening adventure was also ironic because it was directly due to my weak-kneed attachment to orchids that I had dreamt up my World Garden idea in the first place. How had this come about? All too easily, I'm afraid.

In 1997 I set off on my travels with £8,000 I had saved by working as a tree surgeon and a further £1,500 in research grants. I left with my college mate Tom Stobbart, the BFG, on what for me was going to be a globe-trotting orgy of orchid study in south-east Asia followed by some hardcore seed-collecting in windy, upland Tasmania, where I was not looking for orchids but those potentially hardy woody plants I so adore.

Tom and I eventually went our separate ways in Penang — he to continue diving, no doubt relieved to be free of my orchid obsession; me to feed the habit further by studying orchid husbandry. My non-orchid researches then took me on to Tasmania and mainland Australia, where, after a couple of years' travelling, note-taking and securing the necessary phyto-sanitary certificates to send my hardy seeds back to England (and finally having had my first snog at the age of twenty-three!), I thought it was time to come home. I decided to do so, however, via California, where I wanted to say 'Hi' to the largest single living organisms on the planet: those monstrously impressive Redwood trees.

Awesome though the Redwoods were, they still left me feeling vaguely unsatisfied, and I was soon hankering for a final fix of truly tropical flora before returning to Kent. Secretly, I was also still itching to copy my plant-hunting heroes and make a discovery of my own. So I headed south to Mexico for one last roll of the green dice. It was there, in November 1999, that I had one of those days that changes your life.

In the morning, scrambling through the Copper Canyon in northern Mexico under a clear blue sky, I came across a stunning penstemon whose purple flowers had such a delicious creamy-white throat I almost wanted to eat them. The penstemon really was drop-dead gorgeous and, though I wasn't absolutely sure at the time, my hunch that I had stumbled across a new variety later turned out to be spot-on.

It was later that day, while drying the penstemon seeds I had collected on the tin roof of my hostel, that I also discovered an interesting new genus of harmless-looking British back-packer in wire-framed specs: the Paul Winder. If I hadn't been sitting on the edge of a concrete washbasin out in the yard cleaning the lens of my camera, our paths might never have crossed and things would be very different today. But I was soon deep in conversation with this laid-back, softly spoken fellow Englishman.

'Have you heard of the Darién Gap?' he asked me innocently as we continued rapping late into the night, swapping travellers' tales.

No I hadn't, in fact; but Paul, who then rambled off on his travels again the next day, had planted a seed. Over the next couple of months, while I tried to learn Spanish, the seed began to germinate. And the more I learnt about the Darién's location, climate, geography and recent history, the more I became desperate to go there.

This missing link in the Pan-American Highway between North and South America had been shunned by sensible travellers for years. This was due to the hostilities that raged in a troubled region straddling the borderlands between Panama and Colombia. To the Green Man from Lullingstone, it sounded like pure, unadulterated, orchid heaven.

Thus it was that Paul and I, having stayed in touch via email, teamed up again in Panama City and allowed his thirst for mountaineering adventure and my weakness for orchids to convince us to do what everybody told us not to do: to cross the Darién Gap on foot, dodging its gangs of marauding militias, bootleggers, bandits and assorted damned and desperate low-lifes.

As people back home in Britain might have seen on the television news bulletins or read in the newspapers in 2000, the guidebooks were absolutely right and we were simply bloody stupid. Once inside the Darién, almost before I could say, 'Christ, Paul — an *Odontoglossum*!', we were on our knees in the dirt, surrounded by

17

men in camouflage fatigues and staring into the wrong end of their AK-47s. Were we CIA? Were we drug-runners? No, we were idiots. But they wouldn't listen.

For our families at home, it was nine months of torture, made worse by the official line that eventually emerged that 'the two missing British backpackers Tom Hart Dyke and Paul Winder' were presumed dead. Mum never gave up hope; but as the weeks of not knowing turned to months, Dad, Granny and Anya, my younger sister, all became convinced that I had bought it. I still cannot apologize enough to them for the anguish I put them through.

For Paul and me, it was a surreal nine months to say the least. How we would laugh out loud when the guerrillas, bored stiff, would hold a mad, macho competition to see who could jump up and smash their head the hardest against the wooden beam of the shack they were staying in. How we wept, whimpered and went numb inside when they told us how we would be executed if our $5 million ransoms weren't paid. A bullet to the head, maybe. Or a machete to the throat. Or, quite fitting for an idiot gardener, by being buried alive beneath the jungle mulch.

The bewildering cast of captors kept changing — crazies to whom we gave nicknames like the Nutter, Space Cadet, Scarface and, one of the most aggressive, a woman we named the Bitch. There were probably a couple of hundred of them in all, but at any one time it was left to between ten and twenty of them to keep us moving through the forest from one stinking camp to the next.

While still in what Paul and I worked out was Panama, we passed some of the most orgasmic orchid specimens I had ever seen. I never missed an opportunity to point this out to our captors, hoping it would persuade them that our presence on their patch was down to nothing more sinister than silliness. If we stayed in one place long enough, I would always try to plant a garden round our hut or tent and decorate our surroundings with blooms. At one high-altitude camp I even managed to create my very own 'cloud garden'.

Despite the joys of gardening in the clouds, we were caught in a strange, parallel world where abject fear was mixed with high farce — not to mention the revolting parasitic worms that burrowed into our bodies and had to be squeezed out by hand in a mini-volcano of blood and pus. One day our captors would hit us with sticks and tell us we were going to die; the next, to all-round hilarity, Paul and I would perform our version of 'Always Look On The Bright Side Of Life', telling our captors in broken Spanish that it was the British National Anthem.

Our constant fear was that even if the guerrillas didn't carry out their threat to execute us, there was still a strong chance that either of us could be killed randomly in a freak accident. These men, and a few women, though naïvely crafty, were absolutely reckless about their own lives and safety. They were always chucking machetes around wildly or leaving their loaded weapons on the deck with the safety catches off. I'll never forget the time Paul was smoking a cigarette and one of our guards approached from behind and tapped him on the shoulder with the barrel of an M16 rocket-launcher to tell him smoking was bad for his health.

Despite the two years that had elapsed since our release, trying to write about my Darién experiences had stirred things up powerfully — hence perhaps the chilling nightmares. But the World Garden at Lullingstone at least now gave me hope. I believed that, even without any of my beloved orchids in it, by finally building with my own hands the garden that was conceived in the darkest moments of the Darién, I would not only create something beautiful and useful for my family's financial survival, but I might finally begin to lay my guerrilla-shaped ghosts to rest.

# 3

## The World in One Acre

As autumn turned to winter and slowly drained the colour from the trees around the lake, at my desk in the gatehouse I piled on extra jumpers and fleeces and dived into my new gardening adventure with gusto. It was brilliant to know at last what I wanted to do with my life. And my first executive decision, though unusual for me, was really quite sensible.

'For God's sake, Tom, don't blab about this to anyone!' I told myself. 'Not even Granny. Not until you have at least *some* idea what you're talking about.'

Normally I can't stop myself talking; but this felt strangely serious. A World Garden that could bring the visitors back to Lullingstone and get the family finances out of intensive care? I felt the whole project was make or break for me and for the estate, so I really didn't want to cock it up. I had to try to keep a sock in it until I had something sensible to say.

Of course Mum and Dad knew vaguely that I had wanted to create some sort of garden at Lullingstone since returning from Colombia. But could I tell them it was going to be a Major New Tourist Attraction? A venture that would sort our finances for the *next* 600 years? Not until I could answer some of the trickier grown-up questions I might be asked.

Given my brilliant track record with schools (rejected by every one you've ever heard of, I only got into a secondary school because during the interview I spotted some early Marsh Orchids in the grounds and the head was a keen naturalist) and given my brilliant track record with expedition planning (immediate capture, humiliation, ransom demands, death threats, etc.), even with the best will in the world Mum and Dad would have found it hard to believe me capable of such a big project.

After Darién, I think Dad was more convinced than ever that his son was unhinged, not to say a complete and utter nutter. I remember our reunion at Gatwick on the afternoon of 21 December 2000, for example, after we had flown home from South America via Caracas. Paul still had his machete with him and I was in flip-flops because my feet were still so swollen thanks to the burrowing worms. After a huge group hug in the VIP lounge, Mum, Dad, Anya and I were wheeled out to meet the press, who were crushed behind the metal barriers.

'Mr Hart Dyke!' a reporter called out to Dad as we eventually tried to pull ourselves away. 'Were you surprised by what happened to your son?'

Dad turned towards me and smiled enigmatically at the reporter. To me, his look said it all. The terrible truth was that, no, Dad wasn't in the least bit surprised by what had happened to me in the jungle.

Dad, who trained as a forester and spent most of his working life in Africa, has always seen me as somehow a bit 'different'. That doesn't mean we don't get on; but, boy, I must have tried his patience over the years — and being a man who watched trees grow for a living, he has a lot of patience to try. Dad certainly thinks my greenhouse technique is on the maverick side. After the discipline of Gordonstoun and joining the navy at seventeen, he went to Canada to study forestry before heading for Africa, a continent he still adores. I don't think Dad ever played music to his trees in Botswana, but I certainly do in the greenhouse at germination time. Don't ask me why, but I know from experience that Pavarotti and Dire Straits can cause rotting at the base of a newly sown seed, while Warren G and Puff Daddy help prevent it. Perhaps it's to do with the vibrations of drum 'n' bass.

Compared with Dad, and my gardening genius Granny, whom you'll meet later, I suppose I'm what you'd call a bit of a 'gonzo' gardener (though I far prefer the word 'intuitive'). But I still knew I had to have a pukka plan in place before opening my mouth to either of them.

Deep down, I also wanted Dad to see that the son who had been such a flop in school, and who had put the family through so much agony due to his thoughtlessness, was perhaps finally growing up and was beginning to be capable of thinking something through properly from start to finish. I wanted to show him that I might even be able to do him proud one day by keeping things going at Lullingstone when he has gone.

I decided not to talk to any of my green and hardy perennial chums about the garden for different reasons. I knew that if I blurted stuff out before my master plan was clear, in my rush of enthusiasm I might say the wrong thing or, worse, sound uncertain and open to persuasion. They, trying to help, might then convince me my idea was bonkers.

'No, Tom. You don't want to do that! You want to do a proper restoration job. Go on . . . do an eighteenth-century apothecary's garden like they had in the olden days!'

That sort of advice, no matter how well meant, I didn't want to hear. I was determined to create something new and different.

Nor for now did I want to become bogged down in things I didn't understand or couldn't control. Not being the world's greatest business-man — not being any kind of businessman at all, in fact — I couldn't bring myself to think too much at this stage about money, beyond the fact that I knew I would need some, possibly quite a lot, eventually, one day, kind of . . . Well, you know what I mean. Funding the garden gradually from tree surgery and plant sales would be a long haul, I knew. But I had the rest of my life, so what was the hurry? Instead I concentrated on what I knew I *could* do. Getting the chlorophyll bit right. And because that really interested me, back at my desk I was extremely focused.

The continents of my world map of plants, I

decided, would occupy roughly half of Lulling-stone's 2-acre walled garden. Visitors would enter this horticultural wonderland through the circular Moon Gate in the east-facing wall, and wander round, through and over the continents. Inspired by my interpretation of our glorious green globe, they would then be able to visit my nursery and plant-sale area on the other side of the plot, where I would have the opportunity to indulge in my other passion, which is talking about plants.

Before the continents and oceans could be landscaped (with what, I had no idea), the weeds — plus Granny's herb garden and quince trees and Dad's vegetables and apple trees — would all have to be cleared unceremoniously. This would be sad and poignant, as I had grown up surrounded by their horticultural handiwork. But it would also be breathtakingly exciting, given what green treasures I hoped would eventually appear in their place. The sheep fence and two hedges that divided the walled garden in half would also have to come down. But that would be a blast, because I love nothing more than a good chainsaw-and-bonfire session.

Even before broaching the idea with Dad, however, in the back of my mind I knew that my cunning plan had one big potential flaw. I hadn't considered my next-door neighbour Trevor Edwards.

Trevor has been one of our neighbours at Lullingstone for, let me think, oh at least 150 years. Well, OK — twenty-eight years, then: it just feels much longer. He is an eccentric musician, and he has a lease on the south wing of the house where he faces the lake and lives in a lot more comfort and style than Mum and Dad, or Granny and I for that matter. More crucially, though, I remembered that Trevor still had a lease on the half of the walled garden that lay beyond the hedges in the middle. This was the bit where I wanted to have my nursery and across which my plant-intoxicated visitors would need to crawl, begging to be allowed to buy my seeds and plants.

Deep down — or not so deep down — I suppose I knew this meant that half the site for which I had such grand designs actually belonged to somebody else. But over that winter of 2002–2003, I was pumped up by the chlorophyll that was flying through me and, as Trevor never seemed too bothered about his bit of garden, which had once been a vineyard, I refused to be derailed by such negative thoughts.

So no: I didn't think this one through fully and certainly didn't talk to Trevor about it. He may look amiable, but he is actually quite big and can fly off the handle when there's an issue. He can go off pop, fizzing all over the place like a bottle of lemonade that's been left out in the sun too long. I decided I would leave him to Dad, who deals with all the leases at Lullingstone, and I filed the Trevor issue away in the folder marked 'Awkward Stuff To Be Dealt With At A Later Date'.

In a different folder I also stashed my longer-term plans for the estate as a whole. I eventually wanted to extend my world map of plants beyond the walled garden and out across our remaining 120 acres. I already had a budding eucalyptus tree collection on 3 acres behind the house, and I reckoned this would one day make a brilliant additional 'Australasia', where visitors could go walkabout and marvel at eighty varieties of gum tree, which, when not getting hammered by the frost, seemed to be growing like the clappers. I envisaged fabulous banks of rhododendron, camellia and bamboo down by the river, representing China and Asia; and an extension of North and South America doing very nicely over by the lake.

But all this was in the far distant future. My immediate problem was to find a way to cram the world into just one acre in a way that was horticulturally meaningful and would have visitors gagging to come back for more.

Selfishly, I also wanted the thrill of trying to grow some of the trickier delights myself here, outdoors in the open air. Having a cosily protective bio-dome over the walls, as they have at the Eden Project in Cornwall, was out of the question — and not just for planning or financial reasons. For me, the whole point was to find the right provenances and then use whatever means necessary to help my babies survive on our shivering valley bottom. I'm certainly not averse to protecting my charges from the ravages of frost by wrapping them in Dad's old woolly jumpers, Gran's old net curtains, pillows and pillowcases, my old socks and fleeces and, on one occasion, a friend's football scarf. But no bio-dome.

Gardening-wise, then, it was all going to be high risk; and seeing which of the world's plants made it and which didn't would be a fascinating experiment for a plant nut like me. Being the first person in 'tropical' north-west Kent to grow something that either hadn't been grown in Britain before or that other people couldn't grow, was really what it was all about. I expected plenty of plant mayhem and death — and probably quite a lot of egg on my face to make 'the experts' grin with pleasure. But all that would be fine.

The real problem was that the four ancient walls of the garden at Lullingstone actually exacerbate our tricky local climate. When the cold air gets in behind them, it just stays put and gets colder. The Moon Gate does allow some air out, but our 2 walled acres definitely have a microclimate of their own. To have any chance of success, I told myself, I would have to choose hardy plants and, wherever possible, high-altitude varieties with a strong survival instinct.

Climate and weather also meant that, as I sat at my desk trying to play God, I had to be pragmatic in drawing up my land masses. Some artistic licence was called for. The Caribbean islands, with just one hardy plant to their name? Decision made. *Gone!* The high-rise Canary Islands, with loads of hardy plants? I'd put them together in one sumptuous, stunning whole and make the Canaries extra big and something to sing about.

I also wanted a big Africa. This was because it was the only land mass on my world map that I knew I would never be able to represent on a larger scale outside the walled garden if I was ever able to expand the idea later. We simply don't have a good sun-baked area anywhere else on the estate. Even so, given how tropical so much of Africa is, it was going to be a challenge anyway. Thank heavens for all the hardy, high-altitude goodies that Francis Masson brought back from the mountainous regions of South Africa in the eighteenth century. Without them, or the hardy beauties of the Atlas mountains, my world map would have been, to mix a metaphor, stuck up a gum tree.

There are high areas in Uganda and Ethiopia, I reasoned; but there was no way I would ever be able to compensate for the lack of light intensity under the grey skies of Dartford. And how would I deal with the tropics of West Africa and that region's lack of hardy plants? Coffee in pots, I told myself. And the Sahara? Er . . . I would have to be a merciful Creator and allow the continent's other plants to migrate upwards and downwards a bit from south and north to fill in the gap. Madagascar would have to go because people would trip over it; but its plants could sit in East Africa, either sunk in pots or with bare roots as summer bedding schemes.

With Tasmania, though, I felt I could push the boat out. After my four months of research work there for the Royal Horticultural Society and the Kent Gardens Trust, I knew the island well and it boasted a great selection of stunning species, many of whose seeds I had collected and sent home. So I let rip and decided to make little old

Tazzy half the size of mainland Australia.

Hardiness wasn't the only requirement that made the process of trying to choose what to grow so challenging. I wanted plants with a 'Wow!' factor too. With no budget, and knowing I would have to try to grow as much as possible from seed to save money I didn't have, I also needed plants that would strut their stuff relatively young. With just an acre to play with, I wasn't going to have space for plants that had to be 80 feet tall before they showed any interesting flowers, bark or leaves.

Traditional gardeners and garden designers will no doubt be appalled, but at this stage I still had very little idea how 'pretty' or aesthetically pleasing my world map of plants might one day look. This was because I didn't yet know all the plants that would be in it, nor which might survive and how they might then grow. In addition, despite my deep love of plants, I've never had a deep love of arranging flowers and so I've never really been one of those gardeners who say: 'Ooh, doesn't this daisy look great next to that succulent!' I wasn't about to change now. My planting scheme — if I ever got round to doing any planting — would be dictated by Mother Nature. My plants would grow, or crash and burn, in the miniature native lands from whence they came: not on the wrong side of the world just because they happened to look good next to something from another continent.

'Ah! But Christopher Lloyd from Great Dixter always put his Canna Lilies, originally from South America, next to the Foxglove Tree from

China because they look so lovely,' I hear you say. True. But I hoped more conventional gardeners would be gobsmacked by my novel approach.

The now late great Lloyd was brilliant and inspired me immensely with his tropical themes and daring designs, which pitted fiery Cannas alongside gorgeously broad Paulownias from China. Although I admired such audacity, it wasn't really my style. I know most gardening programmes and books on garden design will tell you 'This plant looks very nice next to that one.' But I've always thought the same thing: 'B******* to that!' Some people like being told what to do in the garden. I don't. The planting scheme for the World Garden would draw from nature's inspiration, not planting prettiness, and that was that.

I knew my approach might end up looking too haphazard for some, but I really wanted to stick to my guns and give the garden time to develop. Nor would I opt for staggered planting, I told myself; so it was possible I might end up with some whacking great plants next to some really quite weedy ones.

I also knew that, because of my lack of funds and the experimental nature of what I wanted to do, initially there would have to be a lot of spot planting: one plant of this here; one plant of that there. It might look sparse in the early years — very sparse until I could afford to buy more plants — but I had time, I told myself, to wait and see what survived. If something flourished, I might eventually put in another four in a grouping.

Groupings of plants would certainly soften the overall look eventually, but for now such perfection was far from my thoughts. To be honest, I wasn't too fussed what people might think of the aesthetics. I was just in love with the simple idea of sticking plants on my map in the places they naturally occur in the wild and telling the stories of how they and their descendants reached our shores. It seemed like a goer to me. But would it now pass the Dad test?

# 4

## Home, Sweet Stately Home

Considering we all share the same address at Lullingstone Castle, which is in the village of Eynsford, Kent, it's surprising how little we see of each other. I can go for days without bumping into Mum or Dad, and then only spy them in the distance somewhere, Dad chugging along on his sit-down mower or closing the church of an evening, Mum waving as she drives off to go shopping at Bluewater, which Dad avoids like the proverbial.

The place is so big we've never had to live in each other's pockets physically; but we're not the sort of family to do so emotionally either. The Hart Dykes are famously independent.

When I was abroad, for example, I wrote home regularly at first (and sent Mum a steady supply of seeds which she put in the fridge for my return). But over the three years I was away, I only ever telephoned her once. The second time we spoke on the phone I was in the British Ambassador's residence in Bogotá telling her that I was still alive and that I would be coming home for Crimbo.

It's not that we're not close. We are close. We're just not *that* close; and we all get on with our respective lives. Perhaps it's the result of having so much space around us, or maybe it's a

Hart Dyke thing, I don't know. But I'd actually been a hostage for several weeks before Mum and Dad even started to think that I might be in trouble. Even then the thought only crossed their minds because Paul Winder's father, anxious that he hadn't heard from Paul, made contact with them. Somehow he had managed to hack into Paul's email and learnt that his son was planning to set off into the back of beyond with someone called Tom or Hart or Dyke. Was this me, Mr Winder asked in a chilling phone call, and if it was, where was I? Cue panic stations all round.

Even though I may not see Mum or Dad for days on end, we all look out for Granny (or Crac, as I've always called her, for reasons that I will explain later). She's been here since 1980 and still lives by herself in the north tower of the gatehouse. She will be ninety-three in 2007 and remains extremely independent. She recently bought a new wheelbarrow and rake, and, being bomb-proof, may well outlive both. She is also the owner of a purple mountain bike which she carefully takes out of the garage pretty much every day, even though she hasn't cycled properly for a couple of years. Though Crac has no problem pushing the pedals down, it seems it's the upward movement that makes her knees creak. So she uses the bike as a kind of walking aid, and can regularly be seen with bike in hand crossing the lawn to tend the east-facing borders outside the walled garden.

The weird thing about my next-door neighbour, apart from the fact that she is the person I'm closest to in the world in every sense, is that

Gran actually appears to be growing younger. I'm sure that when she hits 105 her knees will have mended and she'll be cycling once more.

Anyone taking the same walk that she and I take each day, from the arch of the gatehouse towards my parents' house at the end of the drive, would probably find it hard to believe that Lullingstone isn't awash with dosh. Framed by the little church of St Botolph to the north-west, majestic cedars to the north and a trout-teeming lake to the south, the view manages to be lush, magnificent and serene all at the same time. Even I can see how it must reek of real money.

Once upon a time, of course, the estate *was* extremely rich. In its heyday — which actually lasted for several centuries — it was a serious pile; and to most of my friends who live in more modest places, it still looks the business. Of course it *is* the business, and I know how lucky I am to live here. But appearances, as they say, can be deceptive.

The church Dad looks after as warden doesn't belong to us and nor do the trout. The church belongs to the parish and the trout belong to the fisherman who bought the lease on the lake after my grandfather Oliver dug it out in the late 1950s and early 1960s so that he could flog off the gravel. He needed to sell the gravel in order to raise money to split the big house into flats, which in turn were flogged off on leases, so that the nineteenth and twentieth generations of his family — Mum, Dad, Yours Truly and Bristles, as I call my younger sister Anya, though I don't know why — could carry on living here.

35

I've always lived at Lullingstone with neighbours — there are seven other households in all — and sometimes it's like being in *The Archers*. Trevor's former partner once had a helicopter which was normally parked at Biggin Hill but which occasionally made extremely loud landings here in the walled garden when Granny and I were pottering there. I got to sit in it once and was amazed to learn that they used to fly around southern England navigating by road map. They must have been good at spotting road signs from the air, because they always came home eventually. But I always wondered: did they stop at traffic lights?

After the big house was first divided into flats by Grandad Oliver, our ancestors in the churchyard would probably have spun in their graves if they could have seen the tiny space Mum and Dad ended up with and the servants' rooms Bristles and I had as kids. I thought they were fine, but they weren't what previous generations had been used to.

The estate was once deemed grand enough, and our ancestors were rich and well connected enough, that Henry VIII and later Queen Anne, among others, were regular guests here. Anne had so many sleepovers here that she ended up with her own stonking great bedroom and special grand staircase, plus her own outdoor Bath House, all built by my great-great-something-or-other, Percyval Hart, Esquire. In the early 1700s he did the entire place up in 'Queen Anne style' in honour of his royal chum; and it's his perfectly proportioned western façade that blows visitors' socks off today with its serene symmetry (while Mum and Dad get palpitations counting the number of rotten window frames and shutters that need repairing).

Bristles and I both owe Percyval Hart and Queen Anne a big debt of gratitude, for when she and I were kids and it was raining outside, sliding down the carpeted Queen Anne staircase on Mum's tea trays was truly a killer ride. The narrow tread, specially built for the ageing monarch's little legs, made the descent smooth and fast — so fast that you could actually become airborne on the turn at the bottom. I dread to think how far I would have flown on one occasion had I not smashed into some of Percyval's period banisters, which acted as a handy brake.

By the late nineteenth and early twentieth centuries, when my great-grandfather Sir William Hart Dyke, the 7th baronet, was in residence, the estate was in clover. It owned more than 8,000 acres of south-east England, including six farms and a deer park, and bits of it reached as far away as Orpington. It was a serious pile.

Sir William lived well and played hard; and it has always amused me that he and some chums reputedly invented the rules of lawn tennis here in the garden one afternoon in 1875 using a ladder and two barrels for a net. Perhaps this helps explain my own love of badminton.

A close mate of the Prince of Wales, later Edward VII, and a confidant of Benjamin

Disraeli, Sir William also hosted the usual massive shooting parties. As well as a muddy-boot brigade of part-time beaters and pickers-up, he could afford to employ four outdoor staff who lived in and twelve indoor staff to fetch, carry, clean, polish, cook and clear up after him, his wife Emily and their guests. Dad says it was like *Gosford Park* but without the sex and murder, Emily's hobbies being (1) playing the drums, which she once did riding a chariot through the village; and (2) taking in broken chairs from the district which she would then mend and re-cane for people. I don't imagine she did the chair-mending because she needed the money.

When the great-grandparents both died within a few weeks of each other in the early 1930s, they left my grandfather Oliver, the 8th baronet, with a double whammy of two massive sets of death duties to pay because neither had made proper wills — brilliant given that Great-Grandad once helped run the Treasury for Disraeli. This meant that Oliver had to flog off virtually everything — 'At thirty bob an acre!' Dad still screams, tortured by the thought of how much all that land would be worth today.

So, along with the thousands of acres, the flats, the fish and the title of 9th baronet — Dad's brother Derek eventually got that, along with some cash, and promptly emigrated to Canada — the staff all went too. Today Mum has a nice lady called Ivette who comes in to help four hours a week on a Wednesday in summer, and two hours in winter.

For my parents, Lullingstone is quite a place to run, then, let alone maintain properly, and Mum, who recently got her bus pass, does most of the cleaning. That means hands and knees stuff, even when the visitors are around; and includes loos, floors and basins. It also means dealing with blockages caused by everything from sewage to people's hair.

Dad, who will be seventy-nine in 2007, looks after the bookings and usually greets visitors in the porch. He also administers our neighbours' leases and tenancies, and still manages the mowing. The lawn in front takes a whole day, plus the edge trimming and path poisoning; and he has to do it twice a week in summer. When I'm not missing presumed dead, I do what I can to help.

Though Bristles has gone off to Serbia, where she works for the UN on something important to do with arms control, my sister and I love every brick, stone and patch of peeling paint at Lullingstone; and we all feel incredibly privileged that our family has been able to inhabit the same beautiful, sleepy corner of rural England for so long. It was to try to hang on to our home for a few more years that Mum and Dad decided to reopen the main rooms of the house to the public in 1976, the year I was born. Little did they know how tricky it was going to be inviting people into their front room.

# 5

## The Estate We're In

In 1976, with the house open two afternoons a week between Easter and the end of September, 8,139 visitors paid 50p to be shown round Lullingstone Castle by its main living exhibit, Dad. Visitor numbers rose, and in the 1978 season 16,014 people came. Ticket sales, coupled with the small ground rents and service charges our flat-dwelling neighbours paid, were enough to keep the roof on, but there was little cash for fripperies — and there was even less when visitor numbers began to decline, which they did quite rapidly.

After the greenhouse blew away in the 1987 hurricane, for example — it flew over the wall and out of the garden altogether, swept away in the general roof-tile and tree carnage that devastated us that night — Mum and Dad waited two years to replace it. I was already a mad-keen gardener and the new greenhouse, when it finally arrived, was known as 'Tom's thirteenth birthday present'.

I was lucky enough to go to a private school, but only because my great-uncle Boyd, Mum's uncle, had left her some cash. In the early 1980s, when Dad was still away for part of the year earning his living as a forester in Africa, we just about ticked over, but to pay for 'luxuries' like clothes and school uniforms, for a few years Mum had to open the grounds on her free days during the week, charging visitors £1 a time. By 1984 enough visitors turned up each summer to justify Mum's serving home-made teas on trays from the porch, and, from 1986, proper sit-down teas in the gatehouse! She needed the cash to keep things going and would sit out at the gatehouse by herself in all weathers, Crac feeding her sandwiches.

Many of the visitors had known Lullingstone as schoolchildren in the 1940s and 1950s, and they clearly remembered Lullingstone Silk Farm, which was started by my paternal grandmother, Zoë, in 1932. Some people *still* remember the silk farm fondly today, even though the silkworms actually left in 1956. Dad tells me that Granny Zoë, or Lady Hart Dyke as she was known before her divorce from my grandfather, would often give visitors a cocoon to take home in a matchbox, and that in some of the rooms the aroma of caterpillars eating their mulberry leaves was overwhelming. Once smelled, never forgotten, apparently.

Back in the 1970s, though, I imagine visitors came to Lullingstone for more than simply worm-fuelled nostalgia. They came, I believe, because it is such an eye-grabbingly beautiful spot and because they wanted to see how the other half had once lived. Kings and queens had once played here and it was Dad's job to try to bring our family history to life with his stories.

The sightseers could marvel at the impeccable

green of his carefully tended lawn between the house and the gatehouse — but could they imagine the ground beyond the gatehouse as a jousting field back in the pre-motor mower days of the fifteenth century? Then the ground would have been rough and muddy with hoofprints and horsy skid marks, and the air would have been full of the shouts of battling knights and their awestruck retinues. The jousters included our own Action Man ancestor Sir John Peche, servant to Henry VII and a close chum of Henry VIII, who was particularly good at galloping around and knocking his mates off their horses.

Upstairs in the house the visitors could see the spooky old doll that Queen Anne left with the family centuries later when she visited Lullingstone. But could they imagine the ageing Queen slowly climbing the grand staircase on the way to her tiny bed in her enormous bedroom? Even with a backdrop of acres of old oak panelling, shelves full of dusty leatherbound books (few of which I've opened) and many austere portraits of my various ancestors (some of whom even I still can't always name for sure), it's a challenge to take people back in time. It's always struck me how Dad, a tree man by trade and not a tour guide, has managed to be so wonderfully engaging and natural about it. I think his dry, laid-back wit helps. He's brilliant.

People often ask me if opening Lullingstone to the public makes us feel like living exhibits. The answer is no, not really. The place isn't a museum, after all. Even if we can't inhabit all of it, when the visitors aren't around we do still use some of the 'public' rooms for private get-togethers. For Anya and me, of course, it's simply our home.

Aged nine or ten, one of our favourite games was to play hide-and-seek in the pitch black up in Queen Anne's interconnecting bedroom and state room. With my sister's friend Stephanie and my mate Jerry Thornton, who went to St Michael's School in Otford with me and is probably my oldest friend, we used to work ourselves into a state of terror.

Queen Anne's bedroom, complete with empty bed and wigstand, is always very, very cold — ghostly cold, you could say — and it is not a room in which I would ever really want to spend the night. I remember shivering, literally and metaphorically, every time I brushed past the black curly wig Mum had on display there. As a child I was convinced the wig had belonged to Charles I, though in truth I think Mum bought it from a theatrical costumier's in the 1970s. Dad looks a real hoot in it if he ever puts it on.

With the wooden shutters firmly closed, Anya, Stephanie, Jerry and I would crouch and creep through the chilly blackness, either seeking or waiting, petrified, to be found. My favourite hiding spot was over by the Queen's bed, and I can still remember how my heart would thump uncontrollably as the floorboards in the room began to creak and I knew that whoever was looking for me was getting closer and closer and closer . . .

Rather more grown-up and less petrifying are the family Christmasses we still have today downstairs in the Great Hall. We always gather in front of the fire at teatime to exchange our presents, and every other year relations come up from Portsmouth: Mum's brother David, who was captain of HMS *Coventry* when it went down in the Falklands, his wife D (short for Diana) and my cousins Miranda and Alice.

We have dinner on the big table in between the hall and the library, and it's all very jolly — even though the Great Hall isn't exactly what you would call cosy. In fact, it's a bit on the nippy side; and even with massively big logs burning in the grate, you're hard pressed to get the temperature much above frost level.

Of course the best Christmas in Hart Dyke history was the legendary one we celebrated in the year 2000 when my Colombian hosts, still ransom-less, unexpectedly told Paul and me to get lost. Despite this miracle of good luck, Paul and I nearly didn't make it home: for we really *did* get lost in the forest. After nearly a week we had to retrace our steps sheepishly, find our captors again and beg them pitifully for better directions. Eventually it was they who gave *us* money to catch a boat out of the jungle and back to civilization . . . but first we had to find the river.

The celebrations at Lullingstone that Christmas were the best ever, even though nothing here is ever over the top. As Dad had driven us back from Gatwick in the family Daewoo, I seem to remember we actually talked about the weather.

'Oh. And your eucalyptus trees have grown a lot,' said Mum.

Sweet Anya, who has always thought of others ever since she was a little girl, just carried on knitting. She was making me a scarf as a welcome-home present and she hadn't finished it yet.

Back at Lullingstone as night fell on the shortest day — it was the winter solstice — I will never forget my joy as I ran across the lawn in my flip-flops to where Granny was waiting for me at the gatehouse.

'Have you been on holiday?' she said impishly before we hugged and hugged and hugged. Being back again with Granny, it felt as if I'd been in Tenerife for two weeks.

When we all finally gathered in the house on that first night, I hit the Coca-Cola — I don't drink alcohol because I don't like the taste — and Mum made plans for the unexpected guest.

'We'll have to get some extra food in,' she said on the phone to Aunt D, who was due up from Portsmouth. 'Tom's home!'

We also hold a party in the Great Hall every Christmas for our neighbours, and in 2000 I suppose I was the guest of honour. To say I was a bit spaced would be an understatement: I was totally zapped as I tried to readjust to being free again. But I shall never forget the look in dear old Trevor's eyes as I hobbled down the red staircase to join the throng. He was incredibly moved and emotional and just held me tight. In fact, if he had hugged me any more, he would probably have killed me. We were genuinely delighted to see each other.

So Lullingstone is still very much a family home full of warm memories, as well as a slightly rambling survivor from a bygone era, bits of which are open to the public. If you pay us a visit, you will meet the family who actually lives here. Mum and Dad think this personal approach is very important and have never wanted to turn Lullingstone into an impersonal theme park with rides or attractions or gratuitous shops. Perhaps this helps explain why, throughout the 1980s and 1990s, the number of visitors fell so steadily. If Mum and Dad had created a restaurant serving Queen Anne nuggets and Henry VIII burgers, or had put up a Medieval Jousting Ride for the kiddies, they might have been more of a draw. But even if they had had the cash and space, which they hadn't, Ye Olde Fashioned Gifte Shoppes just aren't their style.

Mum eventually had to stop doing her sit-down teas and lose the associated income — and here I must hold my hand up and take some of the responsibility. She was expecting me home around June 2000 and generously intended that I would set up home in the gatehouse. She had even bought me a double bed and shifted the dishwasher to make room for me, but I of course was unavoidably detained.

After Mum closed her tearooms (now my bedroom and sitting room), if the visitors wanted a cuppa they had to walk ten minutes along the lake to the Lullingstone Park Visitor Centre, which is now run by Kent County Council. Even I can see the drawback to that. Visitors simply don't want to amble ten minutes there and ten minutes back for a soft drink and a biscuit.

Mum and Dad knew they needed to find other sources of income, but nothing at Lullingstone is ever really straightforward. Weddings, for example, seem an obvious solution and people are always ringing up asking if we host them. Given the stunning setting of church and house, we're not surprised. But the answer has always been 'Sorry, no.' Given our special circumstances — the need for permission from the parish; our neighbours in their flats; the lack of a suitable place to seat and feed the guests apart from the Great Hall, which is still our front room after all — wedding receptions have always been impractical. Besides which, Mum's kitchen is actually smaller than those in many Victorian terraced houses.

Other requests — by ghost-hunters to search for ectoplasm on the landing and TV archaeologists who asked if they could dig up the lawn — were intriguing, but Dad still declined. He was completely foxed by one lot who wanted to run a knitting course in the house.

'*Knitting?*'

Over the years other initiatives did go ahead, however, and Lullingstone hosted several open-air concerts and plays. I remember a group called the Geoffrey Whitworth Theatre who put on a *Wind in the Willows* by the cedar trees, and even a firework display from boats on the lake which was part of an open-air concert including jazz, classical music and the dancer Wayne Sleep. But fireworks and the rest never caught fire financially, so as our income steadily fell, holding on to what we had became more and more of a struggle.

Money-wise, 2002 was a particularly bad year. The visitors, by now paying £5.50 a time, hit rock bottom that summer; and when Dad totted up at the end of the season, our income was virtually flat-lining.

'This really can't go on,' he tut-tutted, more gravely and pensively than usual.

So as I prepared to wow him with my World Garden idea that winter, I felt a keen sense that it really *had* to work. I also reckoned Dad would be happy to hear of any suggestion, bar nude celebrity stock-car racing on the lawn, that might potentially be a long-term earner.

When I finally sat down with him and Mum in the den off the Great Hall, the first thing that struck me was how relieved they both seemed when I confirmed out loud that, yes, I definitely saw my long-term future here on the estate. I've always been extremely lucky that Mum and Dad, in their restrained English manner, are ultra-cool as parents. They never put any pressure on me along the lines of: 'One day, son, all this will be yours . . . *so bloody well get your act together!*' But I sensed that hearing of my commitment to the place, despite my track record, gave them a boost.

In truth I had known since I was small that I wanted to stay here and be part of the place for as long as I possibly could. It's where I belong. But if I hadn't wanted the responsibility, as Uncle Derek hadn't, and if I had preferred to go off to some far-flung corner to work in an orchid-rescue centre or whatever, Mum and Dad wouldn't have batted an eyelid or tried to stop me. That's part of their magic. But it was a relief for them to know that, even though Anya had flown the nest, so long as the sums could be made to add up their plant-nut son was staying put. The Hart Dykes of Lullingstone weren't finished just yet.

My biggest worry was that the World Garden idea would simply be too complicated and bothersome for Dad. A major new tourist attraction? Crikey. He was a lot closer to eighty than he was to eighteen, after all. The walled garden itself would never be the same again either — everything would have to be levelled — and I knew I was proposing a degree of disruption that most men of his age would run a mile to avoid. But as I began to speak, Dad looked thoughtful and receptive.

'Hm. That's an interesting idea,' he said after I'd rattled through the continents, plants and plant-hunters I wanted to feature. He only seemed to hesitate when I mentioned the landscaping of mountain ranges and that I eventually wanted to display at least 10,000 species of plant.

'Sounds . . . *expensive?*' he ventured.

'But I'm going to do it all really slowly, Dad,' I reassured him. 'I'm going to fund it bit by bit. Through plant sales, naturally . . . and through continuing to work as a tree surgeon.'

The fact that I hadn't asked him for any money — the thought really hadn't crossed my mind — helped keep the whole subject safe and low-key. I told Mum and Dad that, working alone, I reckoned it would take me five years to get the garden cleared, landscaped and planted to a basic level; ten years for it to be really chlorophyll-packed.

'Well . . . good luck to you,' he said, possibly unable to object because I had made no attempt on his wallet. 'Let's see how it goes.'

Phew! Dad had taken me seriously and the seed of my idea was free to germinate. All I now had to do was make my garden grow.

# 6

## Money Doesn't Grow on Trees

As a former part-time tree surgeon, I can tell you categorically that money doesn't grow on trees. At the end of 2002 my finances were so dodgy that if I had stopped to think properly about what the World Garden would cost, I would probably have packed it in there and then.

Instead, because the air is so much sweeter and the atmosphere so much more positive here on Planet Tom, I decided to look on the bright side. Yes, my finances were completely dire and nowhere near good enough to launch any kind of gardening project, but, boy oh boy, they were a lot better than they had been the year before.

In 2001, as I had tried to get used to the sensation of no longer being watched by men with guns every time I went to the loo, Mum and Dad had fed me and let me move back into my old childhood bedroom while I readjusted to normality and sweated out the worst of my experiences. This was an odd situation for a twenty-five-year-old man who thought himself pretty independent. After all, I had been away from home for more than three years and had survived nine months as a hostage under sentence of death. Yet here I was back with mummy and daddy and I couldn't even afford to go to the local chip shop.

Apart from late Great-Uncle Boyd paying my school fees from beyond the grave, there's never been a Secret Trust Fund for Tom. Dad's never given me an allowance, not a pound even, and that's always been fine with me. He couldn't afford it; I didn't expect it; and in any case I was grateful to have had so much from Mum and Dad in other ways. When it came to cash, therefore, I learnt early on that I just had to get on and earn my own. But in the first months of my freedom, I was in no state to work nine to five and I did need some pocket money.

I reckon my feeding and watering needs are very modest. Take me to the pub and I'll drink tap water — or lemonade if you twist my arm — and I don't smoke. (Well, not unless I have a loaded AK-47 pointed at my head: I actually smoked 100 cigarettes during my nine months as a prisoner, which was a lot for a non-smoker!) I certainly never buy smart clothes; and I go to a restaurant about once every six months. But after my return I did want to be able to catch up with friends, few of whom live locally, and I needed to be able to get to see the ones who couldn't come to see me. I considered signing on the dole, but instead went foraging in the garage. There, under a pile of dusty old crap, were the chainsaw and climbing gear I had packed away in 1997.

It was by working as a tree surgeon that I had saved up enough to set off on my travels in the first place, so I decided I would see if the chainsaw was still working — and start all over again. Given that I was back sleeping in my childhood bedroom across the landing from Anya's old room, the illusion that my life was going backwards in some sense was now quite vivid.

Still, at least I no longer had to cycle round the lanes of Kent with the chainsaw on my back. Granny offered to lend me her Corsa on condition I kept it spotless and didn't use it to cart tree chippings around, and my wages were now up from £5 to between £8 and £10 an hour.

I was extremely grateful for any work I could get in that first year of freedom; but I still had to fit it in around serious sessions at my desk, belatedly writing up my notes for the Royal Horticultural Society at Wisley, the Merlin Trust and the Kent Gardens Trust, all of whom had given me research grants. Apart from that, I also had to deal with fridges full of the seeds I'd sent back; and so by the end of 2001 I realized I had managed to earn almost precisely zilch.

My domestic arrangements received a definite boost, though, in the summer of that year when I felt ready to 'leave home' once more and I moved into the south tower of the gatehouse, which Mum had fixed up for me. With her old tearoom tables flat-packed in the cellar, the tower consisted of two big rooms and a big kitchen, plus some battlements you can climb up to via a ladder if you want to fly the flag or pour boiling chip fat on invaders.

It was the first place I could really call my own; it meant I was now Granny's official next-door neighbour, she being in the north tower on the other side of the arch; and it really was the business. I didn't even mind that I couldn't afford to furnish it; nor that I had to share it with the cigar-smoking spectre of one Lieutenant-Colonel G. W. Meates, rtd.

So far as anyone in the family can tell, Colonel Meates is the only person to have lived properly in the south tower since it was built back in the year dot. During the Second World War, while nearby Biggin Hill and Dartford were bombed senseless, the army were all over the estate training and planning and in and out of the gatehouse too. But before my arrival, the colonel was its only full-time inhabitant. He died in 1985 and his mortal remains were found in the sitting room, sitting exactly where my sofa is today. He died alone and had been there for some time, Mum says. Though I've never seen the colonel's ghost myself, so many people claim to have experienced him that I don't think Colonel Meates has properly left the building yet.

People apparently encounter him in stages. Stage one is the Fried Breakfast Stage when, even though I may be on melon and a can of ginger beer, they catch the strong smell of burnt bacon and sausage coming from my bedroom, which is where his kitchen used to be. There's been no cooked breakfast in my bedroom for years, so how or from where the smell emerges I don't know, but some friends have experienced it strongly and been seriously freaked by it.

The next stage is down to the late colonel's smoking habits. Out of the blue people claim suddenly to get a very strong whiff of cigar smoke, usually in the sitting room where he died. At the next stage, apparently, the old boy 'manifests' himself in person. Some friends, like poor Graham and Roger, have chosen to sleep outside in their cars in winter rather than kip down on the floor and brave an encounter with the colonel or with any of the other ghosts who appear in various corners of the house and grounds from time to time.

Me? I'm not really bothered. Though I've definitely picked up some strong smells of this and that, like Dad I'm not susceptible to ghosts. Mum, on the other hand, is very sensitive and knows all about Colonel Meates.

I didn't know the bachelor colonel well when he was alive in this world (he's now in the churchyard), but even as a child I could sense that he wasn't exactly Mr Happy. Mum feels there was something distinctly Mr Unhappy about him and that this is perhaps why his spirit hasn't yet departed.

To be honest, I'm far more intrigued by the extraordinary thing that happened to Mum one night when I was still a prisoner in the Darién. Dad was away, the house was empty and Mum was in bed when the door of her bedroom suddenly flew open. Quite literally, she says, a wind blew in. This wasn't the ordinary wind you might expect in a draughty old house, but a blast of really warm, scented tropical air. Though it was freezing in her room, Mum soon found she was almost sweating.

'It really wasn't a dream, Tom. I was

absolutely wide awake when it happened,' she insists.

We worked out that this event must have occurred in late October at a crucial time for Paul and me: before we were released, but after the guerrillas had obviously decided, or been given orders from on high, that we were not to be executed after all. Mum was convinced the gust of tropical wind was a sign that I was coming home, though she is far too level-headed ever to begin to try to explain who or what sent it. In any event, I suppose you could say it was prophetic, and it certainly reassured Mum.

Though Paul and I have ruminated endlessly on why we were suddenly released, our best theory is that in the end the guerrillas simply couldn't find a justification for executing us. Though a couple of them, the evil Bitch and her ugly boyfriend Goofy, clearly wanted any excuse to kill us, we had spent so long with the group, and they had spent so long observing us so closely, that we believe they simply decided that we were what we said we were: an idiot orchid-hunter and a mountaineer. Oddly enough, Mum had a repeat performance of the door incident in early December — as it turned out, the same day we were released.

Ghost or no ghost, by the beginning of 2002, as I was settling in to my new life with my invisible lodger, my finances got a small boost when a TV company was mad enough to offer to take me orchid-hunting again, only this time in Papua New Guinea. The horticultural aim was to find a new species of orchid to name after my hugely influential Granny Crac — and my other aim was to avoid being captured by any unsavoury types I might bump into. Having failed on the first count but managed the second, the modest presenter's fee I pocketed was very handy.

It was also at around this time that I stumbled on another means of supplementing my meagre tree-surgery earnings. Despite having a faint stammer that kicks in at odd moments, when the words seem to crowd together on my tongue, I found I was beginning to be in demand as a public speaker.

My first gig, unpaid, was talking to the Kent Gardens Trust, which had been kind enough to give £600 towards my researches in Tasmania and then patient enough to wait ages for me to report back. It was arranged that members of the Trust would come to Lullingstone and I would speak inside the church of St Botolph, the patron saint of the traveller.

This was a very new experience for me, but at least I was on familiar ground, surrounded in the tiny Norman church by the shrines of several ancestors and the incredibly ancient stained-glass windows that I had grown up with. I was a little nervous, I admit; and I knew that given my special organizational skills there was little point in trying to write a proper speech and read it out. I would probably either lose my place or start to gabble. So I just had a quiet think about what I wanted to say and went for it.

The church was packed with expectant faces, most of them at least thirty years older than mine; and, amazingly, no one walked out. People who shared my passion for plants seemed genuinely interested in what I had seen and what I had to say about the potentially hardy, woody plants of upland Tasmania; but nearly everyone seemed even more intrigued by my later adventures and I was asked dozens and dozens of questions.

Afterwards we walked across the lawn and went over to the house for supper. I rather enjoyed myself — it was a very jolly evening and not uncomfortable at all, and it gave me the confidence to say 'yes' when other local groups started inviting me to speak to them. I rapidly became a regular on the WI village hall lecture circuit and I even decided to invest in a projector.

I would show my planty slides and then churn stomachs with various travellers' tales — including how, on my sponsored expedition to Siberut, in the Mentawai Islands off Sumatra in Indonesia, I was once obliged to eat a still warm-blooded, fully furred raw rat. Starvation had nothing to do with it. It was simply to avoid offending my two guides, who had just caught the rat by hand and offered it to me as a delicacy. Without them to guide me through the rainforest, there would have been no orchid-hunting. So I ate, or tried to eat, what I was given, to my hosts' hysterical delight.

My guides, to whom I had given $125, were certainly quite a pair: two bare-footed brothers, aged six and nine, the younger of whom was already on cigars. Nor was there anything innocent about the way the older boy despatched our snack using pliers and a knife. With the rat still wriggling, quick as a flash he pulled out its teeth. Having yanked off the claws, he soon had it chopped into three, a piece for each of us.

'Tom! Tom! Tastes like marzipan,' they chorused, grinning from ear to ear.

No, actually, it didn't taste like marzipan at all. It tasted like still warm-blooded, fully furred rat, which was precisely what it was, and I was soon gagging and choking as the fur got stuck in my throat and the boys plied me with water to help me get it down. Needless to say, I then had dysentery for about six solid weeks. Or not solid weeks.

'Enjoy the tea and biscuits afterwards,' I always tell my now retching WI audience.

The great thing about speaking in public is that I *love* talking about plants. In fact, sometimes it's hard to stop me talking about plants. But there was another lure. Some of the talks now started to pay actual money. Admittedly £30 a pop wasn't a fortune; and as the fee also had to cover my preparation time and petrol, tax exile was not an immediate issue. But after my first really big paid talk — nearly £100 from the Sheffield Orchid Society — I remember thinking 'Yesssssssss!'

With my focus increasingly now on the World Garden, I reckoned that if I could only give five such talks a day, every day for a year, I could hire people with diggers and lifters and get the garden built in no time. As it was, working alone, the Green Man was going to have to talk to an awful lot more WI groups and orchid societies, and generate a heck of a lot of plant sales, to get the garden, excuse the pun, off the ground.

But with Dad's nod of approval, as 2003 marched on my days and nights were at least busy and I felt I was moving in the right direction. During the day I would be outside restoring my derelict greenhouse or tending my gum trees in what I hoped would one day become a eucalyptus collection of national importance. By night, if I wasn't writing up my Darién experiences in *The Cloud Garden*, I was out on the road talking to rooms full of elderly ladies.

At first it was a strange sensation trying to talk with authority about woody plants and orchids to gardeners who, to judge by their weathered hands and faces, had many, many more years' experience and knowledge than I had. I was still only in my twenties, after all. But then I did have one enormous advantage over all of them. Ever since I was three I had been taught by the most brilliant gardener of all: my grandmother Crac.

Not only is Granny an incredible teacher, but, as I have said, she is also the person I am closest to on this earth. As it happens, she was also the person whose horticultural handiwork had so inspired me in the walled garden I was now intending to turn back into a blank canvas. For all of my life the garden had really been her domain and I felt far more nervous at the thought of telling her of my plans than I had when approaching Dad. I felt I needed her permission to proceed and I wasn't really looking forward to asking for it.

# 7

## Sap Rising

It's no exaggeration to say that Granny is the most influential person in my life. Mum isn't jealous of our relationship — far from it: she's always encouraged it. But my friends, especially those who have never met their own grandparents, can find it hard to fathom.

To me, of course, it feels entirely natural. Nevertheless, I realize how lucky I've been to see Crac virtually every day that I've been at Lullingstone, and how unusual the bond between us is. Despite the age gap — at the time of writing I've just had my thirtieth birthday, while she's already into her tenth decade! — we're more like best mates or pals than grandmother and grandson.

For example, when it comes to serious girlfriends — not a frequent topic of conversation for me, I admit — I'm still more likely to pop round to Gran's to discuss what to do about so-and-so than I am to go to the house and talk to Mum or Dad. Gran is so on the ball she should charge for her advice. Even if I don't always follow it to the letter, I always listen. She's still very wise and totally switched-on about relationships, which is pretty cool when you consider that she did her courting in the early 1930s and in 1935 married a naval officer who later became a country rector.

To outsiders Granny must appear very quiet and shy. She's certainly very independent and comfortable in her own company, and this last trait is definitely one I've inherited from her bit of the gene pool. We also share a single-mindedness, a kind of horticultural tunnel vision, if you like, that kicks in whenever we're near plants or out in the garden. The garden is where we belong, and it is where our relationship took off one Wednesday afternoon — I'm told it was a Wednesday, anyway — when I was three years old.

Back then Crac was still living at Lavenham in Suffolk. Though already well into her sixties, she would drive down to Lullingstone every morning, leaving home at 5am and putting in a full day's hard graft in the garden before driving all the way back again. Extraordinary? Perhaps; but then she is descended from a line of strong-willed adventurers.

In the late 1970s Granny took it upon herself to renovate the walled herb garden, which had been derelict for twenty years. A right jungle it was too. Single-handedly she had to dig out and burn all the old tree roots, stumps and all. I was awed by her feats of strength, often breaking off from playing with my soldiers and cars in the mud to gaze at her heaving some massive bit of nonsense around and then giving it what-for with her pickaxe. Then one afternoon she produced a small packet of carrot seeds and my life hasn't been the same since.

'I think it's time you started your own garden,

Tom,' she said. 'Why don't you plant some seeds and see what happens?'

Though the edges of the memory are hazy, I can definitely still picture us together in the garden, digging over a square of earth measuring 4 feet by 4 feet, a little away from Dad's vegetable patch. After digging it over together (with Gran helping massively of course), she handed me the packet of seeds.

'Now then, Tom, you've got to divide them into three.'

I tried as best as my little fingers would allow, and with her help planted three equal rows of seed, which I then covered with topsoil. After that, there was nothing to do but wait. And water. And wait some more.

The lack of instant results probably explains why vegetable-growing isn't a top activity for the average three-year-old. But for some reason I didn't forget about the carrots or lose interest in what the seeds might do. I was gripped in fact; and I liked the thought of being a proper gardener like my granny and my dad. For days I checked the soil for signs of life. When the first specks of green finally did poke through, it was as if I'd just seen a garden elf.

'Gran!' I screamed. '*Carrots!*'

At that age, the appearance of the minuscule green shoots seemed to be an act of pure magic. I had created life, or something like that, and I was really, really excited. I'm not embarrassed to admit I still feel that same rush of childish glee today when I get something to germinate. I've moved on from carrots (with no nicely coloured flowers, they're actually very boring to grow: bang 'em in, cover 'em up, job done), but the thrill of germination has never left me.

Nowadays, of course, there's a lot more aggro involved with the sort of stuff I try to germinate. Some of my more temperamental, high-maintenance babes from extreme climates can be absolute so-and-sos. A lot of Australian seeds, for example, need two or three sessions of frost, then baking weather, to kickstart the process; and I might have to ferry seeds back and forth between freezer and fridge a few times to con them into thinking they've lived through a couple of harsh southern hemisphere winters, before whacking them over the head with a burst of really hot greenhouse. Trying to trick seeds into germination like this — or 'stratifying' them — is great fun and hugely rewarding. It is when it works anyway.

Other seeds might respond only on sphagnum moss doused with rainwater. And some even need the chemicals in smoke to tickle their fancy, replicating the regeneration that occurs in the wild following a bush fire. Lighting bonfires in the greenhouse always gets everyone worried sick when the smoke starts billowing out, but sometimes it's the only way I can get a seed to germinate, particularly some South African varieties. Smoke treatment pads work well, of course, and are a lot easier on the eyes, throat and lungs, but they're not nearly so much fun.

Trying to put into practice things I've seen in the wild makes my approach to germination fairly experimental and maverick, but there is far more to it for me than intellectual curiosity. I still find there is something magical — mystical even — when a seed decides it's ready to live large and all that amazing potential bursts forth. It's a killer moment; and given that it all comes from a piece of matter that can be so tiny and dust-like and apparently inert, seeing it happen still blows the wind up my skirt.

But there are other thrills associated with being a horticultural midwife or Dr Frankenstein. Collecting seeds from a plant that has interesting features — bark or leaves or flower-bud shape, say — and then waiting to see if these translate into the individual progeny you have coaxed into the world is also a blast.

I realize this must make me sound like the Compleat Gardening Anorak, but when you have the germination bug like Gran and I have, gardening makes you feel a connection to the planet and the life that springs from it that is way beyond words. I can't even begin to thank Gran for revealing this to me. Her simple act of introducing me to the joys of gardening was a gift that didn't so much change my life as determine its course entirely. So Gran and her carrot seeds have a great deal to answer for.

In 1980, when I was four, she came to live with us permanently at Lullingstone, moving in to the gatehouse next door to Colonel Meates of fried-breakfast fame. She had been a widow since 1971 and must have been happy to be so close to us. Anya and I were certainly delighted to have Gran as a permanent fixture in our childhood. Selfishly, it meant my gardening adventures just got better and better.

My little square bed was soon bursting with cast-offs from Gran's main borders: herbs, Chasta daisies, dainty blue *Veronica gentianoides*, roses and peonies. I had some nice flowers, plus the carrots of course; and there was always a bit of lettuce and radish too. I remember how hot and mouth-wateringly fiery the radish tasted straight from the ground.

Seeing that my interest in gardening wasn't a passing phase and that I was keen to spend every moment I could outside, Mum and Dad let me expand. By the time I was going to primary school, I had access to the border by the south wall as well. At that age I also loved having little bonfires, and the hours of daylight between school and bed were basically spent either digging, planting, hoeing, weeding, watering or burning. The toy soldiers I used to play with while watching Gran work were more or less abandoned, though sometimes I might bury one and stick a plant on top. We're still digging them up today.

Gran always had a huge selection of corking plants on the go, and there was always masses for us to talk about and masses to do when I came home from school and ran out to see her. If we weren't tending our plants outside, she and I would be inside her cosy sitting room on the second floor of her tower chatting about plants. With its old grandfather clock and wind-up songbird by the window, I loved scoffing tea and Crac's legendary cream cakes in her neat and tidy den. She'd serve me chocolate muffins and sponge cake, and while she sipped her tea I would gulp down glasses of cold ginger beer or milk. Everything in Gran's sitting room was always so well organized. Letters waiting to be posted were always laid out on her desk, just so; and when I grew taller she even stuck a bit of pillow on the wooden beam for when I bumped my head.

We would talk about plants and plan what we would do in the garden the next day, and our intense conversations were only ever interrupted by *Newsround* or, on Fridays at 8.30pm, *Gardener's World*. The gardener Geoff Hamilton was an immense figure for both of us and Gran often took notes of what he said. But neither of us was too shy to say when we felt he was wrong about something.

Even today Granny and I can still chat for hours when we meet in the garden. Obviously I had told her about my Darién experiences, but she and I had never really discussed how she felt when I was missing, presumed dead. Mum says Granny was very positive for the first few months, but towards the end, when the official line from the Foreign Office and from Colombia and Panama was that Paul and I were now 'permanently disappeared', Gran's optimism, like Dad's and Anya's, began to drain away as she tried to accept the inevitable. When eventually I flip-flopped across the lawn towards her as dusk fell that midwinter day and she stood illuminated in the doorway of the gatehouse, I thought we would hug each other to death. We didn't need to say very much at all. We just basked in our happiness and relief.

When I went to see her early in 2003 to show her my plans for the World Garden, however, I was expecting a bit more of a discussion. What I wanted to propose was, for me, a big deal. Gran had worked so hard for so many years to resurrect and revitalize this area of garden on the estate, I imagined she would be sad when I told her that the herb garden she had tended so lovingly for nearly two decades would have to be cleared. But she didn't bat an eyelid.

'Oh, Tom! This looks really exciting,' she said, peering at my sketches and planting plans.

This was really great news — and not just for me. I was happy that Granny wasn't upset; but she, then in her eighty-ninth year, was also quietly relieved, I think, that I was making it easy for her to withdraw gracefully from a responsibility that was now too much for her. So the conversation I had been dreading actually turned into a really cool chat about gardening . . . before branching off into an amazing *Boys' Own* tale about the exploration of Lake Chad, of all places.

Yes, Gran thought the World Garden was a great idea from a horticultural point of view. But as I ran through it with her, I could see her becoming more and more enthused by my stories of the Victorian and Edwardian plant-hunters whose exploits I wanted to celebrate.

'Oh, Tom. Would you like me to draw them for you?' she offered excitedly.

I jumped at this suggestion. Gran was a very

gifted botanical artist as a young woman, and her skill with pen and ink had never left her. Her delicate drawings of George Forrest, David Douglas, William Lobb and the others would look great on the signs I would put up for visitors.

Gran, I discovered to my surprise, felt an almost personal connection and empathy with these derring-do nutters from a bygone era. But it had nothing (or very little) to do with nostalgia or with the glorious green cargo they brought back to Britain. It was because these men's curiosity, bravery and adventurous spirit reminded her so strongly of two of her own uncles, Boyd and Claud Alexander, both of whom perished while adventuring a long way from home.

'Look,' she said, rifling along her bookshelf and pulling out a couple of old volumes. 'Have you seen these?'

Gran handed me a work called *From the Niger to the Nile*, written by my great-great-uncle Boyd. He was the balding ornithologist whom I could probably thank, genetically speaking, for my own prematurely receding hairline, and about whom I had heard many snippets down the years. I knew he had brought back stuffed birds galore to his place in Cranbrook, and that he had built his own boat in which to cross Lake Chad. I had even seen his portrait at the Royal Geographical Society. But I had to confess that, along with a lot of other books, I still hadn't read *From the Niger to the Nile*.

'Oh, you must one day. It's just up your street.'

Published in 1907, these dusty volumes told the story of the epic west-to-east expedition my great-great-uncle led across the heart of Africa to survey the area around Lake Chad, before pressing further east and trying to find a water route to the Nile.

'He wasn't a plant-hunter, more of a bird man,' said Gran matter-of-factly. 'But he was certainly an adventurer.'

The more Gran told me about her uncle's exploits, the quieter I became. I began to feel humbled and more than a little foolish. Hearing how Boyd's party had yomped and canoed into relatively uncharted territory in a spirit of pure exploration, I couldn't help but recall my own silliness and selfishness, blundering blindly into the Darién so I could look at a few flowers. However, we did have something in common: I wasn't the only family member to have run into trouble on foreign shores. Boyd's misadventures, moreover, were easily a match for the daring exploits of any of my plant-hunter heroes.

A captain in the Rifle Brigade, Boyd had set out in February 1904 with his brother Claud, a long-time travelling companion from the Cape Verde islands called José Lopes, a Captain G. B. Gosling and a certain Mr P. A. Talbot. Their starting point was the Niger delta and the plan was to cross the heart of the continent to survey the marsh area around Lake Chad, mapping and noting as they went. At the time it was described as one of the last great journeys of African exploration.

By October, however, Claud had contracted enteric fever and died. Despite losing his brother, Boyd pressed on with Lopes, Gosling and Talbot, and the four did sterling work unlocking some of the final mysteries of what had once been Africa's mighty inland sea. From Lake Chad, Talbot returned to England, but the others continued eastwards. Gosling was the next to fall ill. He contracted blackwater fever and died in 1906, leaving Boyd and Lopes to take the Kibali River and try to find a water route to the Nile.

They did precisely that and made it back to England in one piece, where Boyd wrote and published his book. But he had itchy feet, and with Lopes he sailed back to Africa again in 1909, at least partly in order to visit the grave of his brother Claud.

'But he didn't find it in the way he intended,' said Gran, who by now had me hanging on her every word.

This time it was Boyd's luck that ran out. He got caught up with some local troubles and was murdered in a ruck at Nyeri. According to Gran, French soldiers then retrieved his body and carried it to the British military headquarters at Fort Maifoni, where Boyd was eventually buried next to his brother Claud.

'Of course your mother and father visited the graves,' said Gran, explaining how Mum and Dad had made the trip when they were in Nigeria.

I gulped silently and felt a small shadow passing over me. Granny's tale had touched a nerve. How would Mum and Dad have been able to visit or even find *my* grave if things had turned out differently in the Darién? Once more I felt a flash of shame at the anguish I had caused my family and the aggravation I had caused the authorities. It was time Tom made amends and proved that he wasn't a reckless twit after all.

# 8

## The Craic with Crac

I didn't want Granny to feel banished from her old kingdom, but taking over responsibility for the walled garden from her meant she had one less thing to worry about. It still left her the 100-yard border that runs outside the garden down to the orangery, and I'm delighted to say she is still fit enough to work there to this day.

Her current patch faces east and gets a fair amount of sun until about 1pm. It can be pretty windy too; but despite the buffeting you'll still see her purple mountain bike propped up there most days, Gran's tiny frame neatly scarfed and hatted, rubber duck boots on her feet. She still wields the hoe or even a pickaxe on occasion, and given her age she's got to be crackers. But that's not why I've always called her 'Crac'.

The name comes from 'crac-oo', which is the funny noise members of my family make to one another in the house and grounds at Lullingstone. We've done it since I was a child, and visitors often find it a bit odd. But we do it for two reasons. One: we probably are a bit odd. Two: distance. A high-pitched sound really will travel through a big house, up the stairs and along the corridors to announce one's arrival, and it can also battle its way across a windy garden and allow us to communicate without having to bellow or blow whistles at one another.

Over the years Crac and I have developed some sophisticated variations on the basic 'crac-oo' noise. By subtly changing pitch and lengthening the note we can make it mean very different things — like 'Come here', 'See you later', 'What time's *Gardeners' Question Time?*' or the more frequent 'Have you seen my trowel? I think I left it over by the Himalayas.'

Well, perhaps it's not *that* sophisticated. But if Gran can't see me because one of us is behind a wall or shrub, it's still very handy. 'O-o-o-o-o-o' means 'I'm over here.' If we want to say 'See you later', it's a much more sorrowful, drawn out 'O-o-o-o-o-o-o-o-o-o-o-o', akin to the howling of a wolf. Newcomers who spend any time with us often end up trying to join in, but they usually get it wrong and think 'crac-oo' is really 'cuckoo'. Which maybe it is. But it works for us.

Though Crac is my mother's mother, Granny is herself a Hart Dyke by marriage. This is because, as Mary Alexander, she decided to park her matrimonial wheel-barrow alongside that of a sailor-turned-rector, Eric Hart Dyke, who was a distant cousin of Dad's dad, Oliver. That means that their daughter Sarah — i.e. Mum — is also a distant cousin of Dad's, and that when they married in 1974 a Hart Dyke married another Hart Dyke. Apparently Mum's great-great-grandfather was the younger brother of the baronet who was Dad's great-grandfather twice removed. Or something like that. What I know for sure is that Mum and Dad had never heard of each other as children, let alone met, and Dad first spied his fiancée-to-be in a framed photograph on top of Granny's piano at Lavenham when he was invited there for tea one afternoon.

'Who *is* this lovely lady?' Dad drooled in all innocence, Mum not being present at the time.

Mum and Dad had a blind date in 1972 at somewhere called the In and Out Club in Piccadilly. This sounds pretty dodgy for them, but the In and Out is in fact the nickname of the Naval and Military Club, which is all frightfully proper. When Dad was next home on leave from Nigeria, where he was working for the government forestry service, they had a formal date: lobster at Manzi's in Leicester Square and a Brian Rix farce.

'Very fitting,' says Dad drily, referring, I think, to the farce and all that has happened since.

Mum and Dad tell me I was 'made in Nigeria'. Nevertheless, I burst forth into the world here in April 1976, the year they reopened the house to the public. Given how hard they had to work shepherding visitors around, and that in the early days Dad had to keep scooting back to Africa to earn a living, it's not surprising I became so close to Granny, especially given our shared love of plants. For me and Anya, Gran was the best babysitter ever.

After the packet of seeds incident, her influence on me as a gardener grew stronger and stronger. It really is because of her, and the setting at Lullingstone, that my boyhood and adolescence revolved entirely around stuff that's green and grows in the ground.

Computer games? Hopeless. I just don't get them at all. Football, rugby and hockey? Not really that interested. I did once play rugby at school, but I made sure I ran so fast no one could catch me because I didn't want to be tackled. When I got into the hockey team, I had a habit of breaking my sticks: at least three ended up as matchwood because my co-ordination was on a par with my organizational skills.

Oddly, though, I did once score a spectacular goal in hockey entirely by accident. We were playing Hurstpierpoint School in West Sussex, I think, and I was standing idly in my own half when the ball came rolling towards me. Having nothing better to do, I took a massive backswing and walloped the life out of it in the general direction of the Hurst goal. By some miracle fluke, it rocketed a good 50 metres and smashed into the back of the Hurst net. No one was more surprised than I was.

I did also develop a genuine love for badminton, which I still play today (I'm actually not bad); but on the physical activity front as a kid I was most happy climbing trees or working in the garden with Granny.

Gran, who was entirely self-taught as a gardener, passed on to me an encyclopaedia of plant lore that she had assembled from personal experience. I just lapped it all up. When it came to horticultural matters, my brain was like a thirsty sponge. I suppose it still is. I seem to be able to absorb any amount of greenery that's thrown at me.

Granny's influence can also be seen in the

types of plants that have excited me over the years. Gum trees, for example. In her herb garden, Gran had two *Eucalyptus gunnii*, or Cider Gums, and I was always very drawn to them. They are the commonest variety, but very interesting none the less.

'Aborigines ferment the sap to make cider,' Granny told me.

The idea of drinking the contents of a tree seemed intriguingly wacky when I was small, and though Gran and I never actually fermented any sap, it was directly thanks to her and her Cider Gums that I started to develop my own passion for eucalyptus trees, with their shiny-glittery leaves, weird peeling bark and the tendency of some of them to grow so fast it's like a horticultural explosion of blue, green and silver.

My interest took some years to blossom fully, if you'll pardon the expression, but it became a really absorbing hobby when I was at college and, later, when doing research for the RHS and Kent Gardens Trust in Tasmania. But orchids? They got under my skin from the start.

I spotted my first at the age of seven when going to St Michael's School in Otford, just down the road near Sevenoaks. My time there was a disaster as far as school-work was concerned, but seeing Bee Orchids, along with Common Spotted Orchids, Pyramidal Orchids, Common Twayblades and Man Orchids was a major epiphany. I was bitten by the orchid bug and bitten bad. Happily, I was able to infect my hide-and-seek chum Jerry with some of my enthusiasm, and he would join me on clandestine orchid-hunting sorties through the undergrowth in the school grounds.

These were quite an adventure, for most of the orchids at St Michael's were to be found on a patch of chalk down-land called The Warren which the headmaster, Mr Cox, had firmly decreed to be out of bounds. On hands and knees, and keeping our heads as low as possible, Jerry and I would slip away from the main buildings at break and crawl SAS-style through the tall grass. I was determined to show him the Bee Orchid's amazing ability to mimic randy female bees by looking and smelling like their insect counterparts. I think Jerry enjoyed himself, but we were both regularly stung so badly by The Warren's red ants that Jerry's orchidaceous interests never really recovered.

Between the ages of eight and thirteen I was also seriously into counting orchids. Not only that, but I would fill entire notebooks — dozens of them, in fact — with endless observations about where I had seen them and what I had noticed about them. An obsession? Quite possibly, though I still prefer the term 'passionate interest'. I would also read voraciously about orchids.

Today, of course, I can see that counting flowers obsessively from the age of eight onwards was pretty weird, or a little unusual anyway. No-one I know did the same thing at that age (nor at any age for that matter), but I felt I was on a mission. Bluntly, it was to count these glistening jewels wherever I could get to them on foot during the school holidays.

Crossing busy trunk roads like the A225, which sprints through the woods behind the house, then wandering alone along the verge, wasn't very usual for a boy of eight either, but Mum and Dad just let me get on with it. They were extremely cool about my orchid-inspired disappearances and I imagine their conversation went a bit like this.

'Er . . . where's Tom today?' Dad might ask nonchalantly after breakfast, having tripped over a trowel or fork I'd left lying around.

'Oh, he's out. He's taken his notebook,' Mum would reply.

'Ah. So he'll be back tonight, then?'

'I expect so.'

Armed with my notepad, clipboard and pencil, I would walk along the roadsides marking down 'Xs' to represent individual flowers in the magnificent colonies of Man Orchids. I knew roughly where to find them because I'd already done an initial recce passing in the car with my parents. Though Anya and I would often play in the garden together, I would be lying if I said she shared my passion for orchids or even plants in general. She was always supportive, but never what you would call horticulturally endowed and she never joined me on my jaunts along the busy A225.

However, thanks to her incredibly sweet nature as a child, when I was ten I managed to rope her in for a mega-counting expedition I was planning up on Lullingstone Park golf course. The course lies to the west of the estate and I was in thrall to the glorious purple-pink haze of Pyramidal Orchids I could see up there, not to mention the Bee Orchids and the main event: Lizard Orchids, which to me smell like a packet of Refreshers from the newsagent's, though others insist they smell more like goat hair.

For me, this was a serious expedition and I got little sis to help me unravel masses and masses of string to mark out a huge triangular slice of meadow. It must have covered 3 acres in all, and my aim was to note what orchids were in the ground and to say whether they were growing singly or in clumps. I also wanted to measure the biggest ones and note the flowers with the darkest colours. Using yet more string to lay out smaller grids within the big one so I didn't wander back on myself and count the same flowers twice, I then walked up and down exceedingly slowly, counting and noting as I went.

Poor Bristles was dumbfounded. She stayed the course for about a day and a half before becoming more or less catatonic with the sheer tedium of my endeavour.

'Tom! I've *got* to go home! This is *so* boring!'

I had taken my sister over the horticultural edge . . . and she never wanted to see another orchid as long as she lived.

What's wonderful about Anya is that even as a little girl she was always thinking of others before she thought of herself. This trait has come to the fore as an adult in her jobs with various charities and now in her work for the UN in Serbia. In a fit of my own generosity, I once tried to show her how much I appreciated her. I wasn't, alas, successful.

It was for one of her teenage birthdays — I can't remember which one — and I decided to buy her a present that I was sure would blow her socks off. We were in the house when I told her that I had something for her, and her eyes lit up with surprise and joy. Anya was slightly nonplussed, however, when I then led her outside and round to the back ditch behind the house, home of my developing arboretum. Her face then fell when she realized that Tom's present wasn't going to be something that was wrapped in coloured paper and tied with a ribbon.

Then, when I showed her my gift with a flourish, the poor girl's jaw hit the ground.

'It's a *Eucalyptus nicholii*,' I beamed, pointing to the Willow-leaved Peppermint Gum I had planted and labelled in her honour. It had come from a nursery near Sevenoaks and was, as far as I was concerned, ecstatically exciting. How couldn't she be blown away?

'Um. Great. Thanks, Tom,' she said.

'It's from the tablelands of mainland Australia!' I enthused.

'Really.'

'Yes! And it can put on four feet of growth in a single season!'

'That's nice.'

This was the last time I ever gave my sister a plant for her birthday.

I couldn't really understand Anya's lack of interest that day, nor the crippling boredom that led her to abandon me on the golf course. Not being the slightest bit bored myself, I simply kept walking slowly and counting orchids for another week.

Looking back, I'm not sure *why* I did it — I certainly didn't tell anyone about it — but I did love keeping records, which, as you can guess, I still have in my bedroom somewhere. Who knows: in twenty years' time, when someone wants to know the precise number of fragrant orchids that were growing in a 3-acre patch of north-west Kent in the summer of 1986, my research might be extremely valuable. Or not.

The first cultivated tropical orchid I was given came from Wisley and was a present from Granny. It was a super-gracious hybrid Slipper Orchid, or *Paphiopedilum*. She later fed my habit by taking me to orchid shows and flower shows across southern England. I loved these days out alone with Gran, even though I was always the youngest orchid lover at the show by several decades.

I also remember visiting the Hampton Court show aged thirteen or fourteen with the parents of a friend, though I can't now recall who that friend was. Despite the human-shaped blank, I know I was clutching my pocket money and desperate to buy my first *Odontoglossum cordatum*, a Colombian stunner, or even an *Encyclia cochleata*, the Cockleshell Orchid, a pulchritudinous Panamanian orchid. These beauties would have cost around £10 probably, which was a fortune to me then; but Granny or Mum had offered to treat me.

The one I really wanted was the *Odontoglossum*, with its spidery, coppery-red flowers, because I knew it would be relatively easy to grow. There was nothing very easy, however, about trying to buy it when you're thirteen years old and have difficulty pronouncing Latin and seeing over the stall. At first, the grown-up growers at flower shows wouldn't take me seriously. They either thought I was trying to be a smart alec or that I had been set up to ask about an exotic plant by my parents. However, as I began to ask searching questions about husbandry, they realized the weird kid was for real. Despite my pronunciation, they usually twigged what I wanted too.

As soon as I got home with my new prizes, I would run upstairs and add them to my collection. Unfortunately, my north-facing bedroom up on the top floor wasn't ideal for efficient orchid husbandry, but I made do as best I could. In front of my little bedroom window, I had managed to construct my own version of a greenhouse by pushing a couple of tables up close, behind which was a standing area with fan heaters beneath some plastic covers which were drawn up like curtains. So that my plants caught all the available light, as many of them as possible were dangling in pots on bits of wire that I had nailed to the wooden window frames and ceiling. It was while I was banging up another large black plastic pot of bark one day with a mallet (I couldn't find a hammer) that Dad heard the noise and came tearing up.

The scene of horticultural horror that met his

eyes left him dumbstruck. With my tables, plastic sheets and bits of wire, my bedroom looked like a shanty-town hovel. When Dad had recovered, he asked me what was in the big black plastic pot.

'Bark, Dad. For my orchids.'

I explained that I was trying to grow *Cymbidiums* and *Pleione formosana*, an orchid with funny little pseudo bulbs that produce a deliciously pink-and-white flower followed by a richly veined broad leaf. Not for the last time, Dad wasn't sure what to make of his son.

Generally I stuck to hybrid orchids in my bedroom because they were more tolerant of beginner-ish conditions in a room that was naturally dark. Not daring to leave the lights on during the day when I was at school in case I burnt the house down, I decided instead to keep them on at night when I went to bed. This made getting to sleep tricky, but I'm sure the orchids benefited.

To boost the intensity of the light, I hung up as much white material, like old sheets, and mirrors as I could scavenge from around the house. I also stuck reflective white polystyrene panels to the wooden bookshelves with UHU glue. Watering my plants and keeping the pots of bark moist was also a challenge. Although I tried to protect the floor with dustbin liners, there were plenty of leaks and spillages.

After the initial shock, Mum and Dad were extremely cool about the whole operation and didn't say a word . . . until the humidity I was managing to generate began to cause health and safety problems for the rest of the house. Normally, any humidity I managed to drum up was soon dispersed when I opened the door on to the landing, but the atmosphere in my bedroom was still sufficiently damp to rot all the wood in the ancient window frames. When one pane eventually fell out in its entirety, sending glass crashing down on to Mum and Dad's bathroom roof below, my patient parents decided that even they had had enough. It was time that (a) Tom had his own greenhouse and (b) that he went away to school.

# 9

## School Daze

Securing my first greenhouse at the age of thirteen was a doddle compared with finding a school that would take me after I failed every subject at Common Entrance. All I had to do to get the new greenhouse was to wait for the hurricane of 1987 to carry off the old one . . . and then wait another two years for Mum and Dad to get round to organizing a replacement. Given the carnage caused by my indoor orchid-growing, Dad was happy to see me and my orchids out of the house.

The new mini Crystal Palace, a brilliant birthday present, went up in the walled garden. It was 7 feet high by 8 feet wide, and about 15 or 16 feet long. To me it was Heaven on Earth. Or compacted earth and hardcore, anyway. While other thirteen-year-olds might have been dreaming about Madonna or Kylie Minogue, or about being in a band, the greenhouse was my playroom, nightclub and crib rolled into one.

Dad's onions and tools were also supposed to be stored in it. But it was soon overflowing with my own plants and planty paraphernalia; and as my orchid collection expanded exponentially, the only safe place for Dad's tools was outside. So, er, out they went.

As in my bedroom, I did all I could to create

the best growing conditions. I had two heaters and even a fan to keep the air circulating. The fan was especially important at night, I told Dad, because of all the bacteria that were on the prowl.

'Bacteria?' His eyebrows furrowed.

'Yup,' replied the thirteen-year-old me with total confidence.

'What bacteria?'

Granny may have kickstarted my interest in gardening, but I had now developed my own intense curiosity and a hunger to learn everything I possibly could about plants and horticulture. I had a growing reference library of books, catalogues, magazines and journals which I studied for hours, and I'd read about bacteria that went on the prowl at night in a magazine.

If only I had been able to tackle the Wars of the Roses, maths and geography with the same energy, I might have caused Mum and Dad far fewer headaches. But school-work never interested me. To be honest, I don't think I have the right sort of brain for it. I loathed, dreaded and blanked out all exams; I tuned out of nearly all lessons apart from biology (and even then there was never enough plant action); and I found most school textbooks quite literally impenetrable — especially in the growing season. If I revised, say, C. S. Lewis the night before an exam, by the time I sat down the next morning to take the test I would have forgotten not only the title of the book but what it was supposed to be about.

It was no surprise to any of us that after Common Entrance my final report from St Michael's read: 'Failed. Missing in orchid land.' Or words to that effect.

Crashing in every subject — and there were a couple I didn't even turn up for — didn't do my confidence much good at all. Worse, it made it nearly impossible for Mum and Dad to find a school that would take me. We went to Gordonstoun, where Dad had been, but they politely asked about my results and Mum and Dad had to say I didn't actually have any.

The interview at Stowe, in Buckinghamshire, was even more humiliating. To engage with the headmaster who was interviewing me, I asked if he had any Fly Orchids in the grounds. He looked at me as if I'd just arrived from some far-distant, plant-filled planet. Which I had.

'No,' he replied, sounding flummoxed.

Of course he was quite wrong about this. I'd recently read a fascinating article in one of the RHS magazines about the amazing Fly Orchids to be found in the grounds of Stowe school. My interviewer presumably didn't know about them or didn't want to waste his time showing them to me. I decided on the spot that I didn't want to go to Stowe even if they offered me a place — which they didn't.

Mum and Dad didn't stress about the rejections or pressurize me, but I did have a rotten feeling in the pit of my stomach when we drove down to Romsey in Hampshire to visit Stanbridge Earls, pretty much our last hope. The stream of rejections had made 1989 a lousy summer and I didn't want to blow this interview too.

Luckily, the flower gods were smiling on me that day. The headmaster, a Mr Moxon, turned out to be a brilliantly enlightened chap who knew all about my hopeless academic record and didn't bother to dig it all up again. Instead of probing me on maths and literature, he asked neat questions about how I might contribute to school life and what I might be able to do to help other pupils. Blimey — this was different. But it was his last question that swung the interview.

'So tell me, Tom . . . what are your hobbies?'

Hobbies? No one else had ever shown any interest in what I might enjoy doing with my life when I wasn't in the classroom. Needing no prompt, I hit Howard Moxon with the Full Orchid Monty. In contrast to previous headmasters Mr Moxon leapt out of his chair.

'Really?' he said, looking genuinely enthusiastic. 'Did you know we've got Common Spotted Orchids in the grounds here at Stanbridge?'

Wow! This was my kind of school.

'Would you like to see them?'

As Mr Moxon and I left his study, I could see Mum and Dad wondering what on earth their maniac son was going to do next. But the head and I really clicked. We went out into the grounds, to a marshy bit of land that was completely sodden underfoot, and we talked and talked. I fired Latin names at him and told him what conditions his Common Spotted Orchids needed. He was certainly impressed; but more importantly for me, he was interested. I then delivered my killer blow.

'Look, Mr Moxon! Look at this! And this!' I had spotted some early Marsh Orchids and Mr Moxon, a keen naturalist, knew I meant business. He looked at me and smiled. I was in.

Stanbridge Earls, I now realize, was geared towards helping kids with learning difficulties, some of them quite severe. But at the time I knew nothing about learning difficulties. Mum and Dad had never tried to label me as having dyslexia or dyspraxia or dyscalcula or whatever; at the age of thirteen, as far as I was concerned and as far as Mum and Dad were concerned, I was simply Tom who could reel off and spell Latin plant names with no problems at all, but who might then forget much more straightforward stuff in English.

I don't know whether you would call that dyslexia or eccentricity, but there is definitely something going on up top that sometimes makes it hard for me to concentrate. Though I have become much more focused and better organized as I've grown older, at thirteen I was really all over the place if you took me out of my natural habitat. Nevertheless, when it was time to go to Stanbridge in the autumn, I fitted in really well.

Having said that, I never really bonded deeply with many of the guys there. I was certainly seen as different. This was partly because I never felt the need to smoke cigarettes to be part of the gang, and partly because I never really gave any thought to girlfriends. Girlfriends? Why would I bother with Camilla when the school had a brilliant Camellia bed that was gagging to be dug and titivated?

I noticed the flower borders running alongside the school's swanky sports hall as soon as I arrived, and especially the border outside the weights room. These borders and their plants seemed to call to me in a way that the kids at Stanbridge didn't. So without asking permission, one lunchtime I simply got hold of a kitchen fork from the dining hall and began titivating. To me this felt the most natural thing in the world, though the head groundsman obviously thought I was completely bonkers. Was I on detention or something? No. I was bent double digging the school's Camellia bed with a fork from the dining hall because . . . I enjoyed digging!

My solo gardening in the school grounds helped establish my reputation as 'Tom Hart Dyke The Slightly Weird Flower Boy'. Being a gardener also meant I was regularly called 'gaylord', the usual silliness of thirteen-and fourteen-year-old boys. But I didn't give a hoot and, more importantly, I never felt that I was bullied or teased. If I was, it never upset me.

One day when I was working on the Camellias with my stolen kitchen fork, a stocky boy called Savage came sauntering past from the sports hall where he'd been playing something convention-ally boyish like squash. It was raining, I recall, but I was still happily forking away.

'Look at this,' I said to Savage, pointing to a small earthworm that was wriggling around in the mud.

Savage was deeply unimpressed.

'Fiver says you won't eat it,' he sneered.

Poor Savage! He had no idea how determined I can be when a £5 note is at stake. That little earthworm was down my throat faster than you could say 'Lumbicus terrestris'. I didn't chew it, I admit: I just swallowed it whole as fast as I could. But Savage was still gobsmacked, not to say grossed out.

'You're a freak, Hart Dyke! A freak!'

He took a while to pay up, but when he eventually did I used his fiver to buy a *Cymbidium* hybrid called Cooksbridge Pinkie for my collection. It had sweet pink flowers, not surprisingly. No, I've never eaten an earthworm since Stanbridge — although I did unknowingly consume dog when I was in south-western China. This was disturbing when I saw the empty cages afterwards and realized what I had eaten.

While I was away at school, back at Lullingstone Mum had inherited responsibility for my orchid collection and spent hours traipsing back and forth from the house to the garden in all weathers, faithfully feeding and watering and checking that the fans and heaters in the greenhouse were in working order. I was always in a hurry to get home from Stanbridge to see how they were doing. (And to see Mum, Dad, Bristles and Granny too, of course.)

Each year in the holidays, Granny would take Anya and me to stay in a little house she still had in Chagford on the edge of Dartmoor. We'd bomb down the motorway, Granny at the wheel with Polo mint in mouth, and spend a really nice week lapping up the landscape, with a few garden and nursery visits thrown in to keep me quiet.

Granny, who was well into her seventies by now, was still amazingly fast on her feet. I remember where the river burbles over the boulders in a steeply wooded valley near Castle Drogo, and Anya and I desperately trying to keep up with her as she leapt nimbly across from rock to rock.

No trip to Devon in early summer was complete without forays on to Dartmoor itself to hunt for Lesser Butterfly, Heath Spotted and the elusive, green and minute Bog Orchids. Because the moors were so rich in flora at that time of year, even Anya seemed to enjoy our orchid odyssey. Oblivious to the usually grey skies and drizzly Devon rain, Granny also let us run free across the moor, our hands reaching down to pluck cotton from the cottongrass that brushed our knees.

Back at Lullingstone Granny would also take me out on garden jaunts, just the two of us. Usually we'd visit places within a couple of hours' drive. Stuffing sandwiches and cartons of Ribena into the door pockets of her car, and with Gran's Polo mints on the dashboard, we'd set sail for Sissinghurst maybe, or go to the less formal Emmett's Gardens at Ide Hill, near Sevenoaks, with their stonking collection of exotic trees. Gran spent a lot of time *in loco parentis*, but she never had to tell me off. Sometimes she would politely suggest, though, that I might want to talk a little less or be a little less energetic. Whatever could she mean?

It was during my teenage years that I first began to become competitive as a gardener, and dear old Crac was responsible for this too. Possibly realizing that my own efforts were beginning to overtake hers in the garden, an element of rivalry developed. It wasn't sharpened pruning saws at dawn, just a bit of friendly competition as we both tried to grow hardy plants with exotic looks — the ginger relations, in particular *Roscoea*, being some of her favourites. Subtly we began trying to outdo one another. Aged fourteen or fifteen, the serious plantsman in me was beginning to emerge to spar with the more experienced, gifted plantswoman in Granny.

'Ah, Tom,' Gran would say with just the faintest note of triumph in her voice. 'You haven't got an *Arisarum proboscideum*, have you?'

'No, Gran, I haven't got a Mouse Plant . . . But I don't think you've got a *Platycodon grandiflorus* 'Mother of Pearl' Balloon Flower, have you?' Touché!

This was a great way to garden: very competitive and quite on the edge as we tried to best each other. Perhaps it gave me the taste for taking risks that I was going to test to the full with the humdingers I hoped to grow in the World Garden. When I was still in my teens, though, my competitive streak was most evident during a brief flirtation with giant pumpkins.

It was Gran again who steered me towards something called Dill's Atlantic Giant — a

94

positively nuclear variety — and I remember nearly snapping my back in two trying to get one particular monster into the back of the Corsa so we could take it to the autumn vegetable and flower show at Eynsford village hall. This brute was truly massive and we could only shift it on a trolley. I thought the produce table was going to splinter when we finally got it on display. Tragically, we didn't win or even get the thing weighed because the competition that year was for giant *marrows*. In fact I had known the contest was for marrows and had tried to persuade them on the phone to have a separate class for pumpkins, but to no avail.

Disappointed, we lugged the beast back home. It was so tough and woody there was no way we could have eaten it. Instead, I vented my frustration by using Dad's hacksaw to rip the top off and a huge machete-style kitchen knife to gouge out some eyes and evil jagged teeth for Hallowe'en. The Atlantic Giant loitered outside all autumn and winter, staring at us malevolently from the bench in the garden, refusing to rot. It only started to go soggy in the spring.

My fetish for growing giant veg was eventually rewarded with second prize for a marrow. The secret? Dig a whacking great offal pit about a metre deep and bury loads of chicken intestines underneath the plant. The only downside — apart from the foxes, which can smell offal a mile off — was having to go to the butchers in Eynsford and Farningham to collect bucket loads of the insides of things. Holding my nose, I amassed sacks full of revolting-smelling gunge from across the district, and once even got my hands on some trout innards from the fishermen at the lake.

Mixed with manure, this offal gave my veg the best possible start in life. The little plants would go in the ground once I was sure the frosts had finished; and presuming I hadn't been outfoxed by the foxes and my plants managed to produce some big yellow female flowers, I'd select one or two per plant, as close to the main root as possible, and then, once the fruit had developed, lay some straw carefully underneath them. The other trick was to bung some hosepipe under the plant at the roots and attach the free end to a Pepsi bottle or milk container filled with Demerara sugar and water. I figured that if I liked sugar, they might like it too. With this sugar solution continually pumping into the marrows, they grew and grew and grew and I produced some absolute whoppers. To pile on the pounds and get them as solid as concrete, I left them in the ground until the last minute before the show.

If I was ever away at a friend's for the night, Mum would gallantly fill the feeding bottles, though I never dared ask her to put out more lambs' intestines. I did myself once try powdered fish and bonemeal, but the foxes liked that even more. Digging and digging and digging but never being able to unearth anything solid drove them nuts, however.

Back at school, I was missing my orchids badly. So I decided to sign up to do the Duke of Edinburgh Award and, along with hiking and stamp collecting, made orchid husbandry one of my pet projects. This allowed me to bring my plants to school and commandeer Stanbridge's old greenhouse. It was perfect for me, but did nothing to lessen my reputation as The Boy Who Likes Flowers. It would have been more acceptably manly if I'd brought in a collection of flick-knives or been The Boy Who Likes JCBs. But I really *did* like flowers and I began to think that my interest and knowledge could eventually lead to a proper career. If so, I knew I would have to pass some exams.

No-one ever told me I was thick and I didn't particularly think I was. I just wasn't wired to do conventional academic schoolwork. There were some poor guys at school with much bigger issues than mine who sometimes didn't even seem to know what day it was. But passing an exam was not something I had ever managed before and it was going to be a challenge. Luckily, some of the determination I had shown in my plant-growing seemed to be spreading into other areas of my life and, aged sixteen, I decided I was fed up being Tom Hart Dyke The Flower Boy Who Always Fails.

With an amazing surge of concentrated ambition, I decided not only to turn up and sit nine GCSEs, but I decided I was going to pass them too — even subjects like chemistry in which I had little knowledge or understanding. My main interest in chemistry was seeing the explosion that follows when water is poured on to lithium. In lessons I always tried to keep back a bit of lithium to flick down the bench into a basin when someone was running the tap.

As you might imagine, the revision of all subjects became a major sweat. In the fifth form I spent five solid months — and the Easter holidays in particular — doing something I'd never managed to do before: studying. I can't say I enjoyed it, but to show how determined I was, I didn't even go out into the garden during those Easter holidays. I literally just sat inside and swotted.

No-one, least of all my parents, had told me I ought to work for my exams. This was something that came from inside me. I wanted to prove that I *could* pass an exam if I really, really wanted to. I knew Mum and Dad would be delighted if I managed it, but this was a personal quest. Growing temperamental plants from seed was also an exam of sorts and I'd passed that test often enough; but sitting down to get a recognized academic qualification felt very different.

I'll never forget the sheer agony that Easter of being cooped up in my bedroom where my orchids had once been, looking out of the newly repaired window and trying to concentrate on my exercise books. It was torture trying to keep my eyes off Granny's Easter-flowering, east-facing border outside.

Nevertheless, I worked and worked and I turned up for every exam. The summer holidays were nail-biting, as much for Mum and Dad as for me. They had seen how much effort I had put into studying things that meant little to me. But, in truth, I had learnt a lot and I kept my fingers firmly crossed.

It was set to be another baking hot August day when the results finally came through at breakfast as I sat in Mum and Dad's tiny dining room next to the kitchen. I hadn't expected to pass nine GCSEs and, naturally enough, I didn't. But I had passed eight. Bloody hell! Mum was ecstatic and I was pretty chuffed too. I told her and Dad I would retake my French and I did. So I did in the end get nine GCSEs. Job done!

Unfortunately all the hardcore swotting had left me all swotted out. When I returned to Stanbridge in the autumn to start my A-levels, I had no appetite whatever for yet more academic work. It was increasingly clear to me and to everyone else that my long-running stand-off with fractions, equations, graphs and essays was drawing to a close. I simply couldn't cope with that sort of stuff any more. The war was lost.

In the summer after my seventeenth birthday in April, I left Stanbridge a year early with two D-grade passes at AS-level and the promise of a place at a college where I could at last do something that interested me: a two-year course in forestry and tree surgery. It was at about this time that I had one of those Meaning of Life chats with Dad under the cedar trees.

'Any idea what you want to do with your life, Tom?' he asked, sitting on top his mower, the motor idling.

I knew that after college I wanted to see the world; but I also knew this was the wrong answer: 'seeing the world' wasn't a long-term career option with earning potential.

'Well, I've always fancied having my own nursery,' I said, admitting something that had been at the back of my mind since I was ten.

'Sounds like a good idea,' said Dad, before chugging off again across the lawn.

Having a nursery had felt like a good idea when I was ten; it had felt like a good idea when I was seventeen; and it felt like an even better idea throughout 2003 as I pressed on with my plans for the World Garden and slowly began to realize how much money I was going to have to earn in order to buy all the exotic plants I wanted to display.

Funnily enough, though, the reason I had always wanted a nursery had nothing to do with money. If I'm honest, I wanted one in order to be able to do what I really love: to talk to people about plants and learn from their experiences while passing on some of my own knowledge. Sure, cash would have to change hands at some stage and I would have to charge for my plants. But the most important bit I would give for free: explaining a plant's characteristic and where it came from, and what the new owner would have to do to keep it alive and make it thrive.

As my World Garden plans progressed, I could feel that I was getting closer to realizing my nursery ambitions. I could even see myself standing by the tables, nattering away twenty to the dozen to satisfied customers. But given my organizational skills, would I really be able to create a garden to go with that nursery? 'If you want to do it, just do it, Tom!' I told myself. 'Just do it.'

# 10

## Gardening Beyond the Clouds

As I continued to compile my definitive plant list for the World Garden throughout 2003, the garden that took shape in my mind's eye was a lot less hardy than the one I had envisaged at the end of 2002. In my desire to garden on the edge, I had become increasingly intrigued by trickier, more challenging plants and there were now fewer and fewer dependable toughies on my list. It was all becoming thoroughly 'experimentatious' — and that was how I liked it.

Branching away (sorry!) from the easier, hardier varieties, I knew that if I wanted the more tender souls to survive the winter frosts at Lullingstone they would have to be sunk in pots or sunk with bare roots into the borders under glass. The pots would then have to spend the coldest months jostling for space inside the greenhouse, a riot of greenery packed tighter than a rush-hour Tube train.

I also decided to jump in at the deep end and try to grow the most difficult plants first to gauge how bothersome the garden was going to be in the long term. As I now discovered, plants don't come much more difficult than *Richea pandanifolia*, an awesome yucca-type thing from Tasmania. Should you be lucky enough to grow one in your back garden, if it ever grows big enough to attract 'oohs' and 'ahs' from the neighbours, it will almost certainly be pinched by an ego-tripping plant nut or perhaps even stolen to order. You simply can't put a price tag on a *pandani* as they're so rare in cultivation.

In 2003 I didn't know of any under cultivation in Britain, and as light relief from my desk duties I continued my own attempts to get one to germinate using seeds I had collected in Tazzy. If it worked, it would be an adrenalin-pumping event of global significance (well, for me anyway), even if I would still have to wait ten years or so before having anything big enough with which to wow my visitors.

*Pandani* are, you see, absolute gits to germinate; and despite trying for a couple of years, I still hadn't been able to bring one of my dust-like seeds to life. While attempting to induce germination you mustn't give the little darlings tap water — they do need constant moisture, but it has to be rainwater and slightly acidic; and the sowing must be done on sphagnum moss as no compost seems to work.

So why keep trying? Well, I was determined to see a *pandani* growing at Lullingstone one day. I had the last of my Tasmanian seeds. I had the moss. I had the rainwater. I had the desire. But would I see germination? The seeds simply refused point blank to co-operate, and I eventually concluded that, like some of the yoghurt and cheese in my fridge, they had probably been there too long. Exasperated, I made a note to order some fresher seed from the Australian Plant Society.

Still, it was great to get away from the desk and computer and spend time back in the Venlo, the classic wood-and-glass greenhouse we got second-hand in the mid-1990s from a local psychiatric hospital that was getting rid of it on health and safety grounds. Worryingly, space was already tight inside and I realized I would need much more capacity to cope with the World Garden's winter wimps. I wrote 'more greenhouse space' on my growing wish list of Things To Buy Eventually.

Before I could afford to buy or scavenge another mini Crystal Palace, I would just have to make do, I told myself, and a lot of radical root and branch surgery would be needed to cope with the inevitable overcrowding. Roots would have to be cut back and tops lopped off, and there could be no room for sentiment.

Mine is not a conventional approach, I admit; but my rule of thumb is that if I've seen successful re-growth occur in a plant in the wild — after, say, a storm or a bush fire or very cold temperatures have caused branches to snap off or roots to burn — I reckon I can pretty much do what I like with my secateurs. I learnt this gung-ho approach from Granny, who has a lot of her own ideas and techniques. 'Treat 'em mean to keep 'em keen' is my motto. Well, it is with plants anyway.

Despite my failure to coax the *pandani* to life and my worries about greenhouse overcrowding, the garden was still a blissful sanctuary from my desk, where frustration mounted alongside sheaves of notes and a stack of old mugs of

Cup-a-Soup. Most frustrating was the general lack of written information in most of my gardening and horticultural books on where plants actually come from. So many plants have been in cultivation for so long now that few books today bother to tell you about a plant's origins: where it is native and indigenous and who introduced it to these islands. Perhaps people aren't interested any more, or maybe they simply don't know.

There are, thankfully, some people who do know: in particular Roy Lancaster, an undisputed legend among modern-day plant-hunters. In the stunning *Hillier Manual of Trees and Shrubs*, Roy sets out in detail where plants originated and who introduced them. I was also hugely dependent on the wondrous colour volumes produced by Roger Phillips and Martyn Rix in their stonking Garden Plant series, a photographic encyclopaedia which not only covers origins and hardiness, but shows colour pictures of plants in their natural habitats too. Without these I would have been stumped as I tried to construct my plant list.

Or should I say plant lists? Each continent or region now had its own list, broken down into individual tables for trees, shrubs, perennials/biennials/annuals and alpines. Plants that were national or state floral emblems were also highlighted, and each table was divided into five columns. In columns 1–3 I gave a plant's Latin name, vernacular name and place of origin. In column 4 I started making notes (where possible) on when and where a plant was 'discovered' and who introduced it into cultivation in Britain. Column 5, still largely blank for now, I set aside to record notes on hardiness, price and final planting arrangements in the World Garden itself.

The internet helped solve some mysteries, thanks to all those plant nuts who use it to publish obscure scientific papers and other crazed plant-inspired ramblings. This was especially handy as I tried to work out where a plant I was interested in should actually go in the garden: whether it should be on the map itself as a true species or in my 'Man's Influence' Borders, or MIBs as I now called them.

With roughly 10,000 species pencilled in, including 2,500 cultivars and hybrids identified for the MIBs, and with each plant taking at least half an hour (often much longer) to research, I was beginning to put down roots myself in front of the PC. At least part of my challenge, given the scale of my plot, was to find plants that would display their fascinating features, whether flowers, bark or leaves, when they were relatively young and not too big. I still only had a single acre into which to cram my world.

Occasionally, once I had managed to track down a plant's provenance, I simply decided I didn't want the bloody thing in the garden after all because it was either too big or because it lacked the horticultural wow factor. Painstaking though it was, this virtual spadework indoors was vital, I felt, if I wanted to be able to defend my planting decisions to knowledgeable visitors.

'But that plant shouldn't be there! It should be

over here!' I could already hear people complaining.

Given the prodigious amount of research I was compiling, it also crossed my mind that I should eventually make the World Garden plant list itself available over the net by developing Lullingstone's website. You would have to be the Plant Anorak's Anorak to want to read it (and probably wear an anorak as thick as a duffel coat). But such people do exist. Believe me.

Working out if a plant had been 'influenced by man' or not was also infuriatingly tricky at times. Again, the books told me virtually nothing about who had made this cross or that cultivar. Admittedly this is a grey area of horticulture that provokes endless heated debate even among people who are interested in such things. You enter this field at your peril.

For example, consider the crazy conundrum posed by a plant that has grown in the wild — a *Buddleja globosa* (the Orange Ball Tree), say — and whose seed has been collected in Chile or Peru and then brought back to the UK. In Britain, more often than not the seed will come up differently from the way the parent plant appeared in the wild.

'Look! Look!' cries the grower, barely able to contain his excitement. 'The flower's much grander and a deeper shade of orange! What's my nursery called? I'll name it after that!'

And so something called 'Bob's Bottlebrush Cottage Garden Cultivar', or whatever, is born. When that gets registered, or when Bob registers it himself by sticking the name on his labels, it suggests to some people that '*Buddleja globosa* (Orange Ball Tree), Bob's Bottlebrush Cottage Garden Cultivar' is some kind of spanking-new variant. But has it really been 'influenced by man' when all Bob has done is cart it halfway across the world and stick it in a Gro-bag in Biggleswade? Not necessarily. To my mind, the plant grown in cultivation has simply taken on a different form, and generally you have to assume it would have done so in the wild too, regardless of what Bob did at Bottlebrush Cottage.

Then what happens if you get a 'sport' — a genetically unstable freak plant that has wonderfully variegated leaves or whatever? A 'sport' is part of a plant that deviates from the rest, and almost all sports must be propagated vegetatively. If you get a sport of a big-flowered plant that already looks different from what the seed collector saw in the wild, would you in the wild get a different form which then becomes a sport . . . or has that difference been induced in cultivation?

A good example of the sort of knotty question I was wrestling with concerned the gracious *Lavatera* shrub called 'Barnsley', a mallow relation from southern Europe. This is a sport that originated from a cultivated version of a plant that had been collected from seed in the southern Mediterranean. Should I put something like that in my Man's Influence Borders or should I put it on the world map itself, somewhere in sunny southern Spain or Italy? I eventually decided to stick Barnsley in the MIBs opposite the Med. Am I right? Gosh! I think so.

And what about plants that occur naturally in Britain, like the contorted hazel that was found in 1863 by a chap who was rootling in a Gloucestershire hedge? Should that go in my MIBs because, although naturally occurring, it's only been found once in the wild and you have to graft it to a normal hazel root stock to get the contorted version, and that graft is done by man? Help! With the hazel I decided it *would* go in the MIBs. Even for a dedicated plant nut, though, going through such hazel-inspired contortions was a nightmare. And no, I don't recommend you try it at home.

Happily there were many clear-cut decisions. My pioneering plant-hunters, without whom Britain's parks, gardens, patios, windowboxes and Homebases wouldn't be the same — and without whom there would be no Chelsea Flower Show or Hampton Court Flower Show each year — more or less leapt out of the bushes and demanded to be included. Occasionally I would even imagine myself introducing them to visitors on a guided tour of the finished garden. Naturally, for this imaginary tour the garden was fully planted and in flower, dear old Trevor had vacated his half of the plot and my nursery was packed with satisfied customers.

'Meet Captain Cook's travelling companion, the great Joseph Banks,' I would tell my visitors. 'He really was the granddaddy of plant-hunters . . .'

And so of course he was. A founding member of the Royal Horticultural Society and its president for forty-two years, he set up the world's premier botanic gardens at Kew. As if that weren't enough, he more or less invented the notion of plant-hunting by sending out teams of professional collectors from Kew to the four corners of the world. He also did an enormous amount to help make Britain a leading power by arranging for the transfer of commercial crops between her various colonies. While some may debate whether this was a good thing for all concerned, no-one can dispute Banks the botanist's bravery, determination and importance.

In a way I felt I had grown up with Banks, Granny having spoken to me about him constantly ever since I was old enough to push a wheelbarrow around. He didn't just bring back hundreds and hundreds of specimens, however. With Cook he literally redrew the map of the world for the Europeans, discovering land masses that their contemporaries back home simply didn't know existed.

Banks established himself early, surveying the Newfoundland coast for seven months in 1766. Then, when the *Endeavour* sailed out of the English Channel on the afternoon of 25 August 1768, he set off on the three-year voyage that was to revolutionize Britain's and the world's knowledge of botany.

Travelling as Captain Cook's plant man, he endured seasickness, hypothermia, scurvy, shipwreck, cannon fire, hostile natives and malaria; had to eat (among other things) shark, albatross, dog, vulture, rat and kangaroo. But, boy, did he find some plants. He collected 125 new species, including *Gaultheria mucronata*, just from a bitterly cold Tierra del Fuego on the southernmost tip of South America; and during a six-month circumnavigation of New Zealand — the first European to visit — he sourced 360 specimens, including discovering *Phormium tenax* (New Zealand Flax), cultivars of which are rampantly common in gardens and nurseries today because of their tropical theme.

His most famous collections were made exploring the eastern coastline of *Terra Australis*, where he amassed hundreds of new species, including Eucalyptus, Acacias (called 'wattles' in Australia), Grevilleas, Callistemon (Bottlebrush), *Brachychiton acerifolius* (the Queensland Flame Tree), *Telopea speciosissima* (Waratah, the floral emblem of New South Wales) and *Leptospermum scoparium* (Tea Tree).

So old Banks was definitely *the* man. Though nothing he brought back was ever grown — it was all dried and pressed herbarium samples — he ended up with a genus named in his honour — *Banksia* — and it was one of these, *Banksia integrifolia*, that I decided I would plant in the World Garden. Why? Well, it's pretty frost and alkaline tolerant, for a start.

Francis Masson, Banks's protégé as Kew's first official plant-hunter, was another who demanded his place in the sun in the World Garden: in Masson's case on the southern tip of what was going to be my Kentish sun-baked continent of Africa. Over the two decades from 1770 he made many clandestine, death-defying expeditions across South Africa, during which he

110

was chased by convicts, forded treacherous rivers in a cart, suffered severe dehydration and almost got killed in the British Cape Town riots. But it was all worth it because Masson, a Scot, brought back a veritable Garden of Eden to these shores, including a favourite of mine, the great white Arum Lily (*Zantedeschia aethiopica*). Who can resist that enormous, glowing, purest white waxy flower?

Masson also introduced the King Protea (*Protea cynaroides*), now the floral emblem of South Africa: a scorching, spiky plant with a conical, 1970s punk haircut that can thrive in Britain in a pot of well-drained ericaceous compost; not to mention the deliciously fragrant Belladonna Lily (*Amaryllis belladonna*). Arguably his most overwhelmingly fabulous import was the striking Bird of Paradise flower (*Strelitzia reginae*). Though it's an extremely popular conservatory plant, I still wanted one in the World Garden and bunged it on my list.

Masson, though few might now know his name, opened European eyes to one of the most floriferous, biodiverse places on the planet and I knew I could only ever hope to do justice to a tiny part of his legacy. For it included Gladioli, Cineraria, Streptocarpus (Cape Primrose), eighty-eight species of Cape Heath, nine different Kniphofia (Red Hot Pokers), Agapanthus, Ixia, forty-seven Pelargoniums, Lobelias, Watsonias, Haemanthus and Oxalis. What a guy.

Nowadays, of course, South Africa has extremely strict controls on the collection and export of seeds, so I was really grateful that Dad, on one of his trips back to Africa at the end of 2001, had stocked up with loads of packets of Protea seeds. He was able to buy them quite legally before he got on the plane at Johannesburg airport and had a rather easier time with them than Masson.

He also had an easier time acquiring the seeds than I did trying to germinate them, for they required me to start a serious fire inside the old lean-to greenhouse. The aim was to fill it with smoke. To create a proper fug, I burnt piles of dried eucalyptus leaves and soon had thick, noxious clouds billowing out of the greenhouse doors and windows. I was choking, my lungs were burning and I couldn't see through my streaming eyes, but this is what you have to do sometimes when you are serious about getting a Protea to germinate and do its stuff.

With the greenhouse thick with smoke, I doused my pots with a fine cloud of water from a hand-held spray, hoping that the smoke particles would be absorbed into the mist and eventually soak down into the compost; the aim was to recreate the conditions the seeds might experience in the wild after a bush fire. I also sprinkled some of the ash on to the surface of my pots and then simply hoped for the best. Admittedly it was all good fun — but a heck of a lot of effort given that only one of the Protea seeds ever germinated.

Over in my North American continent, meanwhile, I planned to pay homage to David Douglas, the fir tree man and, like Masson, a Scot. In the 1820s and early 1830s, this son of

112

Perth made a series of ground-breaking trips across the Atlantic, in particular to the rugged, plant-rich Pacific north-west.

Douglas braved tough mountainous terrain, skirmishes with hostile locals, freezing nights in wet, mossy forests and numerous capsizes on torrential rivers (he once lost almost all his seed collections, specimens and diaries) but he still managed to introduce more than 200 new species, including some now hugely famous crackers like *Ribes sanguineum* (the Flowering Currant), which is so desirable in the spring garden. And let's not forget *Lupinus polyphyllus*, one of the main ancestors of our modern garden Lupins. Or *Garrya elliptica*, that great evergreen shrub that livens up the winter garden, first with its catkins and then with purple-brown fruits on the female plant.

In 1826 the daredevil Douglas dazzled the world with something he had found in the foothills of California — the annual *Eschscholzia californica*, or Californian Poppy, which is now the state floral emblem. But the really important thing about Douglas was that he became Britain's 'Mr Forestry'. His finds were not restricted to the merely ornamental; in an era of rampant industrialization and commercial expansion, some of them had enormous value too. Majestic timber-producing trees changed the face of the Victorian landscape: *Pinus radiata* (the Monterey Pine) is now to be found in the biggest cultivated forests in the world; *Picea sitchensis* (the Sitka Spruce) now forms the basis of the forestry industry in Britain; and then there was the towering, columnar *Abies grandis* (Grand Fir). Without the *Pseudotsuga menziesii* (Douglas Fir), which hails from south-west British Columbia and central California and reaches heights of up to 400 feet, large parts of the British landscape just wouldn't look the same today.

Douglas, who lost the sight in one eye, came to a mysteriously premature end in Hawaii on 12 July 1834 when he apparently fell into a hole that had been dug to catch wild cattle and was gored to death by a trapped bullock. There was talk that he had been having an affair with the wife of an ex-convict, and that it was the aggrieved husband who had pushed him in, but murder was never proved.

The plant-hunter who spoke most directly to me and whom I most wanted to celebrate in the World Garden was of course the mad Scotsman George Forrest, who made seven plant- and seed-collecting forays to Yunnan in south-western China between 1904 (the same year my great-great-uncle Boyd set out from the Niger delta) and 1932. Forrest had such a massive influence on our garden flora it's hard to understate the importance of his discoveries or the number of plants he introduced to cultivation.

Once in south-western China, he set off with his Winchester gun and his dog, his porters and his mules, the latter loaded down with plant presses, camping equipment and huge supplies of rice. In the heavy rains of the monsoon they battled swollen rivers, as well as cold, fever, hunger and even some local tribal wars. It was during one of these that Forrest had to flee for his life, hiding by day and travelling by night. In the end he was hunted down and fired at. Luckily, he was quite a short man, and the two poison-tipped arrows flying his way only penetrated his hat. Had he been any taller, he would probably have been killed.

After surviving the arrows, Forrest then managed to spear himself through the foot when he trod on a farmer's bamboo booby trap. He wrenched his foot free before eventually hobbling to a mission house where he found refuge. Once recuperated, he continued his plant-hunting — and just as well for the rest of us. He collected thousands and thousands of samples and seeds, from every altitude and climate zone. He even trained locals to collect plants and seeds on his behalf. Each plant was pressed dry in paper, and was then given a 'Forrest' number which corresponded to his detailed notes describing its habitat, locality, latitude, longitude and altitude. These were then packaged for shipment to Britain. Seeds were also sorted, dried, given a number and packaged too.

In all, Forrest collected more than 30,000 specimens, including an amazing array of rhododendrons and many new species of primula. One of his most famous treasures was *Primula vialii*, or the Orchid Primula, to which I decided I would give pride of place in the World Garden, next to my Asian waterfall. If I ever got to the stage of building an Asian waterfall, that is.

On the other side of the world I wanted to celebrate the achievements of William Lobb, a Cornishman who on 7 November 1840 set sail from Falmouth for Rio de Janeiro. He was employed by the powerful Veitch Nursery but was a famously poor note-taker. Nevertheless, it's known that he visited many regions in South America, including the Organ Mountains in Brazil, where he discovered orchids, passion flowers and begonias. In Chile he found *Berberis darwinii, Embothrium coccineum* (the Chilean Firebush) and *Nothofagus antarctica*; this last, I decided, would look great on the Patagonian tip of my South America when it was created.

Most famously, from Chile Lobb also reintroduced to cultivation in Britain the Monkey Puzzle tree. With its tall, cylindrical trunk, which is covered in coarse bark like an elephant's hide, it creates a silhouette a bit like an umbrella. Who can fail to be blown away by its majestic crown of spidery branches, which are, in turn, endowed with huge cones and stiff, pointed evergreen leaves? It's an absolute killer to look at and desperately endangered in the wild. And I wanted one. Or three.

Back in Europe, I was drawn to the early achievements of the Tradescant family, a father and son team who operated in the late sixteenth and early seventeenth centuries. In particular I was interested in John the Elder, who was believed to have lived between 1570 and 1638 and hailed from Suffolk. To my mind he was really the first plant-hunter to be influential. Employed by the Earl of Salisbury at Hatfield

House, he travelled all over: from the Low Countries and Arctic Russia to what used to be called the Levant, or Middle East, and North Africa. He collected seeds and bulbs wherever he went and was particularly famous for introducing the tulip to Europe from Turkey.

Though I am someone who would always rather be outside in the garden than stuck indoors at a desk, and although the process of armchair plant-hunting was slow and frustrating, I reckoned that the more planning and planting detail I could pack into my virtual World Garden on screen, the fewer problems I would encounter in the muddy offline garden, as it were. I was also quietly pleased with myself because for once in my life I felt I was really thinking something through properly from start to finish.

# 11

## Prest a faire

Our family motto '*Prest à faire*' means 'Ready to serve' or 'Ready to do'; and by the end of 2003 I was more than ready to do the fun bit of turning my dream garden into a plant- and boulder-strewn reality. In fact I was *desperate* to get my hands dirty. But there was still a mountain of virtual spadework to be completed at my desk before I could pick up a fork for real and start making my own indelible mark on the Lullingstone landscape.

With the complex (and at times brain-numbing) planning of the World Garden's plant list romping away nicely, I did occasionally allow myself to look up from the PC long enough to think about what lay ahead. And I didn't entirely like what I saw. Was I *really* going to be able to do everything by hand myself in the garden, funded by plant sales in summer and the odd talk to WI groups over tea and biscuits? Maybe Dad was right. Maybe I *was* a bit unhinged.

Slowly the truth dawned that if I was serious about making this garden happen, I would soon need some serious help and some serious money. Sponsorship perhaps. Or even Lottery funding. How else could I hope to pay for contractors with their whopping great digging machines? Or the lorryloads of whacking great boulders that I wanted? Not to mention someone to help me clear the wilderness that was developing to choke the walled garden that would be home to all the plants I had so painstakingly chosen but didn't yet have the first penny to buy? It was all beginning to feel overwhelmingly daunting.

Still, with a motto like 'Ready to do' to live up to, how could the Green Man chuck in the towel? I even started to wonder how my forebears had coped when they had undertaken major works on the estate. But unless there was a plant or horticultural link — concerning the dating of the cedar trees, say, or the landscaping of the vista in front of the house by old Sir John Dixon Dyke — I was more than a bit hazy about what any of my ancestors had actually done when they were 'ready to do'.

Though I had been brought up on an estate that was up to its ears in history and over the centuries had been home to some prolific 'doers', my own grasp of their 'doings' was at times tenuous. This has caused some of my more excessive friends to despair — Richard Reeves, for example, the Bog Orchid hunter from the New Forest who also happens to be a hardcore history nut, tears his incredibly long hair out whenever he thinks I'm being flaky about the details of my antecedents.

'You just take it all for granted, don't you, Tom?' he says, shaking his mane in disbelief and flapping his arms in despair.

Rich has a point. And it was now time, I felt, for Tom to get back to his roots — no pun intended — to see if he couldn't learn something from all that had gone before. I began to pump Dad, Mum and Granny for all the information they could give.

When I was younger, Mum and Dad had never rammed the details of our family history down my throat — and just as well, given my attention span for things that aren't green and that don't absolutely fascinate me. In school, for example, probably the most useful contribution I ever made when Henrys VII and VIII came up in class was: 'Oh. I think they used to come over to our gaff for jousting competitions with the relations!'

'Yeah, sure, Tom,' my classmates would chorus. 'Now shut up!'

I also remember a geography lesson at Stanbridge Earls when the teacher asked us to draw the fronts of our respective houses and count the windows. After a couple of minutes all my friends had finished and put down their pencils, but I was still scribbling away feverishly.

'Hart Dyke! Have you finished yet?' snapped the teacher.

'No, sir.'

'Why not?'

'Still counting the windows, sir.'

'Oh yes,' he said, remembering that I was that boy from the castle.

Long before our house acquired all those windows (it was during a major makeover in the eighteenth century), we reckon that Henry VIII, being a close chum of our ancestor Sir John Peche, *was* a regular visitor here. But did that make me feel more connected than my classmates to the blood, guts and intrigue of English history? Not at all. When I was small, I really did spend every minute in the garden, and conversation with Mum and Dad at mealtimes revolved around plants — not what Sir John might have done to help his monarch when accompanying him to the Field of the Cloth of Gold in 15-0-something-or-other.

On the rare occasions I did actually look at the portraits of my ancestors when I was younger, I knew vaguely who most of them were and when they were born, but their lives remained remote, abstract concepts. Though I realized I was descended from these chaps with weird clothes and stern gazes, there wasn't a plant-hunter among them whom I could plug into. I certainly couldn't relate to any of them in the way that I related to Granny, say, who was out in the garden with me every day doing stuff.

The first bit of family history I remember Dad telling me was that I am named after an eighteenth-century bloke called Sir Thomas Dyke and that my sister Anya was named after his wife, Anne Hart. Thomas Dyke was an ironmaster from Sussex whose marriage to Anne brought loads of money to Lullingstone, along with a title. He was certainly a 'doer' and I can still see his handiwork around me today — the pollarded trees up on the golf course are a constant reminder of how hard he worked to maintain and re-enclose the medieval deer park. But the notion that he was a flesh-and-blood relation? Bit remote, really.

What has never, ever felt remote is the physical

sense of connection I feel with Lullingstone *the place*. Though I am not a religious person in any way, I feel a connectedness with every stone and tree on the estate at an almost spiritual level. My roots are here and they go deep — but they go into the ground rather than into the past. I feel I belong at Lullingstone like nowhere else and I've always felt this way.

Like all good things, Lullingstone started small. With careful feeding, watering and nurturing — not to mention some pretty canny marriages over the years — the estate was able to blossom and grow. I've described how radical root and branch surgery was needed in the twentieth century to ensure the survival of the house and estate and our family's continued presence here. But what about the early days?

After burying my nose in some of the research carried out by my ghostly house guest, Colonel Meates (research carried out when he was alive, that is), I learnt that when William the Conqueror was doing his Domesday survey, Lullingstone Ros, as it was then called, was actually pretty modest. Worth just 100 shillings, the estate comprised 120 acres (which is what we're left with today, funnily enough), and included 6 acres of meadow and just enough woodland to keep twenty hogs happy.

My family is actually descended from the first Sir John Peche, who, confusingly, wasn't the Sir John Peche I've just mentioned (nothing is simple here) but the Sir John Peche who bought the place in 1361. He was an alderman in the City of London and must have earned some fairly decent bonuses even in those days. By the time he was pushing up *Bellis perennis* in 1380 and had handed Lullingstone on to his only son, Sir William Peche, the estate had grown to '250 acres of arable land, 3 acres of meadow, 12 acres of wood, 50s. rent and 42 hens'.

Where the pigs went, I've no idea; and nor do I know nearly enough nitty-gritty detail about the rest of my family tree. But then my lot are confusing.

Take, for example, the Sir John Peche who begat us all. As we've seen, he handed the place on to his son, Sir William Peche, in 1380. So far, so clear. But after Sir William Peche pegged out, Lullingstone went to his son, who was yet another Sir John Peche. This Sir John was made Sheriff of Kent in 1430 and was in turn succeeded by his son who was called — you guessed it — Sir William blinking Peche. This second Sir William died in 1487 (he's buried in the chancel of St Botolph's, which I can see from my bedroom window) and he had a son and heir who was born around 1473. If only Sir William had called the boy Bob, things might have been simpler. But no. He was yet another Sir John Peche.

Funnily enough, this last Sir John is one I know more about because he did some interesting things. He not only built the original manor and gatehouse in which I'm sitting writing this book right now, but he was also something of an Action Man and the '*Prest à faire*' motto was his. A courageous jouster, he won what could have been an early pilot for TV's

*It's a Royal Knockout!* when in November 1494 he took part in the jousts at Westminster in front of Henry VII. First prize was a gold ring set with a ruby, and by knocking out somebody called Sir Robert Curzon as well as the Earls of Suffolk and Essex, my forebear won the right to stick feathers in his helmet in the colours of the king's champions. We've still got the helmet over the fireplace in the dining room, but not, alas, the original feathers. Nor the ruby ring, for that matter.

As I've said, this Sir John was big mates with Henry VII's son, Henry VIII, who is almost certain, Dad reckons, to have stopped off here on his way to and from the arch-bishops' palaces at Otford and Knole, and probably also on his way to Hever, where Anne Boleyn lived. Under Henry VII Sir John was made Sheriff of Kent; but his career really took off under Henry VIII. He was knighted after the Battle of Blackheath in 1497, was later made Lord Deputy of Calais, and in 1520, two years before his death, he accompanied Henry to that famous Field of the Cloth of Gold.

Now, if I'd dug deeper into the archives instead of into my flower borders when I was in school, I might have been able to tell you more about my ancestor's contribution to this attempted peace summit on the other side of the English Channel and more about the sumptuous tournaments that were held there with the aim of ending the fighting between England and France. But I didn't, so I can't, and I'm sorry about that. All I do know is that Sir John was too busy jousting, looking after his monarch's interests in Kent and doing whatever it was he eventually did on the Field of the Cloth of Gold to have any children. Or perhaps he was unable to have children. Or maybe he was gay and didn't want children. Or maybe he was gay and *did* want children but wasn't allowed to adopt in those days. Who knows. Either way, the estate passed via his sister Elizabeth to his nephew, Percyval Hart; and it is at this point in my family saga that I recommend you put the kettle on and get a hi-energy snack from the biscuit tin. For Sir Percyval Hart was the first of no fewer than *four* Percyval Harts to run the place. Depending on what source you read, some of them had one 'l' and some had two. But let's not go crazy.

Like his uncle Sir John Peche, Percyval was also a local fixer for the Royal Family. As Chief Server and Knight Harbinger, he worked for four monarchs in all: Henry VIII, Edward VI, Mary I and Elizabeth I. There is an impressive life-sized triptych of him in our Great Hall, painted when he was eighty in 1575, in which he stands next to his two surviving sons, Sir George Hart and Francis Hart. It's a killer painting and the three of them look down on us to this day when we're sitting in front of the enormous fire.

As a kid, I always thought Percyval just looked like Henry VIII because he was so big and rotund and had the same beard. Today, though, I am more sensitive to his enormous presence and demeanour. Despite the royal connections and his own fifty-year reign at Lullingstone, this great big barrel of a man was humbly preparing for his impending appointment with the Man Upstairs. '*Expecto horam libertatis meae*' says the inscription on the hourglass on which he rests his pink hand: 'I await the hour of my liberation.' Powerful stuff.

Having some experience myself of feeling that the hour of my own liberation was imminent, I imagine he and I could probably have quite an interesting chinwag about mortality and such things were he around today. I hope our imaginary chat might conclude with the observation that whether we live in Dartford or the Darién Gap, whether our parents are royal harbingers or scrofulous harlots, whether we are rich and well known or poor and miserable and anonymous, one day we will all end up as plant food and taste exactly the same to the plants.

As I mentioned earlier, it was Percyval Hart, Esquire, great-great-grandson of the mighty first Sir Percyval Hart, who Queen Anne-ified the house. But the serious money didn't arrive until he died and his daughter Anne married my namesake Thomas at the beginning of the eighteenth century.

Sir Thomas Dyke, the wealthy ironmaster, certainly had aspirations to, if not delusions of, grandeur, and he proceeded to spend, spend, spend. He changed the name from Lullingstone House to Lullingstone Castle — even though the place looked more like a house than a castle — and he sank mile upon mile of fencing to maintain his massive deer park and mark out his territory. This, and the Ice House he built to keep his meat fresh, were major status symbols in

126

his day, akin to being royal.

It was when one of the fenceposts was being driven into the soil and hit something hard that the remains of a Roman villa were discovered on the estate. However, it wasn't until the 1950s when the cigar-smoking Colonel Meates was poking around that the full extent of the discovery really emerged. Sir Thomas's men had speared one of the most spectacular Roman mosaic floors ever seen in Britain. Now properly restored (and no longer belonging to us, of course), bits of it depict the 'Rape of Europa by Jupiter' and 'Bellerophon riding Pegasus killing the Chimaera'. But I doubt Sir Thomas, or the deer that ended up on his plate, would have been much bothered by all that.

Sir Thomas's son, Sir John Dixon Dyke, also remodelled the estate and largely created the serene layout that still blows visitors' socks off today. He pulled down the inner Tudor gatehouse that was spoiling his view from the main house, opening up a magnificent vista to the west. He also filled in the moat and dug out a lake to the south. At the back of my mind, I hoped that one day perhaps my own plans to extend the World Garden across the estate as a whole would be equally significant. But perhaps now it was me who was having delusions of grandeur.

In any event, Dixon Dyke's alterations left the estate looking as pretty as a picture; and it was this sumptuous pile that eventually came to my great-grandfather, Sir William HD, when he became the 7th baronet in 1875.

He and Great-Grandma Emily, daughter of the 7th Earl of Sandwich, lived in considerable, not to say excessive, comfort. As fully paid-up members of the leisured ruling class, they knew how to party. Quite apart from her jazz drumming (she even played on horseback at charity concerts and pageants around the county) and her amateur chair-mending, Emily was also a keen photographer (she had her own dark room in what is now Mum's laundry) and she was fêted as one of the best female billiard players of her day.

Sir William, though he reputedly hosted the first game of lawn tennis here and was a prodigious racquets player and shot, was also a serious 'doer' as a Conservative politician. He spent more than forty years in the Commons as the MP for Dartford — 41 years and 170 days, I think — sitting through nine parliaments and seven prime ministers. Tragically, the only words of wisdom I have so far found attributed to him are his apparent comment, recorded in a collection of the stupidest things ever said, that: 'The Right Honourable gentleman has gone to the top of the tree and caught a very big fish!' What he was on about I have no idea. Dad recalls him saying that politicians were basically like bananas: 'They all hang together and are bent!' No comment.

Great-Grandad was a regular Sunday lunch companion of Disraeli, and in 1885 Lord Salisbury made him Chief Secretary for Ireland. As vice-president of the Committee of the Council on Education, he then saw through the

Free Education Act in the early 1890s. Perhaps if he'd spent less time 'doing' politics and more time organizing an orderly succession, his poor son Oliver, my paternal grandfather, might have inherited less of a mess when William and Emily died in 1931 and Oliver became the 8th baronet.

Grandad Oliver was a mechanical engineer by training, and it's all thanks to his determined practicality that we're still here. Quite apart from the financial acrobatics he had to perform so that the Hart Dykes could remain in at least part of the estate, he had another huge challenge in life: trying to keep pace with his first wife, Zoë.

Though I never met Dad's mother, all I had ever heard about this utterly amazing woman convinced me that here was an ancestor whose example I really had to study closely. For if I could take a leaf from her book, I'd have the World Garden built in a trice . . . and still be back home in the gatehouse in time for *Gardener's World*. It was clearly time to pick Dad's brains about my other granny.

# 12

## Zoë and the Worms

In the summer of 1935 an unusual advertisement appeared in dozens of local newspapers across the Home Counties: 'Silkworms starving: HELP!! HELP!! Lady Hart Dyke would be extremely grateful for sacks of mulberry leaves for her silkworms. Will those kind enough to help please send their sacks by post or rail (carriage forward) any time between 1st and 31st July to Lullingstone Castle, Eynsford, Kent? Do *please* dispatch as soon as possible after picking as mulberry leaves ferment very quickly.'

Within days, according to Dad, a mountain of sacks, envelops and brown paper parcels tied up in string arrived at the castle. They came from as far away as Ireland and France and were stuffed with nearly half a ton of freshly picked mulberry leaves. My paternal grandmother knew how to get things done all right.

Zoë, or Lady Hart Dyke as she was known after Grandad had become the 8th baronet, died in 1975, a year before I was born. Despite missing each other through poor timing, I have always known that Zoë, with her thing about worms, was definitely on the slightly crazy side. But her craziness was of enormous benefit to the estate. Lullingstone Silk Farm put the castle firmly on the tourist map, and by showing visitors around herself, she began the tradition that Mum and Dad have continued of making a visit to Lullingstone feel homely and personal.

'She used to have forty thousand visitors a summer!' Dad would gasp as he totted up his own visitor numbers with increasing despair. 'Took over the railway station. Put posters up everywhere. Practically dragged people off the down train!'

In fact, Grandma Zoë actually went so far as to stand in the middle of the railway tracks outside Eynsford Station to make sure the trains stopped for the visitors to get off. So yes — a madwoman and an inspiration to us all. But particularly to me.

Born Zoë Bond, daughter of a Dorset GP, when she was young her family moved to Hammersmith in west London, where Zoë attended that forcing house for female brain-boxes, St Paul's Girls' School. Dr Bond believed girls should have as good an education as boys and not be raised as mere marriage fodder, and he wanted Zoë to develop a mind of her own. She certainly did that.

Though she claimed to have been a hopeless pupil (rotten at maths, she failed the Barclays Bank entrance test and her first job was as a lowly insurance clerk in the City), she neverthe-less had a streak of iron. When she decided in later life to 'undertake the venture of reviving the art of sericulture in England', it was only a matter of time before she achieved precisely that. And all from a standing start.

I didn't really know what 'sericulture' was

until Dad plucked a book from one of the shelves in the den one day and suggested I read it.

'You'll learn everything you need to know about Zoë . . . and more than you'll ever want to know about worms,' he said, handing me a slim blue volume called *So Spins the Silkworm*. 'All over the house they were. Thousands of them. You could hear the worms munching, munching, munching. Always munching they were.'

Written by my grandmother and published in 1949, the book told of Zoë's lifelong infatuation (there's no other word) with *Bombyx mori*, or the mulberry-eating silkworm, and her dream of producing silk fit for a queen. Considering that her interest started when she was four; that her first worm-driven business was launched from an attic in Leatherhead; and that the raw silk thread she later produced at Lullingstone found its way into both the wedding dress of our present Queen and the Coronation robes of the Queen Mother, I devoured Zoë's story with increasing interest and at times incredulity.

In fact, the more I read of Zoë's mad mission in life, the more I realized my own ambition of trying to create a major new visitor attraction from a standing start wasn't so batty. It was only a garden, after all; and it wasn't as if I had livestock to care for or was trying to do it while the estate was being bombed senseless, as it was in Zoë's day during the Battle of Britain.

I also realized that my own 'passionate interest' in plants in general, and orchids and gum trees in particular, was quite in keeping

132

with Zoë's major obsession: rearing silkworms from eggs and then hand-reeling silk from the resulting cocoons. Indeed, by the standards of my family, I told myself, I might well be a plant nut. But if I was, I was a perfectly 'normal' Hart Dyke plant nut.

At about the same age that I was germinating Crac's carrot seeds in the walled garden, the grandmother I never met was living in Dorsetshire, as she called it, hatching out silkworm graine in a chest of drawers outside the door of her nursery (and that's nursery as in Peter Pan and Wendy, rather than the sort of nursery I was intending to build). As with my own early bedroom orchids, Zoë's attempts at egg husbandry were so successful that her mother went bananas when the first batch hatched out and a knot of hungry worms were soon crawling over a drawer full of Zoë's clean clothes. My grandmother had her 2d pocket money docked and was ordered to put it in the collection plate the following Sunday.

After the Bond family moved to London, Zoë's interest in worms intensified and was given a huge boost when she discovered a free source of their staple food: a whacking great mulberry tree in the playground of her school in Brook Green. For the period — the years leading up to the First World War — Dr Bond had quite advanced notions about women's place in society, and after St Paul's he sent Zoë abroad to finish her education: not at a silly girlie finishing school where she would learn deportment and flower-arranging, but to the Collège de Jeunes

Filles in Saumur, to continue her practical studies on the banks of the Loire.

Just as I hated being separated from my orchids when I was at Stanbridge Earls, so Zoë was now deeply put out by the college's 'no pets' rule. She suffered definite worm-withdrawal, it seems; but she was a crafty so-and-so and hatched a plan. When her attractive best friend Margaret, who had 'boy-conquering dimples', caught the eye of a young townie called Georges who had relations in the south of France, Zoë's silkworm antennae twitched instantly.

Zoë knew that sericulture was well established in the south of France, and not for the last time she used her considerable powers of persuasion to get her own way. She managed to convince the smitten Georges that if he really wanted to get into Margaret's good books, he'd write to his relations down south and request a supply of . . . eggs!

Thus it was that, under cover of darkness, my grandmother and her best friend climbed out of school one night for a midnight assignation with a smitten twelve-year-old in a shrubbery in Saumur. Georges kept his part of the bargain, handing over a grubby envelope, and for his efforts he got a peck on both cheeks from Margaret.

Back inside the Collège de Jeunes Filles, Zoë did all she could to avoid discovery and to create the right conditions for her teaspoonful of tiny grey eggs to hatch. To keep them at a constant temperature she put them in a box which she took to bed with her . . . and then wore the box intimately about her person during the day.

'I was terrified of crushing them at night as I was ever a restless sleeper,' she recalled. 'I will not dwell upon the difficulties I experienced whilst wearing those eggs, sufficient to say that the gymn. class almost turned my head grey. Until that time I had been one of M. Lally, the instructor's, star performers, but now I was scared even to climb a rope or vault over the horse; in fact I was too terrified to do anything at all. Monsieur was annoyed but put it down to 'Love'. As a nation I found the French prone to attribute everything and anything to this tender emotion!'

When the eggs finally hatched, Zoë was 'nearly sick with excitement', but the challenge now was to find regular supplies of fresh mulberry with which to feed her wriggling larvae. Not having seen a single mulberry bush near the college, she had thought this one through too. Cannily, she had written to her father complaining that she wasn't getting enough exercise in France. Might a bicycle be a good idea for his daughter? At Dr Bond's request, Zoë was thus allowed to acquire two wheels on which to make daily tours of the district in search of mulberry trees and her worms never went hungry. The developing silk cocoons Zoë then set in paper cones which she hid in the stove in her bedroom.

The silkworm habit then continued on Zoë's return to England, where she started work in the City and lodged in a big old house in Earls Court. Her landlady, whom she called 'Honey-bunch', was exceedingly laid-back about all the intensive worm action; and as the spring mulberry rush approached, Zoë was given a boxroom on an upper floor for hatching purposes. The tree in the playground of her old school still provided fresh leaves, but friends and admirers were now bringing mulberry sprigs and branches from Kew and further afield. Her family of 200–300 larvae were stuffed full.

Marriage to my grandfather Oliver then followed after the couple met by chance at a dinner party to which Zoë had been invited at the last minute to make up the numbers. They settled in a large modern house outside Leatherhead, but there was little sign of 'tender emotion' in Zoë's description of early family life there. Like many of her social class at the time, she was not what you would have called a mumsy kind of mum. In her book, she didn't even name Grandad — or indeed Dad or his brother Derek or their sister June — referring merely to 'my partner and I' and their 'young family of two boys and a girl'.

She said it was a happy time; and perhaps it was by the standards of the day. But as Dad recalls, the three siblings were very much part of the children-should-be-seen-and-not-heard generation, cared for by a succession of nannies, housekeepers and cooks. Washed and polished, they were occasionally presented to their parents for inspection before being promptly returned to the nursery. Or, rather, nurseries: the house in Leatherhead had one for the day and one for the night.

'It was very much a case of life behind the

green baize door for us children,' Dad recalls wistfully.

With a team of domestic helpers at home, Zoë was able to hang out with Leatherhead's other ladies of leisure. When they weren't discussing menus with their cooks or running their households, they 'played golf and tennis, rode and swam, in a gay group'. Tied to the sink she certainly wasn't; and once Uncle Derek was at boarding school and Dad was at a day school in Leatherhead, my grandmother had even more time on her hands. She obviously wanted more from life than simply to be part of a 'gay group' of sporty housewives, however; and, inspired by the Chinese proverb that says 'Patience and perseverance turn mulberry leaves into the silken robes of a queen', she set out to do precisely that.

Zoë hatched her first serious batch of eggs — 5,000 or so bought from a London store — in the attic in Leatherhead and convinced her cook to allow her into her own kitchen long enough to 'stifle the chrysalides' — which, I soon twigged, was Zoë's polite term for 'moth murder'. She performed this act by putting the chrysalides in a biscuit tin and then bunging it in the oven. 'I contented myself with popping in every half-hour to examine the cocoons, Cook watching me with such an evil expression that I thought it wiser to dine out that evening.'

Armed with a hand-reeler bought for 7s 6d, and buoyed by the number of silken cocoons she had produced, Zoë now pushed the boat out and ordered a whole ounce of eggs — between

30,000 and 40,000 of the tiny beggars, apparently — from a company in Turkey.

Soon worm production had outgrown the Leatherhead attic completely; and because Lullingstone was now empty following the death of my great-grandparents, Zoë decided to take over three large rooms in the castle and use them as a hatchery. She drove over here every day as Lady Hart Dyke, wife of the 8th baronet.

Zoë's success at hatching so many thousands of worms on the trays she made herself from stretched muslin created new problems, however. First, she needed massive quantities of mulberry — hence her begging adverts in the local press. Worse, the kitchen oven in Leatherhead was now far too small to murder the number of moths she was producing. Or it was if she didn't want to lose her precious Cook. Zoë needed another oven and she needed a big one.

'Eventually, dead to all shame and decent feelings, I hit upon the brilliant idea of seeing our local baker about it,' she recalled. 'The poor man was simply *horrified* at my suggestion, and I took nearly a whole morning to wear him down, but eventually he promised, rather miserably, to do the fell deed in his bread ovens the following Saturday night after baking Leatherhead's bread.'

Yet again Zoë found herself involved in secret nocturnal operations involving worms. Though light to carry, her thousands of cocoons were extremely bulky when packed into sacks with straw, and they simply wouldn't fit in her little car for the drive from Lullingstone to the baker's in Leatherhead. 'In the end I borrowed a small lorry from Eynsford, and, packing my sacks in it, I covered them over with rugs, and away I drove. I had to drive myself, as the baker had sworn me to secrecy.'

My grandmother arrived at the back of the baker's at around midnight, just as the bread was being taken out of the ovens. She was quite overcome by the glorious smell of freshly baked bread, she said, and was in a state of great excitement when she plonked in her cocoons for frazzling. But would the poor baker's nerve hold? 'After half an hour, I asked for one oven door to be opened, so that I could test a cocoon.' This was a big mistake, it seems, for a foul stench of lightly cooking silkworm moth now filled the bakery and Mr Baker went ballistic. 'I honestly thought the poor man would die on the spot, and it was quite a while before I could calm him down,' wrote Zoë afterwards.

It took the baker and my grandmother a full six hours to stifle all her cocoons. Heaven knows what favour my grandmother had to promise the man, but as dawn broke she crept away an exhausted but happy woman. 'Cautiously, I drove home, and, parking the lorry near some trees in the garden, I crept into bed. The secret was well kept . . .'

The Hart Dyke family eventually moved to Lullingstone and Zoë now shifted production up a gear by importing serious quantities of reeling machinery and silkworm graine from Italy. After Oliver had converted the laundry at Lullingstone to house the reeling machines, the silk farm was truly motoring.

Thanks to Zoë's driving energy and unquenchable ability to draw attention to herself — not to mention her uncanny skill in getting other people to help her out for free — the enterprise grew in fame and capacity. Intrigued visitors started to arrive by train and coach; and they all wanted tea, which Zoë duly laid on in the stables. All was going swimmingly, in fact, until one year thousands of her worms caught a disease called flacherie, which was caused by eating fermented mulberry leaves. She also got clobbered in 1936 after ordering 4,000 mulberry bushes from the government of Palestine. Alas, along with the rest of Kent's fruit trees, the bushes were hit by a killer late frost, Jack deciding to pounce on 29 May that year.

Zoë was far luckier, however, when she invited Queen Mary to the farm. The Queen was the patron of the Silk Association of Great Britain and Ireland, and my grandmother managed to persuade Dartford Rural District Council to work overtime to sort out the castle's bumpy drive. Men and machines steamrollered the approach for four whole days and nights to make it smooth enough for the village's royal visitor. Volunteers from Eynsford then scrubbed and polished the house until it 'smiled again', as Zoë put it, while gangs of men weeded her mulberry plantation. My grandmother's chutzpah knew no bounds.

Judged purely by its fame and prestigious clients, as opposed to its balance sheet,

Lullingstone Silk Farm went from strength to strength. Zoë ordered another 15,000 mulberry bushes from Milan to plant over a further 15–16 acres, in addition to the 5 acres of mulberry she already had. And it was at about this time, following the abdication of Edward VIII, that a discreet enquiry was made to her by the powers that be. Could she and her team produce 20 lb of raw silk for the robes which Queen Elizabeth (our late Queen Mother as was) would wear at the Coronation in 1937? Yes she jolly well could . . . but only if she and her girls worked round the clock. Which they did, reeling for twenty hours out of twenty-four for two whole weeks. Zoë's dream of using perseverance and patience, as the proverb said, to turn mulberry into silk fit for a queen was well and truly realized.

The Second World War, I've always been told, brought out the best in many Brits, and it certainly did nothing to dampen my grandmother's fighting spirit. In the summer of 1939, the War Office descended on Lullingstone to make a film in the park to drum up recruits for the ARP service. This involved teams of nine to twelve gunners manning anti-aircraft batteries. Despite the terrific racket, Zoë still hatched in record numbers.

Nor was her desire to spread the word about Lullingstone silk dimmed. On the eve of war, she ignored advice and took a stand at the Applied Arts and Handicrafts Exhibition in Malvern, where her cocoon posies went down a storm. She was also promoting a material she had invented called 'silk tweed'. This made use of all her waste silk and was, she said, 'light yet warm, uncreasable and gay'. She sold hundreds of yards of the stuff at Malvern and reckoned she would have sold hundreds more yards if the exhibition hadn't been forced to close early because of Mr Chamberlain's inconvenient announcement on 3 September that Britain was now officially at war with Germany.

By the following spring, with the Phoney War over and proper hostilities now raging, the estate, which was not far from Biggin Hill, became home to a variety of military units. As Zoë put it gamely: 'Conditions that spring of 1940 were a little difficult, as the Air Ministry had disguised part of the grounds as a decoy Fighter Station. We tried fervently to be patriotic as we watched the last dummy 'plane being wheeled into place, but our knees wobbled somewhat at the fair prospect of getting an extra quota of bombs.'

Naturally she took in evacuees; and she also offered the silk farm's output to the Ministry of Supply to make parachutes. The boffins tested it and said it was more than up to the job, but the farm could produce only enough silk for 200 parachutes. As she said, if the government had done more to help her by reducing the tax on imported mulberry bushes, perhaps she could have made a bigger contribution to the war effort.

As Nissen huts sprang up all over Lullingstone, Zoë also found herself running a canteen in the Great Hall for members of an artillery battery. She did this for two years until numbers were so great the NAAFI had to take over. But nothing got in the way of my grandmother's worm-rearing. And it was only when actual bombs started sending plaster and glass crashing down on to the hatcheries that numbers were seriously affected. Even so, Zoë would dragoon squads of willing uniformed helpers in to assist in shifting the egg trays and clearing up the debris.

Zoë was more worried that her silkworms might be harmed by the gas being used by a company of Royal Engineers who were involved in secret chemical warfare experiments on the estate. 'I had heard that geese were not affected,' she recalled, 'but this was not quite the same thing. I fled to Major Morland, who was in charge, and explained the position. He managed not to laugh, but his eyes twinkled as he assured me no gas would be released anywhere in the vicinity of the silkworms.'

It was also at this time that my grandmother learnt the handy skill of how to kill a man using just a short length of stick. This she mastered courtesy of a Royal Army Medical Corps battle school that had also set up shop in the grounds. She was deeply in awe of the man in charge, a Major G. Petty, who 'had the difficult task of turning out men who were a mixture of prize-fighter, commando and nurse'.

Major Petty was a firm believer in teaching fighting skills and self-defence, he said, explaining to my grandmother that these were vital for his men, who were generally unarmed. This point was never lost on the enemy, who often sought to take advantage. 'The Major then proceeded to instruct me how to kill or disable a man with the aid of a short stick, and when I learned how to do it neatly in the [sic] matter of seconds, my respect and admiration knew no bounds.'

No doubt the confidence that being able to kill a man with a bit of stick gave my grandmother helped her in her business career. But why had she gone into the silkworm business in the first place when she could have spent a leisurely life playing tennis and golf as part of a 'gay group' of other Leatherhead housewives?

As she had told exhibitors at the Home Life exhibition in Brighton in 1938, which she had been invited to open and where she was awarding the prizes to the winners of the Exhibition Window Dressing Competition: 'If a woman tries to run a business, people have three explanations for her peculiar action. Firstly, she is doing it to support a family, or perchance a drunken male relative; secondly, she has been crossed in love, and is trying to forget the distressing incident by hard work; thirdly, she is a mannish type — all tweeds, collar and tie. What people seem to forget, or perhaps do not understand, is that some women like business for its own sake, and enjoy it tremendously; I come under this category.'

As I thought about all the things I now had to do in the World Garden, I found my grandmother Zoë's example truly inspiring. But there was a disturbing footnote to her story on which I tried not to dwell.

Though she was profiled in *Time* magazine in

1937 as being a veritable human dynamo — which she plainly was — she was so determined to make her sericulture dream come true that she lost sight of the pounds, shillings and pence. At one stage she was even sending silk cocoons to Italy for reeling and then re-importing the raw silk, thus paying two sets of import duty, one in Italy and one in Britain, not to mention the cost of freight, insurance and the reeling itself. This meant that Zoë was paying 48s 6d a pound to produce silk thread when the average price at the time was just 10s a pound.

The lesson was clear. Zoë was a marvel all right. But all dreams have their price and, as a businesswoman, my dynamic grandma was nothing if not a walking financial disaster area. I let that be a warning to me.

# 13

## A Class of My Own

Grandma Zoë's great good fortune — apart from being strikingly beautiful, hugely persuasive, inexhaustibly energetic and married to my grandfather (who had a degree in engineering and could assemble and fix her reeling machines) — was to have vast reserves of charm and cheek. She'd invite royalty to visit Lullingstone, or badger the local railway people to shuttle trippers to the castle, with the same determination that she set about that poor bloke with the bread oven in Leatherhead.

When required, she could also be extremely focused. She taught herself about the science of sericulture, for example, by travelling up from Leatherhead to the Natural History Museum in South Kensington every day for a month to copy out in longhand the only textbook the museum had on the subject: the translation of a work by someone called Count Daldano.

Later, when she wanted egg supplies or advice on the practical or commercial side of silk production, she would skip off to Milan and gaily secure introductions to the people in the industry who mattered. Faced by tedious hassles and bothersome bureaucrats while trying to source mulberry bushes or machinery from abroad, Grandma Zoë always seemed to know of

146

a little man somewhere who would fall under her spell and get things sorted. She'd write shamelessly to an ambassador she vaguely knew here, or to a military attaché she'd once met there, and she usually secured the help she wanted.

Perhaps the fact that she was a woman in business at a time when this was still unusual made men take note of her. Maybe it was her striking appearance — in photographs, she always seems to me hugely confident and beguiling. Or perhaps people were simply bowled over by the hardcore worm action and were happy to help. My own hunch is that Grandad's title and the Lullingstone Castle address did no harm in helping open doors and made it harder for people to refuse her. Indeed, back in the days of deference I imagine Zoë could have got away with murder in the mulberry bushes if she had wanted to.

For me, the World Garden was a challenge every bit as daunting as anything Zoë had tried to achieve. I would need the same level of determination to make it happen, but there was a world of difference between our personalities and our network of social connections.

'Have you seen the Queen recently, Tom?' is a question I've been asked more than once and my answer is always the same.

'Jeepers! No!'

I have nothing against the Queen, God bless her; but I've never met any member of the Royal Family and I can't recognize half of them on the telly. Though generations of Harts and Dykes and Peches would shudder to hear me say so, I'm not even very interested in royalty. The Queen seems pretty cool and does her best, from what I see on the news, but that's about the sum of my interest.

Oddly, when visitors and even some people who know me see me working out in the garden, even though I'll be wearing one of my old jumpers or fleeces and a tea-cosy on top, they sometimes seem unable to differentiate between me, the big house and the portraits inside it. It's as if they imagine that secretly I must be ever so grand and that my family must be on Corgi-stroking terms with Her Maj. Worse, they also imagine I have an army of helpers to do my weeding and watering — 'Can't you get the servants to do that, Tom?' — and that all my friends must be well-connected chaps who also live in stonking great piles and are part of an exclusive club called 'The Landed Gentry'. Well, they haven't met my mate Richard.

Zoë and some of my grander ancestors might be quite shocked to see how modestly, socially speaking, their Hart Dyke descendants live today. Not that it bothers us, but my parents don't 'entertain' in the grand tradition as they've never had the time or the money. Nor do they hunt, fish or shoot. On the very, very rare occasions I am invited to supper with them at another stately pile or to a Christmas party, I rarely feel in my element and am often unsure which knife and fork to zoom in on first. Being left-handed doesn't help; but that sort of etiquette simply isn't on my radar. Nor do I own a dinner jacket, in case you were wondering. I still borrow Dad's old one when I have to.

Sitting at table in someone else's big house, I'm far more likely to want to gaze at the vases and what's in them and wonder about the orchids in the greenhouse than make social chit-chat with the attractive woman sitting next to me. Some people find this mildly endearing for about five minutes, because it marks me out as slightly unusual; but if there's ever a return match, they know I will probably turn up smeared with oil because the Astra has broken down again or I'll come straight from the garden. They doubtless think, 'Big house, no money — fine'; but 'Big house, no money, soil under the fingernails — bit different.'

Socially, my remarkable ability to sometimes forget names doesn't help. It must sometimes seem shockingly rude; but I never mean to be. I was exactly the same in school with chemistry and C. S. Lewis. Plant names are fine; I'm just occasionally hopeless with people — unless they have a serious gum tree or orchid habit, and then I'll never forget who they are.

When I was growing up in the garden at Lullingstone, I was in such a little bubble I was never aware that something called a 'county set' might exist, let alone that the Hart Dykes could have qualified for membership if this had interested them. Which it never did.

My notions of 'class' are also unconventional. I know that many people in Britain are still very sensitive to the notion of 'class' and the mobility between lower, middle and upper, etc. I also know that, as birds of a feather tend to stick together, people often choose their friends by background. But I don't and I never have. Perhaps gardeners never do. I take everyone at face value and work on the sole principle that if someone's a cool bloke and I trust them and get on with them, and they get on with me, great — let's be mates and have some fun. Perhaps I am naïve, but in friendships, I just go for it. So far, my instinct has rarely let me down.

People — especially people from backgrounds similar to my own — find this approach slightly unusual, to say the least. 'Who's this plant nut going to talk to next?' they wonder. When I have randomly met others with similar family set-ups to mine — big house, no cash; or even big house, lots of cash — I've never felt any special connection with them. Sometimes they must look at my parents and then at me and think: 'Crikey! Where did it all go wrong?'

Seeing strangers' reactions to me can also be an eye-opener. I might be chatting to someone of any age or sex about gardening, say, and everything is relaxed and fine until they begin to get an inkling of the set-up here at Lullingstone. Once they realize we've got a lake, quite a few trees and Queen Anne's bedroom, almost imperceptibly their attitude and tone can begin to change and they become somehow more attentive. I find this fascinating. It's as if they suddenly feel they have to respond to me differently. But with the Green Man they really needn't bother. Lullingstone remains a thoroughly work-orientated place, not a social centre.

Dad, don't forget, was a proper tree man.

So when it comes to class, I have no idea which one I am and I couldn't care less. I do find it quite funny that one day I might end up *Sir* Tom Hart Dyke, the 11th baronet, because the 10th baronet, my cousin David in Toronto, Uncle Derek's son, has no kids. But *Sir* Tom? As I said, bit of a hoot really.

I'm incredibly grateful to Mum and Dad for bringing me up in what I think is a very straightforward, open-minded way. It means that though I'll never be as smooth an operator as my networking granny Zoë, or have regular Sunday lunches with the prime minister of the day like Great-Grandad William, I have a wide group of brilliant friends. They are, to put it mildly, a fairly mixed bunch.

One has run a fish-and-chip shop; another was a car-jacker until he ended up inside; and a third is a seriously sensitive soul who is deeply into ley lines. What my closest friends like the Big Friendly Giant Tom Stobbart, Richard Reeves, Gum Nut Steve, Gum Bark Geoff and Laurence 'Bat Man' Dell all have in common, however, is that, like me, they have some serious horticultural issues they will be working through for the rest of their days. And that's why we get on.

I bet many of my ancestors would have been blown away meeting Richard, for example. They might even have taken a while to recover. But I love Rich dearly and he is, quite simply, a legend. As well as extremely long hair and long arms, he has an amazingly pale complexion. *Really* starchy. To look at him you would think he's

151

either on drugs or drink; and having spoken to him, probably both, plus some extra things he's found growing by the side of the road. But like me, Richard is as clean as a whistle and I think his complexion is down to his unusual diet.

Richard lives exclusively on chips and Tesco Value lemonade — although at Lullingstone he has thrown caution to the wind and picked at a bowl of Coco Pops. This highly selective menu doesn't necessarily make it easy to cater for Richard when he comes to stay. In fact, it's a bit of a nightmare if I buy the wrong sort of chips or cook them in the wrong sort of way or buy the wrong sort of lemonade. It *has* to be Tesco Value, the really cheap stuff, or he won't touch it.

'Cup of tea, Rich?'

Forget it.

Mercifully, the chips can be any length, but they have to be cooked in vegetable oil in a certain way and for a certain time or Rich won't go near them. A connoisseur of the deep-fried potato, Richard Reeves is probably one of Britain's leading authorities on chips and chip shops.

Despite the fact that he looks like a creature of the night who hasn't seen daylight for several years, the times Rich and I spend outdoors in the fresh air, crawling through the New Forest searching for Marsh Helleborines, Heath Spotted Orchids and the extremely elusive Bog Orchid, are the best ever. I will never forget a really serious session of hardcore bog action in the New Forest with him in the summer of 2001. It was a baking hot day, and we went squelching on hands and knees through a stinking, sinking quagmire of Creeping Willow and smelly-leaved Bog Myrtles, hunting for my first-ever *Hammarbya paludosa* or Bog Orchid. It was truly brilliant. It was also hugely competitive as we slithered over the ground like a couple of swamp creatures and tried to be the first to spot one.

The other day Rich took me down 30 feet to the bottom of an old Roman well at Kevington Hall, near Orpington, home of my inspirational friend Jon Jackson. We were looking for treasure, said Rich, and we should have had oxygen with us but had to make do with a couple of cycling masks. Unfortunately, when we were both blue and purple in the face at the bottom of the well gasping for air, all we found were some plastic eggs of the sort you stick under a hen's backside to make her lay.

Richard is a genuine inspiration and genius with an encyclopaedia for a brain, whose day job is working in the library of the New Forest Tourist Information Centre in Lyndhurst. Like me, he has a thing about Latin plant names, and we'll often try to catch one another out. For example, I'll ask him the Latin for some chalk downland species up on the golf course because I know it's exclusive to Kent and, as there's not much chalk in the New Forest, he'll probably be stumped.

'What's the Latin for 'Lizard Orchid', Rich?'
'Dunno.'
He'll counter by asking me the Latin for some incredibly obscure water-loving marsh dweller

only found in a 3-metre-square spot near Brockenhurst.

In fact, we can bicker for hours about his beloved native plants and my desirable exotic or 'alien' plants, as he describes them dismissively. If I dare suggest that something like *Rhododendron ponticum*, now a seriously invasive pest in the New Forest, was once native to Britain (as can be proved through the fossil record), Rich explodes with indignation.

I suspect strongly that Rich (who always wears combat trousers and army boots — I've literally never seen him in anything else) takes his interest in Latin plant names to extremes. I'm convinced that as a hardcore punk-metaller, he even screams them out at the top of his voice while head-banging in the mosh pit at gigs. No drug could ever give you that kind of high. Thank God.

'Did Richard ever spend any time in a remand home?' Dad asked the first time they met.

'No, Dad, I don't think he did.'

'Are you *sure*?'

Mum and Dad, having accepted that I am slightly different, have grown to adore Richard, who is also slightly different — even if his idiosyncratic views on the history of the development of the Lullingstone estate can be a little too 'extensive' for Dad at times. It's not geomancy, exactly; but Rich can — and does — go right back to the Druids to give us chapter and verse on the spiritual significance of Lullingstone growing up beneath a hill and by a river. He also knows his kings and queens backwards and what colour socks they wore. As I said, a legend.

I met Rich during a joss-stick session (more of which later) when I was a student at Sparsholt College in Hampshire. The college specializes in training people to work in what they call land-based industries — everything from fish farming to floristry and animal welfare, or the 'Fluffy Bunny Course' as we all called it. Rich was doing Game and Wildlife Management and I was studying Forestry and Tree Surgery. Sparsholt, whose gem of a campus is surrounded by the blissfully rolling chalk hills of Hampshire between Winchester and Stockbridge, was basically the Dog's Bollocks. Although it was a very sensible and well-organized place, for me it was a riot from start to finish.

After Crac, Mum, Dad, Anya and of course Lullingstone itself, the friendships I made during the two years I spent there have easily been the most influential thing in my life. Any assumptions about how I might have turned out evaporated the second Mum and Dad dropped me off at Steele, the hostel on the edge of the campus where I lived in my first year, and I fell in with a fascinatingly diverse crowd.

After school I had made the conscious decision *not* to study horticulture. Without wanting to sound cocky, on a two-year course I would probably have known much of the syllabus already. Forestry I didn't know much about and about tree surgery nothing at all. By studying for a First Diploma and National Certificate and then getting NVQs in things like spraying with chemicals, shinning up trees with ropes and wielding a chainsaw, I reckoned I would at least be able to earn a living afterwards.

Some of my fellow first-year students on the First Diploma Forestry and Woodland Management course were excessive. Indeed, I think only 40 per cent of them passed the relevant modules in that first year and a couple were expelled.

Some were definitely unstable. Take, for example, a chap I shall call Dope Dave, who spent the entire first year catatonically stoned. Just walking into his room was a major health hazard given the fug of burning weed; and if the passive cannabis-smoking didn't knacker you, there was always the danger of tripping over one of the comatose bodies of his friends who were slumped on floor, chair, bed and bog.

Despite being 'bonged out' for an entire year, Dave did find the energy to take part in at least one leisure activity: creeping up on fellow forestry students when we were in the minibus on our way to tree-cutting exercises . . . and viciously knee-capping us with his small but extremely effective home-made shillelagh. As we were generally in the sitting position in the minibus, our knees were always horribly vulnerable to his painful attacks.

Though Dave and I shared an interest in the music of De La Soul and in playing badminton, I never had any desire to smoke his weed. Drugs interest me even less than alcohol. However, as a means of protecting myself from a knee-capping and to blend in with the crowd, on a trip home to Lullingstone I took the precaution of making my own cracking giant of a shillelagh. Where Dave's was about 7 inches long, I chose a massive 2-foot length of heavy hornbeam from Trevor Edwards's hedge in the middle of the walled garden and made myself a monster. I even painted it black and decorated it with woodlouse and millipede motifs; and I made sure I always had it near me on the minibus just in case. Happily, the mere sight of it was enough to deter attacks and I never had to wield it in anger.

Given Dave's smoking habits, his reaction when the Sparsholt authorities allowed the planting of a 4-acre field of cannabis in the college grounds was predictable. The cannabis was meant to provide hemp for the horses that were cared for by the college's equestrian students. Naturally, it was an entirely inert strain and lacked the necessary chemicals to give smokers any kind of high. But that didn't deter Dope Dave and his bong-buddies from descending on the field like a swarm of locusts to smoke themselves stupid.

In no time our forestry intake earned an appalling reputation. As the nice chap who taught us tractor-driving announced with regret one day (shortly before having some kind of breakdown), my group was the most disruptive, unreliable and badly behaved the college had ever seen. He had a point. As well as Dope Dave, we included a hopeless kleptomaniac who was wanted by the police for car and bicycle theft, as well as a number of day-release students who never bothered to turn up. When they did, it was only to roll the quad bikes, jack-knife the tractor and trailer or set off the fire extinguishers.

In the second year, when I was studying for a National Certificate in Arboriculture (that's tree surgery), things had calmed down a bit. I had moved into room number 6 in Flint hostel (where everything was colour-coded blue, in contrast to the green of Steele), and I had started to forge some genuinely brilliant friendships with people on other courses. These included Steve Godber and the Hipstarrr, aka Paul Bamford. I'll never forget the first time the Hipstarrr walked into my room. He was holding a pot of compost in his hand and he just looked at me and screamed at the very top of his voice: '*GERMINATION!!!!!!!!!!!!*'

He was throwing down a gauntlet, and if he wanted a germination competition . . . he could have one!

I had wasted no time in transforming room number 6 into a tropical rainforest, much as I had my bedroom on the top floor at Lullingstone. With the radiators whacked up to full volume and soaking-wet towels laid out on top of them, the humidity was such that I was even producing deliciously lush aerial root growth on my *Monstera deliciosa*, better known to students and bedsit dwellers as a cheese plant. This, along with my yuccas, orchids and a really nice Marmalade Bush from Ecuador (*Strepto-solen jamesonii*), thrived in the steamy heat — despite my habit of hosting some extremely intense joss-stick sessions. While Dope Dave had filled his bong with weed, I burned nothing more controversial than incense. But I did so in almost industrial quantities, challenging my badminton-playing friends Sye, Steve, Tom Stobbart and Spud Gun Rog to eye-streaming endurance contests.

It was during one of these massive sessions that I first met Richard Reeves, and the ritual was always the same. Before 'baddy' or 'badders' as we called it, we would congregate in room 6, lay a towel at the foot of the door and light up, filling the room with thick, billowing clouds of sweet-smelling incense smoke. With rasping coughs and streaming eyes, the aim was to see who could last the longest before demanding to be let out to breathe again.

It was during one of these joss-stick sessions that we nearly lost poor Steve Godber in what would have been an unusual incident even for Sparsholt — its first case of spontaneous combustion. Steve, who was on the college's Sheep Management course (attended by a massive three students) even though he seemed to have no natural affinity for sheep whatsoever, had got hold of my can of Lynx deodorant. Perhaps through boredom, or maybe to ward off the smell of sheep, he decided to spray his entire body extensively from head to toe and at close quarters, at the same time as sparking up another joss-stick with a lighter.

There was an amazing 'Whomp!' as the flammable deodorant vapour suddenly ignited, creating a large ball of flame in front of Steve's upper body.

Luckily he failed to catch fire himself, and by

159

way of relief I seem to remember he, Sye and I then adjourned to the sports hall for a mega session of badders. We'd often play from 6pm right through to 1am, and I loved these marathons. I even organized a club at Sparsholt and got us playing in the Hampshire County League against colleges from Southampton and Winchester. We had such a good time it really didn't matter that we lost every single match with the exception of one game of doubles that Toby Sherwood and I managed to sneak against a team whose name I've completely forgotten.

Despite the intense pleasure generated during badders, which also involved Richard Reeves, Tom Stobbart and Dan The Man He Who Can, games often degenerated into racquet-smashing brawls — particularly if the dysfunctional 'Car Jacker' was playing.

Nothing really fazed my friends and we were well known in the hostel for our mild eccentricities. Anya, having met some of the crew and heard how batty life was in Flint and at Sparsholt in general, tried an experiment one day when she rang me up for a chat.

'Flint,' said a bored voice after the hostel's communal phone had been ringing for about a week.

'Hello,' said Anya cheerily. 'Can I speak to Thomasina Tittle-Penis, please?'

The person who answered didn't bat an earlobe.

'What room?' came his matter-of-fact reply.

'Er, six,' replied Bristles.

'Hang about. *Phone for Thomasina Tittle-Penis, room six!*' yelled my fellow Sparsholtian.

Freed from the constraints of academic work which had always reminded me of what I couldn't do well, for the first time in my life I was surrounded by people who were passionate about the same sort of things as I was. This was a major revelation and I felt integrated and able to have a proper social life. I even found a part-time gardening job near Southampton on Wednesday afternoons to earn some pocket money.

The people I was friendly with weren't all total delinquents; they simply had one or two more issues than the majority. The fact that I happened to come from a castle while most of my mates were from more modest backgrounds made no difference at all beyond having brief novelty value. Indeed, in the eccentric plant-orientated company of my friends, I no longer felt 'different' as I had in school. How could I when I was mates with someone like Steve, for example, who was brilliant company . . . but not if you were a sheep. I'll never forget how at the end of term, giving a live shearing display in front of proud parents and interested professionals, Steve was so cack-handed he managed to cut off the lower bit of his sheep's ear. This was bad enough — it was dreadful; but did he really then have to try pathetically to stick it back on again with all those people watching? The ear was eventually lost in a sea of blood stained with purple spray-on disinfectant.

It was also in my second year that I developed

a really serious crush on a girl called Chris who was one of the equestrian students. She was very, very pretty, with long black curly hair, and I was smitten, quite unable to sleep for nights on end or even to eat properly for thinking about her. Whenever I did pluck up the courage to talk to her, I was always so nervous I could only ever babble out mundanities. I was never able to ask her out properly and I think the best we managed was a single bus ride to Winchester together.

Of the saner Sparsholtians I was probably most comfortable in the company of the BFG, Tom Stobbart. We met during my second and his first year. Like me, he had long hair, he was the same height (6 foot 2 inches) and was also left-handed. I loved his deadpan sense of humour and how very together he was, and a strong friendship has grown up between us. It was one winter's day in the second year when we were in the library with Sye Man that we all decided to go travelling after college. We chose our destination after a great deal of careful planning and research . . . by gathering around an Oxford Atlas, agreeing to open it on page 46 and going to wherever happened to be in the middle of the page.

'Yeaaah! Borneo it is!' we yelled in delight, instantly naming ourselves the Borneo Boys.

In the event, Sye was unable to come with us; and Tom, following an unfortunate incident towards the end of term, was himself lucky to be available for any kind of foreign travel at all.

With the sheep-shearing Steve Godber, Tom

and I had been to the Party in the Park in Southampton, an open-air musical jamboree sponsored by a local radio station, Power FM. Because we'd missed the last bus home we decided to walk the 5 miles back to Sparsholt along the main Winchester to Stockbridge road.

Walking through the moonlight on a summer night with my mates after a big party, I was certainly knackered but didn't have a care in the world. That was about to change. As we approached the final bend near the entrance to college, the three of us had spread out in single file, Tom now some way ahead with his Big Friendly Giant strides. Over our shoulders, Steve and I could hear that a car was coming up behind us at a belting speed; when it whooshed past in the darkness like a racing demon, it must have been doing 60mph — not bad on a double white-line bend. The next thing we heard was an almighty skidding and screeching of tyres around the bend ahead of us.

Steve and I sprinted into the darkness, our minds racing and fearing the worst. The car had indeed screeched to an unceremonious stand-still.

'Tom! Tom!' we shouted, desperately searching for our friend. We eventually found him on the deck in the most bizarre position imaginable. After flying over the car and nearly going through the windscreen, Tom had evidently whacked the aerial, gone over the boot and caught the rear bumper. Weirdly, he had landed on his kneecaps and was still in the kneeling position.

Tom obviously had a guardian angel looking over him that night. For not only was he not dead, he was still speaking. As I bent over him, I'll never forget what he said.

'Tom . . . we're going to Borneo!'

He remained in the kneeling position until the ambulance arrived. After he'd been examined in hospital in Winchester, it emerged that it was only his clothes that had been damaged: Tom barely had a scratch on him. Unbelievable. 'Your friend's a miracle man,' said the doctor.

Today Tom is married to Claire — I was his joint best man — and he now works as head groundsman at Windsor racecourse. It's a big responsibility, but then Tom was always very together, even as a student. When we were both saving hard to go on our travels, he managed to wangle a job at Millets in Biggleswade, which entitled him to staff discount on all his camping gear. Good old Tom.

Like Gum Nut Steve and Gum Bark Geoff, both of whom you'll meet later, Tom has helped give me my outlook on life and my values, and I'm eternally grateful to all of them. It was Mum and Dad, of course, who first brought me up to try to be open-minded and to treat everyone with the same courtesy. Their influence and how important it had been really came home to me when Tom and I finally did make it to south-east Asia. It meant I could stop and chat to anyone — a guy living on the street in Indonesia, say, who only had one eye, one leg and no hair and who was begging for 25p a week — and, in less murderous moments, it even enabled me to communicate after a fashion with my gun-wielding captors in the Darién, like M16, Trouble Ahead, Space Cadet and the spooky Whispering Death.

Perhaps if Mum and Dad had brought me up more traditionally and made me more self-conscious or inhibited, I doubt I would have survived my capture so well. I also might have hesitated that winter in 2003 to pick up the telephone and dial a certain number in Derbyshire to ask for advice from a complete stranger who I felt could help me.

'Hello,' I said to the voice on the other end. 'I'm Tom Hart Dyke from Lullingstone Castle in Kent. I'm trying to create a World Garden here . . . Can I speak to the Duchess of Devonshire, please?'

# 14

## Friends in High Places

I found the Duchess of Devonshire's telephone number easily enough — it was printed on the back of a Chatsworth House leaflet someone had left lying around. But hers wasn't the only number I rang at the start of 2004 when I realized that to create my World Garden I now needed some serious advice, not to mention help, both financial and physical.

Chatsworth House, the legendary pile in Derbyshire, is in a different solar system from little old Lullingstone. I learnt, for example, that it had had more than 680,000 visitors the previous year, and I doubted Mum, Dad or Red Indian Reg, who collects our ticket money, would appreciate that many people filing past the sentry box where Reg sits. Incidentally, Reg does have real Red Indian ancestry — and the Red Indian name of Ma-Zakantanka.

In some ways I felt slightly fraudulent even daring to discuss my proposals with the Devonshires. Since 1950 when Andrew Cavendish became the 11th Duke, he and his wife had been at the forefront of the revival of the country house in England, developing Chatsworth into a stunning amenity. It's no exaggeration to say they led the way; and tapping them for tips felt a bit like asking Bob Flowerdew or Geoff

Hamilton how to grow cress on a bit of cotton wool on the kitchen table. But I had to start somewhere, and taking a leaf from Zoë's book I thought: why not at the very top?

I also contacted the Heritage Lottery Fund to see if the transformation work I was proposing to do on the walls of the garden and up at the old Ice House and Bath House, both of which were jungled-out beneath a rampant thicket of greenery, might qualify for some sort of funding. In fact I cast around for anyone who might be able to give me advice.

I even tracked down Jeremy Thorp, the ambassador who had greeted Paul and me when the Colombian Red Cross delivered us, swollen and smelly, to his official residence in Bogotá, where, hilariously, we really were given Ferrero Rocher chocolates on a silver plate!

I had heard Jeremy had left the diplomatic service and was now doing something in the City of London, and I thought he might be worth a chat, given the World Garden's unusual genesis in the Darién. Unlike the $5 million ransom notes the guerrillas made Paul and me write, my email to Our Former Man in Bogotá did get through, but at this stage he was unable to help. (Later though, funnily enough, I was delighted to see him and his charming wife Estella in the audience when I gave a talk at the Brazilian Embassy in London. They didn't mind my joke about the Ferrero Rocher chocs and Jeremy even arranged for seeds from an ancient pine in the garden of the ambassador's residence in Bogotá to be sent to Lullingstone. Good man!)

Thanks to the many months I had spent rooted to my chair in front of the PC, I had a fair idea how much all my plants, seeds and horticultural sundries were going to cost — everything from spades and forks to plant pots, feed and slug pellets. It was mounting up, and I didn't dare look too closely at the really big figures: how much it would cost to turn my rough sketches into a proper technical design from which contractors in hard hats could make the earth move and install all the underground infrastructure; how much I would have to pay for heavy digging machinery; not to mention the tonnes of extra acid soil I would need in China and Japan; plus rocks and labour, and how much it would then cost to market the garden and tell potential visitors that it existed.

Even without precise figures, the whole project was feeling seriously expensive — certainly beyond the spending power of a sometime talk-giver. I started wondering about the possibility of sponsors and whether that would mean having to call my creation the 'John Innes Potting Compost World Garden at Lullingstone' or whatever. Then there was charitable status. Perhaps I could set up some kind of global-gardening-environmental charity to help me raise funds. It was with such half-thoughts blowing around my head like an eddy of autumn leaves that I contacted the legendary 'Debo', as I didn't quite dare call Her Grace over the phone.

'Ah yes, Lullingstone,' she said warmly when we were put through. 'Of course I know Lullingstone. Silkworms!'

Well, at least the Duchess knew I wasn't a prank caller. It was a blessing and a curse, however, that like so many others of a certain age she still remembered Lullingstone for Grandma Zoë's worms. The worms had actually wriggled off in 1956 to spend their days at Ayot St Lawrence in Hertfordshire, which was where Zoë settled after her marriage to my grandfather ended. The worms, or their descendants, then eventually finished up near Sherborne in Dorset when the Lullingstone Silk Farm business was sold following Zoë's death in 1975. My own secret ambition was that one day people might say: 'Ah yes, Lullingstone: the World Garden!' But, as I explained to the Duchess, I was some way from achieving such immortality.

'Debo' listened politely and made encouraging noises as I gabbled. I explained that with no business experience, I wanted advice on the best way to structure a new garden attraction on a struggling family estate. Our roots might go back to the fourteenth century, but the Hart Dykes had no priceless Old Master drawings or oils to flog off or put on show to help us survive into the twenty-first.

'Why don't you come up to Chatsworth, Tom, and have a look around? We can have a proper talk over lunch.'

*Result!*

The magnificent Chatsworth and its acres had always been too far for Crac and me to visit on our days out in her car, and I was incredibly excited at the thought not only of meeting the Duchess but of seeing where Joseph Paxton,

Chatsworth's legendary head gardener from the 1820s onwards, had brought about so many feats of horticultural heavenliness: from his giant rockery and Pinetum, to the tropical splendours of his Great Conservatory, designed with the help of Decimus Burton, the architect behind the Wellington Arch at Hyde Park Corner.

Though the Great Conservatory came down in the 1920s, at the time it went up in the late 1830s it was the biggest such structure in the world: a glass cathedral dedicated to the saintly plant-hunters of the day. Then there were all Chatsworth's modern additions — the Kitchen Garden, the Cottage Garden, the Sensory Garden — with which the Devonshires, themselves mad keen plant people, had enhanced the splendour of Paxton's Victorian vision. I wanted to see them all.

So the Green Man was definitely buzzing as he motored north in February 2004 in a second-hand Vauxhall Astra he had bought for £3,000 with a slice of his Darién book advance. So buzzing, in fact, that he clean forgot to pack a sleeping bag, a toothbrush or any spare clothes. But he did remember to take a hat — a gold-coloured corduroy teacosy, specially chosen for the occasion.

Just as some people buy shoes or CDs, when funds permit I have a weakness for plants (reasonably priced ones anyway), and I indulged my weakness at several nurseries and garden centres on the drive up. This meant that by the time I hit downtown Matlock, the Astra resembled a greenhouse-on-wheels, the rear seats and boot stacked with trays, tubs and a riot of green tendrils, mostly of tropical-leaved herbaceous plants and creepers.

As well as forgetting my toothbrush and a change of clothes, I also forgot to check my accommodation. Thus when I arrived at the youth hostel nearest to the Devonshires' pile, I found it was shut for the winter. Damn! When I'm on the road, saving money (apart from plant-buying) is a priority. I'm a firm believer in *not* spending £50 for a full night in a hotel when I can make do with three hours' free kip in the car at a service station. But a whole night shivering in the Astra now beckoned, and with no sleeping bag I wasn't relishing it.

Seeing a likely lay-by on the outskirts of Matlock, I decided to park up and try to get some sleep. Unfortunately the road was still quite busy with late-night traffic and I felt a little too visible. As I didn't want to risk being moved on by the police for vagrancy in the small hours, I decided to get out of sight and sneak the Astra into the field behind the lay-by.

I quickly snuck the nose of the car in through the gate that had been left open and started to drive into the field, intending to tuck myself in behind the hedge.

Big mistake.

Because the car windows were steamed up due to the humidity pumped out by the leaf transpiration of the plants I had bought earlier in the day, and because it was now dark, I couldn't see out of the car and I didn't spot that the entrance to the field was a fairly major mud bath. Within a matter of yards the wheels of the Astra were slipping and sliding giddily; and cranking the steering wheel from side to side had no effect. Before I could say, 'Tom, you didn't think this one through,' the car and I were deep in the dark brown stuff.

Opening the driver's door, in the dull glow of the courtesy light I could see that I had come to rest in a glutinous bog of mud and manure that had obviously been churned up by a recently departed herd of livestock. The front wheels had smoothed themselves a couple of nice deep ruts in the gunge, and no matter how carefully I tried to edge the car out of them, the wheels just spun and spun.

With my greenhouse-cum-bedroom on wheels marooned, I needed traction. Stepping out into the freezing night air and gingerly squelching through the quagmire, I went back to the lay-by to see what was lying around. A bit of old carpet perhaps? In the light of passing headlights I was just about able to make out some planks and big pieces of flint by the hedge. Brilliant! I was going to be all right.

Loaded up with as many short planks and flints as I could carry, I hurried back to the sinking Astra. I couldn't tell if the field had been home to pigs or cattle or wildebeest, but the stench confirmed I was definitely in the middle of some kind of livestock lavatory area where four-legged creatures had recently been having a vigorous mosh pit stomping session. With great gobs of mud and manure clinging to my DMs, I knelt down in the gunge and arranged the planks and bricks by the front wheels before squelching back into the car and starting her up.

If the rubble would only give me a tiny bit of grip, I reckoned I would have enough traction to get out of the mud and on to the firmer grass I could see tantalizingly in the headlights. Then it would be lights out and bed. Unfortunately, my carefully arranged planks and flints simply sank pathetically into the cream-cheese mud. The car had no grip whatsoever and I was going nowhere.

Beginning to feel slightly desperate, I turned off the engine, climbed out and in the glow of the headlights rearranged my bricks and planks for one last shove. With my hands filthy, wet and freezing, I climbed back into the car, gripped the steering wheel and prayed. Leaving the headlights on had already begun to drain the battery, but the Astra eventually spluttered to life. To get a better view of what was happening at the front wheels, I decided to open my door to peer out as I hit the gas.

Another big mistake.

If you have ever been sprayed in the face with high-pressure farmyard slurry at point-blank range, you will have some idea of what happened next. The boards and flints were entirely useless, and as I hit the gas and turned the steering wheel from side to side to try to get some purchase, the tyres spun furiously, sending a powerful jet of mud, dung and grass all over me and the inside of the Astra.

Realizing I now needed help, I got out and stood in the quagmire. Very tired, cold and foolish, and with the slurry drying on my face and tightening my skin, I rejoined the road and trudged into the darkness to find a friendly farmer. Eventually I came to a lone farmhouse where a single light was burning in an upstairs bedroom, suggesting that the friendly farmer who lived here was just about to go to sleep. Not a great time to call unannounced while streaked from head to toe in liquid manure, but this was an emergency.

'Hello!' I called up pathetically, scared of the sound my voice was now making in the silence and darkness.

No response. I cleared my throat.

'Ahem. *Hellooooo!*' I ventured a little more loudly.

Still no response.

'*Help!!!!*' I cried. '*Help!!!! I need help!*'

The upstairs bedroom window immediately swung open and a woman in a nightdress leaned out.

'Who is it?' she demanded.

I stammered out my apologies for disturbing her so late and explained my predicament.

'Um . . . I'm afraid I think I need a tow.'

The woman in the nightdress disappeared and was replaced at the window seconds later by a man in pyjamas.

'Where's the car?' he barked, not obviously amused.

'Er . . . it's in the lay-by down the road,' I lied, not daring to admit that I had actually driven it into someone's field. But hopefully not *his* field.

'But it's hard standing in the lay-by! Where's it stuck?'

'Um . . . It's sort . . . er . . . ' I could sense I was digging myself deeper in trouble. 'Er . . . it's sort of on the edge of the lay-by,' I mumbled, hoping the farmer wasn't paying attention.

'Wait there,' he said.

I stood in the darkness feeling like a complete tit and not a little apprehensive. What if it *was* this man's field and I had lied to him? It didn't bear thinking about.

The farmer came out of his house grumpily and motioned for me to climb into his Land Rover. I gabbled out my thanks and apologies once more; and as we chugged out of the farmyard, his irritation at leaving a warm bed almost seemed to turn to faint amusement when he saw what a mud-spattered mess I was. I made a mental note that I would give this nice chap £20 of the £40 cash I still had left as a generous thank you.

Unfortunately the farmer's air of faint amusement changed to chill menace the moment his headlights lit up the lay-by.

'Where's the bloody car!?!?' he snapped, suspicious and aggressive at the same time.

I wanted the ground to swallow me up.

'Um . . . er . . . well . . . It *was* in the lay-by when I . . . er . . . started trying to turn round in the entrance to the . . . And then, um . . . It's in the field.'

'You've driven it into my bloody field! You've no bloody business doing that! It's private property! What on earth did you think you were doing?!'

I thought the farmer's head was going to explode. He wasn't angry, he was apoplectic; and he proceeded to give me one of the worst rollickings I have ever had, easily on a par with anything the Darién Gap guerrillas ever hurled at me. Despite the freezing night air I was sweating. For a moment I even thought I was going to wet myself.

'Um . . . I can pay for the tow,' I stammered.

'How much have you got?'

'Forty pounds.'

'I'll have that as the recovery fee,' he barked, squelching off angrily to attach a tow rope to the stricken Astra before tugging me free. When I handed over the money and we parted, he did not wish me a pleasant journey.

Freed from the quagmire but feeling more than a little shaky now, I left the lay-by as fast as I could and drove into the night. Apart from the few coins I keep in my dashboard cubbyhole to feed parking meters, I was more or less penniless and completely knackered. I kept driving until I found another lay-by and pulled in, this time with the cosy lights of Chesterfield twinkling at me invitingly from down below. No, I wouldn't be driving into any more fields tonight.

With a frost beginning to form outside the car, and the plants inside continuing to pump up the humidity through high-level leaf transpiration, I was in for an extremely cold, damp night. I couldn't leave the engine running to power the heater for a full eight hours, I reasoned, in case I asphyxiated myself; so once the warmth had dissipated, that would be it: I would just have to

176

pull the tea-cosy down hard over my ears and curl up as small as possible, hands between legs, behind the steering wheel. With the back of the Astra full of plants, I couldn't even tip my seat back, so I spent all night in the driving position, chattering with cold.

To say I woke up frozen stiff would suggest that I got some sleep. In fact I had a succession of fitful dozes, interrupted by bouts of serious shivering in the interrogator's lamp of passing car headlights. When it was light and I could stand no more, I climbed stiffly out of the car and tried to stretch my aching body back to life. What greeted me was a scene of devastation. After the previous night's mud bath in the field, even by my own relaxed standards of cleanliness the Astra was a disgrace. It literally looked like a mobile dung heap, as if I had driven it back and forth through a slurry pit and then sprayed it with extra liquid manure for good measure. There was no way I could visit anyone, let alone the Duchess of Devonshire, in a manure-mobile like that.

Counting my loose change, I realized before I could go in search of a hot bacon sandwich I would first have to find a hot car wash. Looking at the state of my fleece and trousers in the dawn light, I would also have to find a public toilet with running water where I could give myself a hose down. My clothes were also covered in mud and manure.

Having suffered dysentery for weeks on end in various far-flung parts of the world, I know a thing or two about dodgy public lavatories. In fact, I know what it's like to have dysentery and *not* be able to find a lavatory, dodgy or otherwise. But early that February morning, the first public toilet I found in Matlock stood out like a beacon of global lavatorial squalor. It had been open all night and everyone, it seemed, with a variety of challenging bowel conditions and other social issues must have been in there, doing their thing.

A fetid jungle pool and hole in the ground surrounded by gun-toting Colombians would have been a preferable place to take a dump. What is it about that killer aroma of disinfectant, number twos and rank urine in dodgy public conveniences that says: 'Whatever You Do, Don't Touch the Lavatory Seat!' I didn't even want to pull the sleeve of my fleece down and touch the rusty taps, but my clothes and I were in such a state that radical decontamination was called for.

Oblivious to what anyone might think, I took off my trousers and spent a full hour trying to scrape the dried mud and slurry from them and from my fleece. By turns I held both under the tap and scrubbed hard with fistfuls of lavatory paper. I then put my wet trousers back on, ignoring the white streaks of loo paper fluff that now decorated them from crotch to ankle, and went to sit in the car with the heater whacked up to full to dry them out. I prayed I would at least have stopped steaming by the time I met the Duchess at 11am.

The tea-cosy hat meant I didn't have to comb my hair, which after a night in the car was sticking straight out at the back and sides of my head like a comedy wig. I'd have to keep the hat on, I reasoned, and just hope the Devonshires weren't too precious about such things at lunch. Luckily I found an old can of Lynx in the glove box — God knows what it was doing there — and I emptied the can, spraying myself all over to mask the stench. The teeth and killer breath were sorted with a couple of sticks of Orbit chewing gum bought from a newsagent. After following the smell of hot bacon to a nearby caff and refuelling, the Green Man was ready for business and raring to go.

There are two ways to get to our place at Lullingstone and neither is remotely like the approach to the mighty Chatsworth.

To visit us, you come through the arching trees down what we call the front drive, which is actually behind the house, and it brings you to a little clearing down by the river at the bottom. From Easter to the end of October, Reg will be there in his wooden box, taking the money. With the lake to your left spilling over the weir and into the river, you then cross the narrow wooden footbridge. Early in the morning you might have to give way to Trevor if he's out walking his dog Jo, which is short for Josephine (Trevor's quite hefty and the bridge is narrow); or you might bump into one of our other neighbours or even the fishermen who lease the lake and are armed with rods, lines and hopeful looks in their eyes. Either way, sneaking up on the house from behind like this, you won't have a clue what wonders await when you walk round and finally see the front façade (which faces the back drive).

But nor will you be intimidated. Lullingstone is big and beautiful. But it's not *that* big.

Come at us from the other side, snaking along Lullingstone Lane from the village of Eynsford at the bottom of our gentle valley, and you first pass under the orange brick Victorian railway viaduct. Then you pass the Roman Villa and the 18-hole golf course to your right, and immediately on your left you see Dad's rolling yew hedge, which he planted in 1976 and which leads to Sir John Peche's whopping great brick gatehouse, where I live. It's not until you walk under the arch of the gatehouse that you really see the house properly for the very first time.

I've already said how serene and lush and magnificent the place looks, framed by three Cedars of Lebanon to the left and with Dad's lawn spread out in front like a gorgeous green picnic rug, but compared with Chatsworth Lullingstone is really just a cottage. Like the great stately piles at Blenheim and Petworth, Chatsworth is one of those country houses that just hits you in the face: Massive Serious Pile Ahead.

'Wowzers!' I gasped as I motored into the estate along its winding drive. I didn't feel I was visiting a house so much as entering some kind of manicured mini kingdom. Which I was in a way. And a very wealthy kingdom it looked too.

After being knocked out by the honey-coloured magnificence of the exterior of the house itself, I was led inside the private quarters by the Duchess's secretary and was taken to her office, where I waited nervously with a cup of

**The family motto**, *Prest à Faire*, means 'Ready to Serve'. Lullingstone is one of the oldest family estates in England and can be traced back to the time of the Domesday Book. **The Gatehouse**, above, dates from the fifteenth century.

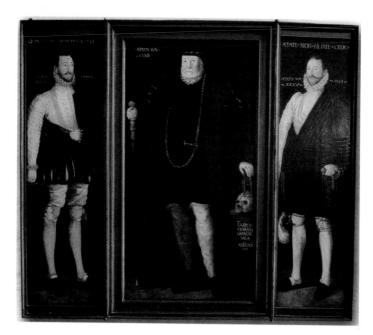

**Family triptych**: Sir Percyval Hart, Kt. (1496-1580), with his two sons, George Hart (left) and Francis Hart (right).

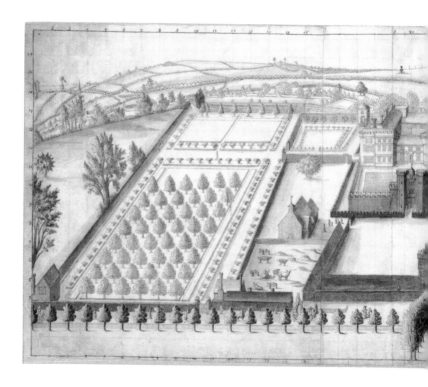

**My great-grandfather**: The Rt Hon. Sir William Hart Dyke, Bt.

**Zoë, Lady Hart Dyke**: My granny with a basket of silkworm cocoons.

**Granny Zoë again**: Zoë, Lady Hart Dyke inspecting camiknickers made with her own silk.

**Seventeenth-century view**: An engraving from before the eighteenth-century alterations, which included the razing of the original gatehouse and filling in the moat.

**Oliver Hart Dyke**: My grandfather.

**Old formal garden (left)**:
Aerial view of the formal gardens at Lullingstone dated 1947.

**The 18-acre fishing lake (above)**: My grandfather Oliver had this former gravel pit excavated and turned into the lake.

**Church (below left)**:
St Botolph's Parish Church in the grounds of Lullingstone Castle contains some of the oldest stained-glass windows in England. St Botolph is the patron saint of travellers.

**Façade (below)**: The present manor house and gatehouse were built in 1497 and have been home to our family ever since.

**Aged eighteen months (right)**: Me in 1977 beneath some of my more imposing ancestors.

**Out in the garden (below)**: Pretending to drive Dad's tractor full of weeping-willow logs in 1986.

**Crimbo 1989 (above)**: Pulling faces in the library with Mum and Anya.

**Orchids ahoy! (above):**
In the orchid house at the Singapore Botanic Gardens in 1998.

**Western Australia (left):**
On a seed-collecting mission with equipment at the ready in winter 1998.

**Collecting seeds (above):**
90 feet up a gum tree (*Eucalyptus pulchella*), seed-collecting in Tasmania with the RHS and Kent Gardens Trust, early 1999.

**Not quite gourmet chefs (above right):**
My superb Indonesian 'guides', who fed me raw rat.

**Gum nuts (above):**
Gum Nut Steve and me in his world-class *Eucalyptus* collection in Oxfordshire.

**Two Toms (below):**
Tom Stobbart and me in Cambodia in the ancient city of Angkor Wat in early 1998. We are surrounded by Tetrameles trees at Wat Ta Prohm, which are wrapping themselves around the ruins.

**Home again (above):**
With the American James Spring (centre), and my fellow jungle captive, Paul Winder (right), in early 2001.

**Moon Gate**: The entrance to the old herb garden, before the build.

**My jungle diary**: Laying out the plans for a garden containing plants from around the world planted out in their continents of origin.

**The Tradescants (above left and right):**
Sir John senior (1570s-1638), and Sir John junior (1608-62)

**David Douglas (1799-1834) (below):** The extensive plant-hunting in North America by this Scot led to the complete and permanent transformation o: the British landscape when he brought back coniferous trees, including the Sugar Pine (left).

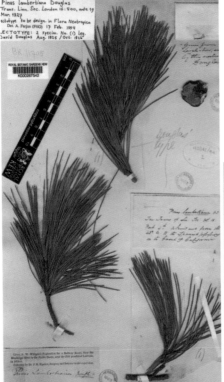

**Sir Joseph Banks (1743–1820) (left):** The father of modern-day plant-hunting, Banks discovered *Phormium tenax* (below) in New Zealand while circumnavigating the world with Captain James Cook.

**George Forrest (1873–1932) (above):** Forrest was a bonkers Scotsman who made legendary discoveries in south-west China, including *Primula forrestii* (right).

**Dad's apple trees (above):**
In full fruit with a bumper crop in late summer 2004, shortly to be felled by Richard Reeves.

**Aerial shot (below):**
A view of the old herb garden taken from the top of the yew tree in the churchyard in September 2004.

**Dutch Venlo greenhouse (above):**
In its original site in the old herb
garden, with *Dahlia imperialis*
bursting out.

**Granny's herb garden
(above):** Looking through
the lovage and opium
poppies to the manor house
and church in summer 2004.

**Pigs (above)**: Me and the pigs Woolly and Red Spider, named after two of the pests that afflict the orchid plant.

**Cutting and shredding (above)**: Friends from my days at Sparsholt College clear the old herb garden site in September 2004.

**Bonfire (right):**
My Sparsholt friends and I
spent the weekend stripping the
old herb garden and burning
the contents.

**Thumbs up (below):**
On 6 December 2004 the
diggers move onto the site.

**Rocks in (above):** Over 340 tons of rock are moved
into place to form the continents of the World Garden.

**Some of the team (clockwise from top left)**: Red Indian Reg, Laurence Dell, Sylvia Halls and Jim Buttress, me and Tony Russell, Vikki Rimmer, Louise Cowling.

**Gatehouse from the World Garden:**
A view from South Africa across the Tasmanian and New Zealand borders.

**The Dutch Venlo greenhouse (left)**: The greenhouse in its new position jam-packed with plants prior to planting out in summer 2005.

**The World Garden from the air**: The whole World Garden, from 300 feet above. I took the photo below from my friend Andrew Pearson's plane in July 2005.

**Palm delivery (above):**
Adrian and the Chusan Palm arrive.

**Totem (right):**
Sylvia and Jim and the totem poles which took nearly a year to get from Bali to Lullingstone.

**Wollemi Pine (above):** Me, Mark Taylor (from Kernock Park Plants) and Dad, with the Wollemi Pine. Dad did the honours and planted up the most ancient species in the garden.

**Above**: *Protea repens*, brought back from South Africa as a seed by Dad.

**Centre**: Me posing on Ayers Rock for a charity calendar for Demelza Hospice.

**Above**: Penstemon 'Crac's Delight', named in my granny's honour.

**Above**: *Eucalyptus caesia* 'Silver Princess', which made history when it flowered for the first time ever in the UK in the World Garden.

**Above**: *Aeonium arboretum* 'Schwarzkopf'.

**Mexico in bloom (above**
Penstemon 'Crac's Deligh
surrounded by dahlias,
yuccas and ferociously
spiny agaves.

**England and Moon Gat
(above right)**: View acros
the UK to the Moon Gate

**Africa and the gatehou.
(left)**: A view across the
north-west African border
in summer 2006.

**New Zealand (right)**:
The North Island of New
Zealand in July 2005.

NEW ZEALAND
(North Island)

Plants native to New Zealand (North) include

Famous Plant Hunter: Sir Joseph Banks 1743 - 1820

**Family (above)**: Dad, Anya, me and Mum at the World Garden party on 16 July 2005.

**Crac's delight (above)**: I surprise Gran by announcing to the World Garden party that I've named the Penstemon in her honour. I dedicated the opening of the garden to my family.

coffee and two digestive biscuits. Why was I nervous? I think I was suddenly overwhelmed by the sheer size and might and solidity of Chatsworth, which I couldn't help but compare with our own little house and financially precarious predicament. I was also aware of the Duchess's awesome accomplishments and knowledge of everything from history and horticulture to hens. But I needn't have worried.

The Duchess, or Deborah or Debo as I think I was invited to call her (I was definitely still a bit awestruck), was amazingly cool. By which I mean she was totally ungrand, and was both welcoming and engaging, as opposed to offhand and haughty. She really made me feel that she was happy to see me. No sooner had I shaken her hand and looked into that famously striking face than I wished I had brought a clean shirt and pair of trousers. For my appearance, I marked myself nought out of ten.

Despite her deeply lined features, the eyes were warm and intelligent and the Duchess seemed to sparkle when she smiled, suggesting that here was a woman of real experience and wisdom who had managed to keep it all together through turbulent times.

After some how-do-you-do pleasantries, she introduced me to Simon Seligman, a walking encyclopaedia on Chatsworth who works for the estate, and suggested I might like to see round the house with him. It was an extraordinary experience, chatting about little old Lullingstone while being led through a labyrinth of polished splendour, the walls and even ceilings adorned with so many overwhelming works of art. Beautifully restored and richly colourful, a host of mystical-mythical godly characters seemed to stare down at me wherever I looked, and I couldn't help but think of the patches of cracked and peeling paint on some of the ceilings back home and how they could do with a lick of emulsion. I thought the ornate barrelled ceiling in Queen Anne's state room at Lullingstone was impressive — I mean it *is* impressive — but Chatsworth was something else.

I was equally mesmerized by the stunning displays of flowers I kept picking up on the nasal radar as we passed and I was already quite breathless with horticultural awe when the Duchess came to find us. There were vases and pots everywhere; and even though it was still only February, the house was a riot of tantalizing, exotic scents. There were pots of tropical plants from the greenhouse, cut flowers, dried flowers, orchids — even including *Phalaenopsis*, or Moth Orchids. I was soon spouting Latin plant names uncontrollably at Debo, who I think began to sense she was in the presence of a slightly unstable plant nut.

Leading me into the massive and beautiful dining room, where the table was laid for lunch, she then seemed keen to step up the campaign and perhaps even call my bluff.

'Do you recognize this?' she asked playfully, pointing to an extensive, intricately painted golden trellis within a gilded picture frame hanging on the wall. It depicted hundreds and hundreds of stunning flower heads.

Hm. Tricky. The trellis was definitely adorned with an eye-popping orchid, but momentarily I was stumped. Then, through the fog of my excitement and anxiety, I recalled the 6th Duke of Devonshire's interest in horticulture and his infatuation with orchids in the mid-nineteenth century. He was a classically passionate aristocratic collector who was hugely influential in popularizing orchids; and I remembered that it was the Bachelor Duke, as he was called, who had first taken on Paxton as head gardener. It was the same Duke who had also sent one of his under-gardeners, John Gibson, to India in search of his favourite orchid.

'Er . . . *Psychopsis p-p-papilio!*' I stammered, beaming at the Duchess and pointing to the gold-coloured trellis with its hundreds of Butterfly Orchids. 'Or *Oncidium p-p-papilio*, as the sixth Duke would probably have referred to them,' I said, sounding like a smart alec.

It was like being a competitive teenager again in the walled garden with Crac and it felt great to be back.

The Duke, who was wheelchair-bound and clearly very poorly, joined us for lunch. Though his speech was slurred through ill-health, it didn't stop him talking, nor puffing on a gasper when they came round after lunch. Despite the amazingly grand setting, the huge table and the lushly coloured high ceilings, lunch was relaxed and informal and even fun. I told the Duke and Duchess about the set-up at Lullingstone and my plans, outlining my modest ambitions for the World Garden and its eventual expansion one day across what was left of our little estate. We talked about the advantages and pitfalls of sponsorship, and the Duchess was completely on the ball with her questions. I came away convinced that in our case sponsorship would be a much better route than trying to seek some kind of charitable status.

The Duchess gave me a signed copy of a book about the gardens at Chatsworth and I presented her with a copy of *The Cloud Garden*, which had recently been published and which would have made clear what a nutter she had just invited to lunch in case she still needed persuading. Not wanting to take up any more of her time, I insisted I would wander round the enormous gardens by myself.

Outside I was blown away by the arboretums, but the key thing for me was to visit Chatsworth's Display Greenhouse. This was the site on which *Victoria amazonica*, the biggest lily pad in the world, had flowered for the first time in the United Kingdom under the beady eye of the 6th Duke and the brilliant Paxton. To test the flotation strength of this monster that emerged on Paxton's lily pond, he famously made his daughter Annie stand on it. The lily's ribs were like cantilevers and, with its organic cross-girders, this amazing feat of natural engineering inspired Paxton's design of Crystal Palace.

I was really touched by the effort the Duke and Duchess made in trying to help me, and a few weeks later I was saddened to learn that the Duke had passed away, the Duchess at his side. The announcement of his death didn't surprise me unduly — he really was very poorly when we met — but it made me think again about our lunch and all he had achieved in his lifetime at Chatsworth. I hoped that in some way as he was preparing for his appointment with his Maker he was able to draw comfort knowing that the sublime views from his window across the Chatsworth landscape would remain the same long after he had gone. I wondered if my own ancestor Sir Percyval Hart had been able to draw the same comfort when he posed for that portrait that hangs in our Great Hall while 'awaiting the hour of his liberation'. And I wondered if one day I would be able to be as optimistic about the future of Lullingstone when it was time for me to face the hour of my own liberation.

As well as seeking advice from the Devonshires, I also renewed contact with Lady Salisbury, of Hatfield House in Hertfordshire fame, which was where my plant-hunting heroes the Tradescants had once worked. Hatfield was another Massive Pile With Serious Garden Attached, and Lady Salisbury held mega open days there attracting tens of thousands of visitors. It was actually Lady Salisbury who had first made contact with me a couple of years previously, when she invited me to give a talk about my own plant-hunting adventures. She had heard of me via Valerie Finnis, who founded the Merlin Trust which had given me a £500 grant to study orchid husbandry in the Mentawai Islands, Indonesia.

I was delighted to be able to ramble on at her

visitors in a marquee during a country fayre in the early summer of 2004, not least because it gave me the chance to see the amazing exotic selection of plants on sale inside. I even got to spend the night at Hatfield — not in a lay-by outside the town but in Lady Salisbury's daughter's four-poster inside the house. No, her daughter wasn't in it at the time. I certainly felt comfortable talking to Lady Salisbury about my World Garden idea, and she later came down to Lullingstone on the train to see how it was developing.

My contact with the Heritage Lottery Fund — I got the number from a family friend — led to a meeting at Lullingstone with a very nice lady who must have thought I was a melon. When I showed her my scribbled plans, she almost fell off her seat. 'But you're not restoring the herb garden, are you?' she said, making it plain there was no way the HLF could help with a 'new development'. I tried to argue that what I was doing was aimed at keeping the whole place afloat, but the best I got was a hint that I might be able to claim help for keeping the walls up.

Restoration of the Queen Anne Ice House and Bath House got a similar response — but only if we provided adequate car parking, adequate access, adequate toilets and a lease on the land for at least fifteen years. I could already hear Dad's blood vessels popping at the very thought and I felt my own brain beginning to seize up. I contacted the Millennium Commission too just as it was being wound up, and was told that if I filled in all the paperwork — and there was weeks' worth of it — I might be eligible for £3,000 to help restore the walls, Ice House and Bath House. Just looking at the bumf was enough to put me off.

Even though these approaches led nowhere, I was still glad I had contacted both organizations. They were supportive of the general idea of what I was trying to do and it was helpful to be grilled by people who knew what they were talking about and put me on the spot with searching questions. I mentioned the possibility of setting up a charity to Dad, but the short answer was 'No.' It was all just too complicated and unsuitable.

All these various discussions made one thing clear: we would have to raise money commercially, either through sponsors or a bank loan or possibly both, and to do either of these things I would need a grown-up business plan with lots of figures in it, plus projections, graphs and probably some equations and chemical formulae too for all I knew.

To this end I approached various financial advisers and on one occasion even a proper merchant bank. Frankly, I hadn't a clue what I was doing in such a world, and this became obvious even to me when one day I found myself in the walled garden with a money man (he was Greek, I think), both of us tripping through the undergrowth carrying bags of sand and cans of spray paint.

The only way I could think of to work out exactly how much soil and rock would be needed to form my contoured continents was to mark them out by hand. Thus, bent double while putting out plants in pots, pouring a pile of sand here and spraying aerosol paint there, we set to work. The exercise was as much use as those planks and bricks had been in the farmer's field near Matlock.

Back-of-an-envelope calculations suggested that the project might be feasible for about £125,000. I had never asked Dad for a penny before, but I now wondered if he would at least agree to raid his savings so we could get some professional help in drawing up a business plan with which to try to raise such a sum. Despite my gung-ho enthusiasm, even I knew that potential business sponsors would need to see more than a few piles of sand and some shrubs daubed with spray paint before agreeing to part with the readies.

# 15

## Branching Out

I also knew I would need some professionally drawn plans which showed my continents shaped and contoured properly to scale, and which detailed the garden's technical specifications. These would have to impress serious types like building control officers and business consultants; and as I didn't have the first clue how to draw on computer, let alone anything about landscape design, access for people in wheelchairs or health and safety matters related to boulders, I started to scout around for someone who did.

One of the first builders I met — he shall remain nameless — didn't get it at all. I thumbed through my jungle diary's grubby pages, enthusiastically explaining how my garden idea had come about and proudly showing him my red biro sketches. But I might as well have been asking him to design a container port in the Thames estuary using Lego bricks and Fairy Liquid bottles. He was baffled.

'Er, OK . . . so, let me see if I've got this right,' he said, making it plain he hadn't got it at all and would rather be trimming his nasal hairs. 'A map of the world . . . plus mountains and waterfalls and ten thousand plants . . . in just one acre.'

'Yup,' I said, as if it was the most obvious thing in the world.

'And I might not be paid for months, because you haven't definitely got any funding in place yet?'

After a couple of fruitless encounters like this, I had a stroke of luck closer to home — just a few hundred yards down Lullingstone Lane, in fact, where there was a smart-looking barn conversion on the edge of the village. It was owned by one of the brilliant local farmers, James Alexander jnr, and it had an interesting tenant.

'Designer chap. Does gardens and stuff. Landscaping. You should try him,' James told me when I visited him in his farmhouse.

I must have driven or pushbiked past the Cart Lodge Design studio a million times, but I had never realized what went on inside. When James finally introduced me to Adam Bailey, the occupant in question, I knew instantly (or hoped anyway) that he and I were going to do great things together. Sometimes you just know — and I did with Adam.

Sitting beneath the beams in his well-lit studio, a pukka, hygienically endowed, dust-free space, I showed him my jungle-stained diary and my A3 and A4 sheets outlining the continents and my plans for watery pathways along which visitors would travel in gondolas. We seemed to click instantly, even though Adam had to point out that, as the land was on a slight slope, actual water-filled oceans might be tricky.

He was far more encouraging about some of

my other ideas. 'Mmm. Interesting. That's a good idea. Brilliant. Mmm. Like it,' he murmured, nodding sagely as I ran him around the world in eighty sentences. Adam was a thoughtful, sensitive soul, but he was also a CAD — i.e. a genius at computer-aided design — and, even more importantly, from the way he was reacting I knew he could see my Darién drawings coming to life in a glorious three-dimensional marriage of rock, soil and greenery.

When I explained that I wanted the continents to look like continents, he actually interrupted.

'Oh yes, Tom. Absolutely. They *must* look like continents . . . and they must be contoured.'

Adam was definitely interested.

'And as the plants are going to be in their natural habitats, we could try to landscape the continents and their coastlines with geologically accurate rocks too . . . '

I swear I saw Adam's pale cheeks begin to flush boyishly and his ginger hair turn slightly redder with growing enthusiasm. Best of all, he didn't fall off his stool when I explained that the project was still at an embryonic stage from the business point of view and confessed that I wasn't yet in a position to be able to guarantee when I would be able to pay him. Nor could I yet draw up a contract without Dad's say-so.

'Could you live with that?'

I prayed silently that Adam was up for the challenge and not about to send me back down Lullingstone Lane empty-handed.

'Oh. And if I'm completely honest,' I stammered, 'there is also the worst-case scenario . . . '

'A worst-case scenario?' queried Adam cautiously.

'Yes. That the garden never actually gets built because we can't raise any money. But that's only a worst-case scenario.'

I felt I had to level with Adam because if things really did go tits-up in the short term, I would be building the garden by hand and it could take twenty-five years.

Despite this unpalatable possibility, I could see that Adam's creative appetite was whetted and that he was cogitating. Was he prepared to devote time to turning my mad vision into a reality without a firm pay day in view?

'Tom, I'm happy to help!'

'That's brilliant, Adam! Absolutely brilliant!' I said, stammering out my thanks.

Endearingly, Adam, like me, has a stammer. I put mine down to the fact that I probably try to speak too fast which makes the words pile up on my spring-loaded tongue. When it's fully loaded, they then spring out in different directions and orders. Hearing Adam's own stutter, I knew that our discussions about plants, rocks and soil were going to take longer than anticipated. But I was still beaming and very nearly yanked his arm off as I shook his hand.

Returning to the castle I was on a definite high and had a warm feeling inside that, finally, I was starting to Make Things Happen. Or at least that I had finally met someone who could start to Make Things Happen. It was a new sensation; and I was so encouraged I immediately told Dad that I'd found a brilliant designer chap who shared my hunch that the World Garden was a really cool, viable idea and who even now was scaling my sketches into a glorious, coherent whole.

'Well, that's good news, Tom,' said Dad. 'What does he charge?'

In the weeks that followed, the drawings that came out of Adam's barn made a huge difference to the way we viewed the project. Professionally presented on draughtsman's paper for the first time, with proper allowance made for wheelchair access, gradients, borders, paths and rocks, the whole project began to look and feel several degrees more serious. What had appeared naïve and slightly bonkers (floating gondolas? I must have been crazy!) was beginning to look as if it was meant to exist for real. Even Dad was growing keener by the day.

Seeing the complexity and intricate detail of Adam's early plans, however, both of us realized that my idea of working solo to create the garden over the next five to ten years using a hand trowel and tape measure was a non-starter. The need to attract more visitors to boost the estate's shaky income was too urgent to wait that long.

'We need a proper business plan now, Tom,' said Dad with a new note of determination in his voice. 'Know anyone who can help?'

Quietly, in my attempt to network like Grandma Zoë, via the local grapevine I had made contact with a chap called Jim Pettipher whose wife Sally had helped with sponsorship at a garden near Tunbridge Wells. It was all very circuitous, but Jim, I was assured, was the fundraiser to find sponsors for the World Garden. He in turn had introduced me to a horticultural marketing wizard called Tony Russell. Knowing that Dad was now prepared to sanction the spending of £5,000 on an initial business proposal, I invited Jim and Tony to Lullingstone.

They thought the project sounded a bit weird and wacky, but like Adam they were sufficiently persuaded by my spiel that they decided it was worth pursuing and agreed to give it some thought. As Jim pointed out, weird and wacky it may be, but given the parlous state of the estate's finances, what choice did we have? He and Tony went away to crunch the numbers and do some research, and they returned to the castle at the end of May to present their findings.

May can be a cruel month in the garden at Lullingstone, the growth surge of early summer suddenly stopped dead in its tracks by a rogue frost. But on the day Jim and Tony pitched up, the castle and grounds looked sublime under a clear blue sky. With bees beginning to bumble through the seductively soft blossom, we decided to sit outside near the cedar trees, the cool scent of the grass freshening our senses. Dad, Mum and I were in suspense, our ears pricked like those of the rabbits on the golf course.

What Jim and Tony told us was both encouraging and exciting — and more than a little scary for people with no experience of major business initiatives. They had taken a five-year view of the project, and reckoned that to create the garden Adam and I were envisaging, we might need to spend as much as £250,000.

*A quarter of a million!* I was reeling and half expected Dad to get up and announce that he had to mow the lawn. Instead, he gulped silently and heard them out.

'Of course you might not need *all* of that,' Jim reassured us, 'and it should be possible to raise what money you do need through sponsorship and other commercial ventures.'

Other commercial ventures? I prayed he wasn't going to suggest weddings and bar mitzvahs. For now, though, the question of how sponsorship might be raised remained suitably vague.

'And it's not unreasonable, we think,' Tony added, 'to expect to be able to raise the number of visitors to around fifty thousand a year within five years. Certainly that should be the ambition.'

*Fifty thousand visitors within five years!* That was the number Zoë had attracted in her heyday. I could hear Dad's mental abacus begin to clatter: 50,000 visitors a year at, say, £5 a visitor. An income of roughly . . . £250,000! That would certainly pay for improvements in the garden and put the estate on a sound financial footing. It had to be worth aiming for.

When Jim and Tony left, things were still a little in the air; but Dad, Mum and I were hugely excited and energized. Dad was most reassured by Jim's view that we would not have to borrow any money because the project would attract sponsors. He had never borrowed a penny against the house and didn't want to start now.

Tony's wider vision of how the garden should be developed and marketed also impressed us.

'All sounds pretty good, Tom,' said Dad, disappearing off to mull things over in the den.

Neither of us had any idea about consultancy fees, but we did know we couldn't find sponsors or market the garden ourselves and so needed the specialist skills Jim and Tony offered. A few days later, Dad made his announcement.

'I like their proposals, Tom,' he said candidly. 'Let's get references on them . . . and see how much they want to carry on helping us.'

To work with us for a year, raising money and promoting a World Garden that could open to the public in 2005, Jim and Tony wanted fees of £70,000. And we didn't have it unless Dad dug into every last penny of his savings. Realizing he was now being asked to put his money where his son's mouth was, he looked even more pensive than usual as he went off to the den to ruminate.

# 16

## Birds of Paradise

'All right, Tom. We'll do it.'

Dad's words sent a jolt of electricity through me. I didn't know whether to pick him up and hug him or tell him to sit down and not be so silly. In any event, it was a pivotal moment when he called me over to the house in early June and announced that he and Mum were prepared to risk their savings to pay Jim, Tony and Adam to get the project rolling.

The three of us sat in the cavernous cool of the Great Hall in front of the empty fireplace with old Sir Percyval looking down over our shoulders, clutching his giant eggtimer and awaiting the hour of his liberation. Mum and Dad's decision left me feeling excited, scared and slightly guilty all at the same time.

Of course I was thrilled and daunted that we were committing ourselves to opening a brand spanking new garden to the public in less than a year's time. But I was also horribly aware that my parents could end up stuffed financially if things didn't work out. Dad was proposing to use all his savings, and that wasn't something I would have wanted to do at his age.

'Perhaps it's not quite so risky, Tom,' Mum said, trying to reassure us both. 'I mean there will be sponsorship. Once Jim starts drumming up interest, I'm sure we'll all feel a great deal less exposed.'

Mum was right. This was a time to be positive and . . . just do it!

With Jim and Tony signed up, and Adam beavering away at his drawing board, the project began to generate a momentum of its own. This in itself was reassuring. Tony was legendary at planting the seed of the World Garden idea out in the media, locally, nationally and in the trade press, and it didn't seem to harm the 'story' that the plant nut behind it was Yours Truly — former hostage and orchidaceous nutter of Colombian kidnap fame.

I also started to shout about the World Garden from the rooftops and gave regular progress reports to the green-fingered of the county via the Green Man gardening column I was now writing in the *Kentish Times*. Grandma Zoë would have been proud.

On the ground, of course, there was naff all progress to be seen. In fact, our half of the walled garden was still no more than a picturesque jungle. I was working overtime in the greenhouse to bring on a variety of seedlings which I hoped would eventually go on show, but there was nothing world-shaped or spectacular for visitors to the house, church and grounds to gawp at: just Granny's two amazing east-facing borders outside the walls and a tangle of fruit trees, herbs and exploding weeds inside — oh, and me with a barrel load of promises that it was all going to be wonderful. One day. Maybe.

Weirdly, none of the visitors seemed to mind

that nothing terribly obvious was happening in the garden. Quite the opposite, in fact. For as summer 2004 warmed up, so did the number of people who were tripping past Red Indian Reg's sentry box and across the footbridge, or coming through the gatehouse arch under my sitting room. Amazingly, numbers were slowly creeping upwards. Dear old Tony was clearly getting our message across.

People were still coming to walk round the house and church, of course, but there were noticeably more of them asking questions about the garden and curious to see what I was doing. I certainly didn't curb my enthusiasm when describing how floridacious everything was going to be come next spring and summer, when I urged them all to return. Despite my positive gushing, however, the place was such a tangle of growth you would have had to be on something stronger than sherry and Sanatogen to imagine it at its blossoming best.

Behind the scenes, Jim and Tony were also looking at other ways for the estate to generate more income. It wasn't long before they raised the dreaded question about weddings.

'Sarah, do you think you could cater for weddings, with the ceremony at St Botolph's?' Jim asked Mum tentatively.

Mum patiently explained the set-up with our neighbours and the parish and the fact that we didn't have enough space to feed and water sit-down guests, let alone put up Portaloos for 300 people.

'Well . . . what about longer opening hours in

the house itself? Or a little more flexibility on the days of the week that you do open?' he then ventured.

What no-one seems to grasp is that when Lullingstone is open, the Hart Dykes are 'open' too and on duty full-on. It has to be that way if we want to give people a personal visit to a family house and garden, which we do. When Jim and Tony made their suggestion, Mum and Dad were knackered as it was. Without more paid help, which we couldn't afford, being open all hours would have finished them off. So weddings or extending the opening hours were not an option. It would have to be the draw of the World Garden that would bring in the extra moolah. I *had* to make it work.

I did, however, suggest we crack on with renovating the Ice House and old Bath House where Queen Anne used to go for a wash and brush-up when she was on a sleepover here. Both ruins were buried under a mass of impenetrable greenery and Jim's advice was simple.

'Pigs, Tom. Get some pigs.'

I'd never even had a puppy, so a pig seemed a bit ambitious and two pigs even more so, given the absurdly long list of Things To Do that was now scrawled in my notebook. Considering that I didn't really even have time to find a girlfriend, why would I want to make myself responsible for a couple of porkers? I promised Jim I would think about it. Which I did during the many hours I was now spending in and around the greenhouse.

The reason I was spending so long under glass was that I really had to accelerate, not to say go nuclear, with my plant-growing if I wanted to have anything to put in the ground to show visitors in a year's time. The result was that I was working like a lunatic, was short of both time and money, and was neglecting my friends more and more.

Because few of my friends live locally, socializing means a couple of hours' drive to get to them and a couple of hours' drive back. That costs at least £20 in petrol; and by the time we've gone for a meal or whatever, I'm looking at losing a large part of the working day and spending the thick end of perhaps £60. I was giving a few more talks than before and so my earnings had risen, but that wasn't really the point. Working alone in the garden, and with the last penny of Dad's savings riding on the outcome of my endeavours, I didn't feel I could decently afford the time away.

Friends might disagree about the extent to which my interest in horticulture is a passion rather than an obsession, but over the years my social life has definitely suffered because of it and it was suffering big time now. Once I get the bit between my teeth, I have to admit I do find it very hard to stop working. Just as I relentlessly used to count Bee Orchids up on the golf course in the school holidays, I tend to become driven by what I'm currently doing and fairly oblivious to everything else. The worst thing for friends is when I ring up an hour before we're supposed to meet and I start to stammer out an excuse.

'Tom — you're not coming to my birthday party, are you?' they say, resigned to the fact that I'm about to let them down yet again.

'No. I'm really, *really* sorry. You see, Jack is coming and . . .'

'Who the hell is Jack?' they interrupt. 'And why's he more important than my birthday?'

'No. Jack *Frost*,' I explain.

It's true that whenever there's a frost heading for Lullingstone, it's action stations as I scurry around getting all the plants inside. Nothing's mechanical or automated in any of my old greenhouses, and turning all the heaters and fans on by hand also takes an age. But letting friends down is a sore point and not one I am proud of. However, the more I think about the extent to which I'm obsessed with plants, as opposed to merely passionately interested in them, the more I suppose I have to admit that my friends are right: it probably is an obsession.

Long before my disastrous orchid-hunting trip in the Darién, for example, I nearly lost my life because of a gum tree. It was a *Eucalyptus regnans*, or Mountain Ash, the tallest flowering plant in the world, and I wasn't concentrating. Or at least I *was* concentrating, but not on what I should have been concentrating on.

It was early 1999 and I was still in north-east Tasmania, doing about 40mph along a remote forestry dirt track in a tiny rented Mitsubishi Colt. Admittedly there were some utterly amazing trees in the area — some Mountain Ashes that were hundreds of feet high — but that was no excuse that afternoon for taking my eyes

202

off where I was going and focusing on one particular 40-foot eucalyptus sapling. I remember looking at it and being struck by how incredibly straight and tall and perfect it was. 'Now that's what I call an amazing tree!' I thought.

Alas, it wasn't an amazing tree for long. Driving on the gravel dirt track was a bit like dancing on buttered marbles, and when I gently (or not so gently) hit the brakes to get a better look I instantly lost control of the motor and found myself careering helter-skelter towards the sublime object of my desire. With a horrendous flip and thud, the car then started to roll into the deep ditch that ran alongside the track, almost tipping over entirely on the gradient before smacking into the perfect tree in question.

I cracked my head hard on something and was seriously dazed. When I came to, the situation wasn't ideal. The sublime sapling was no longer tall and straight but snapped over at an angle of 45° to the ground; and the car had somehow ended up on its side. Miraculously, I hadn't gone through the windscreen and no bone seemed to be broken. So I undid my seatbelt, climbed gingerly out of the driver's window and tried to thank someone, perhaps even God, that I was still alive.

So, yes, I can get a bit obsessed by planty things, and horticulture naturally takes priority over my relationships with humans. I don't imagine it will always be like this in my life; but the plants v. people balance was even sorely tested when I met Lin, my first ever girlfriend.

I was twenty-three and living in Red Cliffs, near Mildura on the New South Wales — Victoria border, and so was she. This was a wine-growing area, and I was funding my continued travels by pruning vines. Lin, who was from South Korea, was doing vine propagation and we both ended up living in the same cool place: Red Cliff Backpackers' Hostel.

I had never given any thought to the fact that I might be a late starter as far as girls were concerned. While first kisses and first cigarettes had preoccupied the other kids at secondary school, they had never bothered me. I was far more interested in digging over the school Camellia bed or tending my orchids in the school greenhouse. There was one girl at Stanbridge I secretly fancied — a willowy, sexy, arty type. But she was a couple of classes above me and far, far cooler, so there was no way I was ever going to ask this Unattainable Dream Girl if she wanted to spend some quality time with me in the greenhouse.

But Lin was different. Lin was a good craic — really, really sweet, and I felt extremely comfortable in her company. We never really went out on proper dates together, though we did once go to the cinema in Mildura to see *The Mummy*. I was in fits of laughter but poor Lin was petrified. By the end she was completely pale, despite the fact she had had quite a healthy complexion before she sat down.

Our relationship did revolve mostly around plants, I admit. I would take her on little outings of two or three hours to see a particular gum tree, and she wouldn't complain. In fact she was brilliant and rather enjoyed our trips out into the bush. She wasn't horticulturally endowed: that was never going to happen and I was never going to try to convert her; but she didn't mind what we did and was interested in anything unusual. If I took her to see a special gum tree somewhere, often it would be in a lovely setting where we could catch up on lost kissing time or share a KitKat or a Twix or something.

I know I had my first kiss with Lin and lost my virginity with her too, but I don't really remember much about either beyond the fact that it was all very sweet. I had never been in a hurry to have that first kiss, but I was glad when it happened. Happily, it wasn't a one-off event and I've managed to enjoy several more since.

In the hostel we shared a bunk bed (me on the top bunk and Lin below) and we slept underneath my hanging gum nuts — no sniggering at the back, please. True to form, I had transformed the room into a giant herbarium. Gum nuts hung from the ceiling and wardrobe, attached by Blu Tack and sticky tape, because I needed them on display for taxonomical reference. The room was also festooned with hundreds of leaf and flower specimens which were being dried before I sent them home. They were all tender, exotic eucalypts, including one monstrously big specimen, a *Eucalyptus caesia* subsp. *magna*, and dear Lin never complained. The gum nuts didn't actually fall on our heads when we were in bed. Instead, as they dried they would simply start to split. I would then just tap the gum nuts on to the table and the seeds I wanted would come spilling out.

Lin and I were together for about three months, and towards the end she said, 'Tom, I know you're going soon . . . all the gum nuts are coming off the bed!'

She was right: it would soon be time for me to move on. It was a sad and sweet moment for both of us. Was I in love with Lin? I don't think so. To be honest, I'm not sure I really know what that would be. But I was definitely very fond of her and it was tearful when we parted. I still cherish her memory and have a sweet photograph of her standing next to a River Red gum tree, or *Eucalyptus camaldulensis*. I remember I wanted Lin in the photograph for scale purposes.

Being held hostage in the jungle obviously didn't do a lot for my social life, nor my love life, though after I was released and made it home I did end up spending a few extremely alternative weeks with the Unattainable Dream Girl from school, who was now an Attainable Dream Woman. It was actually she who wrote to me after hearing of my release, and she asked if I was going to go back to Stanbridge Earls for old Mr Moxon's retirement do. Given that Howard Moxon was the only secondary-school headmaster in southern England who had been prepared to give me a chance, how could I refuse?

'Good orchids here, Tom, eh?' the old boy said when I shook his hand and wished him well in his retirement.

Attainable Dream Woman had also turned up, as arranged, and she and I then fell into spending some really cool weeks together. She was seriously into painting horses and strange photography — she once took a picture of loads of different high-heeled shoes — and was, I thought, very clever. She's now very married but was kind enough to invite me and Bristles to her wedding.

I also went out for several months with one of Bristles' friends from Edinburgh University, an utterly sweet and huggable girl called Nina, whose mother was Thai and whose father was Danish. Nina was totally gorgeous and extremely nice to keep warm with. Though not particularly interested in horticulture, she still agreed to traipse round various nurseries and garden centres with me. On her visits to the gatehouse, however, I would have to close the windows, especially in winter, as otherwise she would shiver and freeze. Nina being a busy, cosmopolitan arty type — I think she worked for the Arts Council at one stage — I would also go to visit her in London when she didn't have time to come down to Lullingstone.

As far as conventional outings were concerned, I remember we definitely went to the cinema once in Islington (to see *Adaptation*, the film version of Susan Orlean's book *The Orchid Thief*) and we had to be evacuated from the cinema because of a fire. We also once went to a wine bar to meet some of her friends. I think I drank Coke and talked a lot about plants to everyone.

After Nina there were a couple of random 'collisions', but generally speaking by early summer 2004, with my days full in the greenhouse and my evenings increasingly spent in village halls delivering talks to audiences with an average age of sixty, the love cupboard was bare.

In some ways I have often longed to be forty or forty-five years old so I can blend in better with the sort of people who are interested in what I have to say about plants and gardening. Though I always have a great time at talks fielding questions and nattering with the audience afterwards, there's not really that much doing in the romance department for a twentysomething male on the WI lecture circuit. But in 2004 all that was to change. And it did so when a charming elderly lady from Dartford wrote to me offering me a Bird of Paradise.

This lady had read one of my Green Man columns in the *Kentish Times* about Francis Masson's adventures in South Africa, and wondered if I would be interested in a plant she had spare for the World Garden. You bet I was interested! The Bird of Paradise was one of the must-haves on my shopping list for South Africa, and I immediately rang to accept her offer and arrange a time to go and pick it up.

Over in Dartford I rang the bell of a small semi, expecting to be greeted by a grey-haired lady of a certain age. Instead I found myself face to face with an extremely nice-looking smiley blonde female of my own age. Was this the wrong house? No. The extremely nice-looking smiley blonde female was the woman's granddaughter. Her name was Louisa and we immediately found we had a lot to talk about. Once we had dealt with the Bird of Paradise (which I discovered could be divided into two plants, which was handy) we started discussing our travels. It emerged that Louisa's dad had been in the Foreign Office and we had plenty of tales to swap. I left the house with one neat Bird of Paradise in a pot and the mobile phone number of another.

Louisa and I started our courtship by text. Though I am not cut out for conventional dates and my pub visits are as rare as the Lizard Orchid in southern England, I seem to remember we went to The Malt Shovel in Eynsford and had a meal together. We certainly both felt at ease in one another's company, and though we were expecting to go our separate ways at the end of the evening, Louisa couldn't resist it when I invited her back to come up and see my 12-foot Echium, or Giant Viper's Bugloss. This is a very rare irritant borage from La Palma in the Canaries, and always an interesting talking point: it injects an acid into the skin that can react to sunlight and give you exploding blisters.

Louisa isn't a horticultural person per se, but she was certainly into gardening and on the propagation front we really did click that summer. I know how challenging, not to say infuriating, I must be to go out (or stay in) with, but Louisa, who works for the Specialist Schools Trust, is extremely patient by nature and adaptable too. With all I now had to do in the garden, this was just as well. But the question was: would I be able to be as adaptable for her?

For now, we just enjoyed our time together and things were busy but blissful. With Adam finalizing his drawings, Jim still trying to raise sponsorship, Tony promoting the World Garden at travel trade shows and my relationship with Louisa beginning to blossom, everything in the garden (apart from the weeds) was rosy.

Or it was until I walked into the house one afternoon to pick up my post. I announced my arrival with the customary 'Cracoooooo' which echoed around the Great Hall, and opened what I assumed was another seed catalogue that Mum had left out for me on the kitchen table. I was right, it *was* a seed catalogue; but this one was also the brochure for something called Plant World. *Plant World!?!*

I blinked, unable to believe what I had just read.

There, burning into the back of my retina, was an invitation to 'climb Mount Everest', 'discover the blue poppies in the Himalayas' and 'walk around the World's Only Garden Built and Planted as a Giant Map of the World!'

*Oh bollocking balls!*

Was my dream of a unique World Garden over before it had even begun? There was only one way to find out.

# 17

## Pig of a Time

The fact that there was already some kind of world map of plants up and running somewhere else in Britain loitered miserably in my thoughts for days. I hit the internet again, scouring the web for any other tourist attractions that might have the words 'world' and 'garden' in the same sentence. I had seen no overall plan or photo of it in the catalogue or on the website, so I couldn't shake off the fear that my own project might appear to some to be a hideous clone. Negative thoughts kept creeping up to mug me. Could a garden be accused of plagiarism? What if I was sued before I'd even lifted a spade? What would happen to Dad's savings?

Though Kent is full of famously visitable gardens, I had convinced myself that I wouldn't have any direct competitors for my interactive plant-hunter's map of the world. On my earlier researches, the only vaguely similar 'world' gardens I had found were one in France — I'd seen an aerial photo of it and wasn't fussed — and one in Morocco where plants from one continent were lumped together but with no apparent shape. But this Devon garden sounded suspiciously similar. Spurred on equally by curiosity and competitiveness, as soon as I had time, I would have to get down to Newton Abbot in Devon and check out Plant World for myself. Jim and Tony, hiding their exasperation, agreed.

Before I could do that, however, I had two very demanding female house guests to settle in at Lullingstone. I had taken Jim's advice and bought a pair of attractive, black-spotted pigs to whom I was offering a temporary stay of execution on their way to the slaughterhouse. They were Tamworth — Gloucester Old Spots, and so that I wouldn't feel too sad when they eventually went to their sausage-breeding programme in the sky, I named them Woolly and Red Spider after two pesky orchid pests. It was their job to clear the mass of vegetation around the Ice House and Bath House and at the same time provide me with copious quantities of free poo. I wanted this natural fertilizer as a base for my own compost. As with lunch, however, I discovered there's no such thing as a free poo.

Although my porkers needed no encouragement to feast on the tangle of ivy, hawthorn and bramble and then defecate wildly, they still needed a lot of attention: pellet-feeding twice a day (with the occasional cabbage or tomato thrown in); a constantly full water trough; a working electric fence to keep them in one place; and quite a lot of chatting up to make them feel relaxed and at home. Judging by their amiable snorts and snuffles, coupled with the amount of vegetation that was disappearing, I reckoned they were in pig heaven.

I must say they were a lot more entertaining than Luss Lass, the black-and-white cat we used to have when I was younger. For example, I'd never realized how ingenious pigs could be — particularly when they had scoffed everything in and around the Ice House and felt, gastronomically speaking, that it was time to move on.

Woolly was particularly frisky. She had the most Tamworth in her (a famously brainy breed, apparently) and was always the first to start trouble. One of her favourite tricks was to put the empty water bucket on her head and then ram the electric fence with it. She and Red Spider would then make a break for it, Steve McQueen-style.

'The pigs are out! The pigs are out!' replaced 'Cracoooo' as the common cry that summer, and many exhaustingly sweaty hours were spent trying to round the pair up and coax them back behind their electric fence. It would only be a few days — or in some cases a few hours — before we spotted them roaming free once more, or before someone called to say that my pigs were now at Eynsford Station attempting to buy tickets to Victoria. On one occasion they even got out on to the A225 and completed a large circuit through the surrounding country before returning home of their own accord in time for supper.

One strange fact I learnt about pigs, however, is that they seem to hate the sound and sight of running water. In any event, when they did escape, they never tried to cross the little footbridge over the river by Red Indian Reg's hut. This at least meant that Dad's lawn was safe from harm. Or it was for the time being.

Knowing what havoc Woolly and Red Spider could cause when they escaped, I was reluctant to spend much time away from Lullingstone. But I had to see Plant World for myself, and with Jim and Tony I hit the road for Newton Abbot. The garden belonged to a plant-hunter called Ray Brown, and I confess I was pretty apprehensive as I paid my entrance fee and prepared to see what he had achieved over almost twenty years on a slice of mild Devon hillside.

Ray's garden, which was already bigger than the World Garden was going to be, was certainly blessed with a more favourable climate in the south-west than we had at Lullingstone. His world map was built on a slope, and had North and South America, plus bits of Europe and Australia roughly in their shapes. Though Ray had a spanking Himalayas, he had no individual Canaries, Ireland or Great Britain; and where he had lawn for oceans, we were planning crushed granite pathways and geologically accurate rocky coastlines.

Ray's contouring was also a little vague compared with our designs for the Andes, the Rockies, and the Drakensberg mountains in South Africa, and he was less rigid than I intended to be about planting. He, for example, allowed plants from North Africa, such as the Atlantic Cedar, to grow in North America. The overall clincher though was that Ray did not set out to tell the stories of the plant-hunters as I wanted to. *Phew!* All in all, I felt I could breathe again — though I was glad Ray's garden was in Devon and not down the road in Dartford.

Ray, who had a healthy gardener's tan, turned out to be absolutely charming. We had a great old chinwag about his delightful garden and about my own plans, and Ray was extremely supportive. I suppose if our respective gardens had been in the same county, the conversation might have been less cheery. Instead we parted on good terms; and thanks to his great growing conditions in Devon, I've since bought loads of seeds from his catalogue and stacks of plants from his nursery.

Greatly reassured, we returned to Lullingstone and I continued to plough through my list of Things To Do. The picturesque jungle in the walled garden was now even more prolific and I knew I was going to have a heck of a job as soon as summer was over getting it cleared in time for the mechanical diggers. Though Woolly and Red Spider were sure to help, I hoped I would also be able to rope in some of my mates (if anyone remembered who I was and was still speaking to me) for some serious clearance sessions.

Though nowadays I try to be better organized and plan ahead properly, the Darién episode had taught me that no matter how well you prepare for the future, the present has a nasty habit of coming up and kicking you hard in the bollocks just when you're not expecting it. And Friday 16 July 2004 was one of those days.

It certainly started blissfully enough. It was glorious high summer: one of those perfect days at Lullingstone that should unwind slowly before you and stretch out in the sun like a lazy cat, then shine hotly and brightly for a few hours before gradually drawing to a close, the house martins squeaking and swooping over the gatehouse, church and house as dusk takes the colours away and the air cools. Instead it ended with Mum and me at Darent Valley Hospital in Dartford, and Anya in the Balkans, all gnawing our guts in worry about Dad, who was lucky to be alive.

At about 3pm he had taken his little table and was sitting outside the gatehouse to welcome visitors who had come along Lullingstone Lane. On the table was his cashbox, which held about £90. I was in the walled garden explaining how brilliant the garden was going to look in nine months' time when I suddenly heard the loud revving of a car engine and the aggressive screeching of tyres on gravel.

Given Lullingstone's location — we're just 17 miles from central London as the crow flies, and well within car-jacking distance of the M25 — I didn't give the sounds much thought. We often get people driving like nutters along the dirt track outside the house, and far worse things happen at night. Quite apart from the visits of the dogging community — and I'm not referring to Labradors: I'm always finding old condoms strewn around — a while back one gang member got torched, literally set on fire, by rivals in the nearby council car park. So screeching tyres didn't surprise me, even though it was a little early for such action.

It was only when Mum rushed into the garden, her face drained of colour, that I realized something serious had happened. Seeing that I was with a party of visitors, she kept it vague. She didn't want to upset them or spread panic. 'Something's happened outside the gatehouse, Tom. Perhaps you could . . .'

I made my apologies and followed at top speed.

'It's your father. He's had an accident . . . He was attacked!' she said as soon as we were out of earshot.

Hurrying towards him, I could see Dad slumped in his chair. As I ran closer, it was clear that he was in shock.

'What's happened?' I said. 'What's happened?'

It turned out that Dad had been the victim of a mugging — the first in Lullingstone's history, so far as we know — and at his age was lucky to be alive. Two men in an estate car had pulled up alongside him and the passenger had wound down his window and said something about the weather. Dad, being friendly old Dad, had replied, and just as the men looked as if they were about to drive off, Yob Number One leapt out of the passenger side, grabbed the cash box and jumped back into the car. Yob Number Two, who was behind the wheel, then hit the gas.

Dad, bless him, wasn't having any of it. When Yob Number Two hit the pedal too hard and his wheels began to spin, it gave Dad the time to get up and grab the handle of the passenger door with one hand and reach in through the open window to seize our cashbox with the other. What a hero!

God knows what these scumbags thought with the face of a furious seventysomething leering at them. But they didn't hang around. Once the car found some traction, it sped off. As it did so, Dad threw the cashbox into the bushes. But he was so angry he didn't let go of the door handle. He was then dragged along the gravel, before being tossed aside like a crisp bag in the wind. Mum found him sprawled on the ground.

We got Dad some rugs to keep him warm while we worked out what to do. Our first thought was to take him back to the house where he could lie down, so I got my car out of the garage and tried to help him into the passenger seat.

Bad decision.

'Aieeeeeeeeee!' he yelped as he tried to swing his leg into the foot well. The poor man was in agony.

I called an ambulance, which arrived within minutes, along with a police car, and Dad was driven off to hospital.

Although he was pretty fit and strong, he had hit the ground with a lot of force and the prognosis wasn't good. The doctors told us he would have to spend at least the next seven weeks in traction, unable to move an inch. Poor Dad had broken a pelvic bone.

# 18

## They Capture the Castle

I had the Darién dream for the fifth time. As on the previous four occasions, I woke up drenched in cold sweat.

'It's all right, Tom. You're safe,' said Louisa, who was lying next to me and was, she told me later, slightly freaked by my reactions. Apparently I had been screaming wildly and thrashing around, and I had even managed to bash her in the face. What had she done to deserve me for a boyfriend? When I told her what I'd seen in my dream, she simply put her arms around me and held me tight.

*It had been sunny this time, and we weren't in the jungle any more but here in the grounds at Lullingstone. The guerrillas remained faceless, but I watched in horror as they lined Mum, Dad and Anya up against the wall of the church. As in previous dreams, Gran for some reason was missing from the scene. Lucky Gran.*

*The guerrillas didn't say anything to me, but the message seeping through from my subconscious was loud and clear.*

*'This is your fault, Tom! You haven't paid our ransom.'*

*The guerrillas had come to the castle for their money; and because I didn't have it, they were going to kill my family.*

'But you can't do that,' I screamed. 'You can't!'

My protests made no difference: they chopped Dad's head off, blew Mum's to smithereens and then shot Bristles. They even shot Lusslass, our cat who had died years ago. I watched this bloodfest unfold paralysed by fear.

'Boy do I have still some issues to resolve,' I realized as I lay in Louisa's arms, slowly returning to the here and now, comforted by the warmth of her touch.

Working on the World Garden and continually fishing out my Darién diary to show people what I was on about had stirred things up, I was sure of that. While I felt this was in a sense therapeutic — I certainly felt that talking to groups publicly about my capture was a healthy form of therapy — all the worrying questions that were now bubbling to the surface over the project's future had somehow become jumbled up with my old fears of execution and death. Would Jim raise the sponsorship quickly enough to get us out of serious trouble? Would I physically be able to get the site cleared, landscaped and planted in time? Would anyone give a damn if I did finish it . . . or would they just think it was a plant version of Legoland? The fact that Dad had been mugged and was now lying immobile in a hospital bed had brought all these anxieties to a head. I was in a state and no mistake, and the Darién wouldn't leave me alone.

Of course I tried not to let Dad know how worried I was about everything when I went to visit him in hospital. Instead I tried to reassure him that Mum and his plant nut son were coping with all the visitors and the lawnmowing and the mail, and I even attempted to cheer him up with progress reports from the horticultural frontline.

'You should see what's happened to my Banana Passionflower, Dad. It's literally gone bananas!' I gushed one afternoon, explaining how this passionate pink stunner, a rarity in cultivation, had suddenly exploded into life and flower. In fact it had shot upwards like a rampant rocket and Dad was tickled to learn that it had actually broken out of the lean-to greenhouse, scampered up and over the 10-foot wall and was now heading for the nextdoor neighbour's herbaceous border.

In truth the Banana Passionflower's eruption really was a horticultural miracle and one of the few bright spots in a horrible summer. Seeing Dad strapped to a hospital bed broke my heart, and I desperately wanted to take his mind off the pain and monotony of being bedridden.

'I actually removed a couple of panes of glass from the lean-to,' I added, reminding Dad how I had originally collected the seed of this climber in Western Australia back in 1998, even though the plant's origins are in the Andes of eastern Colombia.

'It must have liked the direct sunlight and decided to make a dash for freedom,' he said. 'Wish I could do the same.'

'And to think it was nearly a goner in March,' I replied. 'The frost had knackered it. Reduced it to ground level and a sludgy mess of jelly. Now it's eighteen feet long and growing three inches a day. Unbelievable!'

'And the pigs?' Dad asked. 'They haven't attacked Trevor yet, have they?'

'All under control, Dad. Everything is. Red Indian Reg and Kay are helping every weekend, so we're doing fine. Really we are.'

Mum went to visit Dad every single day in hospital for seven weeks. Given that she was also looking after the visitors and the castle too, this was a tough time for her. But she kept going because she had to — a bit like her great-uncle Boyd yomping his way eastwards across Africa while those around him were dropping dead like flies.

'This will get better,' Mum kept reassuring Granny and me when we got together for Sunday dinner, Dad's empty chair at the head of the table a yawning gap, as uncomfortable to look at as a missing front tooth.

I did all I could to help Mum. I even managed to put in about two weeks of 20-hour days in the garden and grounds and at my computer, sleeping just four hours a night. But when I started to get spacey and see purple patches in front of my eyes, I realized I needed to pace myself better or I would conk out completely.

'You must get some rest, Tom, you really must,' said Mum, sounding like a mum.

When I wasn't trying to recapture Woolly and Red Spider as they ate their way round the district, I was either mowing the lawns, or doing the paths, or working in the walled garden from dawn till way past dusk. Before the major autumn clearances could begin, I had to start the painstaking process of picking through the overgrown jungle to identify the shrubs, perennials, biennials and annuals that I wanted to save and transplant into pots or prepared beds outside.

On my growing removals list from the rampant flowerbeds was even one of the descendants of Grandma Zoë's original plantings in 1947 when she had a herb garden here: *Tanacetum vulgare*, or Tansy; and I also wanted to salvage some of the sweet Himalayan Honeysuckle (*Leycesteria formosa*) from the derelict crazypaving paths. Some other specimens were simply too big to shift. So with Louisa's help I began a massive propagation process using cuttings from established plants such as *Viburnum rhytidophyllum*, *Sparmannia africana*, *Salvia rutilans* (Pineapple Sage), *Osmanthus heterophyllus*, *Callistemon linearis* (Red Bottlebrush), *Ficus carica* 'Brown Turkey' (Edible Fig) and many more.

Louisa, in whose company I felt more and more at ease, was a real angel and support, and we 'layered' together extensively. Layering, in case you were wondering, is a neat propagation technique in which you bend the branch of a plant that is too big to be moved, and bury the bend in a trench with a small cut in the lowest part to which you've applied root hormones — the tip sticks out the other side. In this way a smaller, more transportable progeny is produced. And full marks to Louisa for her patience and technique.

Though I wasn't sure I deserved it, many of my other hardy-perennial chums whom I had been neglecting of late also lent a hand. Two in particular sprang to my rescue that summer: two men who are, in their own very different ways, almost as bonkers about plants in general and eucalyptus trees in particular as I am. But then what would you expect from a couple of blokes who go by the names of Gum Bark Geoff and Gum Nut Steve?

# 19

## Gum Nuts

Gum Nut Steve was already a eucalyptus nut when we first met as students at Sparsholt College. He was studying for a National Diploma in Forestry and we clicked straight away. We would often take time out to visit the famous Hilliers nursery in nearby Romsey, where we would drool over the hardy woody plants like two weirdos on day release from a horticultural secure unit.

Today Steve earns his living as a landscaper and all-round tree person; but at heart he's still a forester and has managed to set up a ground-breaking eucalyptus collection near his parents' place in Oxfordshire. He has dozens of varieties and what really turns him on is diversity for 'forestry form'. This means that if a tree is gnarled or wonky, it's out; but if it's tall, straight, looks bloody good and you could turn it into planks with which to make something useful, Steve likes it a lot. 'Good forest form, Tom!' is his catchphrase.

In many ways Steve is a lot like the kind of trees he likes. He's a really straight up and down kind of guy, honest and practical and scientific; and there's not an infuriating knot to be found anywhere in his personality. With Steve, what you see is what you get and I like him enormously.

Steve is also very switched on about growing trees. He studies geological maps and records everything, including temperature and rainfall, to the last millionth of a millimetre, and as far as I can tell he has done so all his life. His brother, meanwhile, is a serious weather enthusiast whose laptop is plugged in to a constantly updated meteorological internet rainfall radar. This came in handy for me one February evening when Steve rang up in a real state.

'Tom! You've got ten minutes to cover your eucalyptus trees and get back inside! *Get a move on*!'

The night in question was certainly cold, but the lake was sparkling in the moonlight and the sky was clear all the way to infinity. I hadn't a clue what Steve was on about.

'You're joking!' I said.

'No, listen . . . it's really gonna *dump* snow on you. Any minute now. Just do as I say. And when it's fallen, get out and shake the trees! There's going to be a hell of a wind afterwards!'

Steve's warning seemed bizarre. Even stranger was that right on cue a thick bank of cloud now began to descend. As if at the command of some terrible vengeful god, Lullingstone was then clobbered by the most violent combination of lightning, thunder and snow I have ever seen in my life and probably ever will see. The heavens did literally dump 4 or 5 inches of sticky wet snow on us in about twenty minutes.

Steve was also right about the following wind that came howling in across the lake behind the house to where my gum trees were already shivering in their freezing frost pocket. If I didn't do something to get the snow off the branches, my budding eucalyptus collection of national importance would soon be no more than a collection of freeze-dried evergreens of no importance whatsoever, national or otherwise. As soon as the snow-burst had finished, I dashed through the white-out to the river's edge and began shaking the boughs of my trees one by one (there were around 300 of them). The snow had already stuck to the leaves like glue and, if left in the biting wind, the whole lot would have been buggered by frostbite or collapsed under the weight. I owed Steve big time.

By the summer of 2004, with Dad in hospital and the World Garden taking all my time and energy, I wasn't able to see Steve nearly as often as I would have liked. But he would still ring up — sometimes even with good news.

'Tom! Tom! We've had a bit of rain,' he'd yell excitedly down the blower. 'Six inches!'

The six inches didn't refer to the amount of rain but the phenomenal growth rate of his beloved gum trees. One of them took on 5 metres in a growing season, which must be a world record; and at one stage Steve's growth rate in a single season was on a par with that of Hawaii. Admittedly he'd cleared the area of weeds and has great growing conditions in his bit of Oxfordshire — an ancient river terrace deposit of acid soil on top of the chalk of the Chilterns. But that's probably more information than you really want.

When Steve and I first used to visit Hilliers,

my own fascination with gum trees was still at the passionate-but-containable stage. I had yet to become so fixated that I could roll a car while gazing at a stunning sapling. But under Steve's influence and that of the Hilliers arboretum, whose collection included some brilliant eucalyptus trees, slowly my fascination turned to a more intense passion.

'*What* an interesting bunch of trees,' I thought, looking round and examining the weird and wonderful way the bark peeled like snakeskin, some in patches, some in strips.

'And just look at this *johnstonii*,' Steve gushed on our first visit, pointing to what was, he said, one of the finest specimens in southern Britain. He was looking at a truly awesome tree; I remember the two of us just standing there becalmed in wonder. We both love the way the *johnstonii* gleams a gorgeous green when it is lashed by rain; and we patted and stroked its fabulously straight trunk and talked animatedly about two of the things that really get us gum nuts going: bark and heteroblasty.

Without getting too bogged down in plant science, I should point out for readers not wearing an anorak that heteroblasty refers to the way foliage develops in two different stages. Put simply, almost all young gum trees have different leaves from older ones. If you're into that sort of thing, it's incredibly absorbing to note the different developmental stages in the same tree.

But hang on, you say: don't lots of plants display this characteristic as their maturing leaves grow and change? Well yes, they do. But with gum trees the heteroblasty is just so distinctive and obvious. As you look up the trunks of some trees, you can actually see the difference between the juvenile and adult stages. It can be so marked it's as if the lanceolate leaves at the top belong to a different tree altogether and that two half-trees have been stuck together. Take *gunnii*, for example, which are common in florists' shops. The leaves start circular, but when they get older they can be anything up to 6 inches long. So yes: heteroblasty really is a blast. For us anyway.

Steve and I are both wowed by the speed at which eucalypts can grow and by their number — there are more than 900 classified species — and our extensive conversations can last for hours, if not days. We talk about the rush of growing gum trees. Getting buds. Being the first to grow something in the UK (around forty or fifty species can prosper in sheltered parts). We talk about diversity of leaf. The smell of the leaf — especially that of the oil-giving *Eucalyptus globulus*, or Blue Gum Tree, which is the floral emblem of Tasmania and whose strong whiff you will know from menthol sweets and Vicks Vapour Rub. We talk about the brilliant flowers. The gum nuts. The fact that it is Portugal that actually provides most of the world's oil, while China is next with 29 per cent and Australia only manages about 1 per cent. So no, you don't want to get stuck in the kitchen with us at parties.

Steve also has a thing about pine trees, and it was this shared interest that could have proved fatal in the spring of 2004 when we got away together for a quick break. Mum was relieved to hear I was only going to the Canaries and not back to Colombia; but as you can imagine, we weren't heading for the beach. I can last about twenty-nine minutes on a beach before my feet start to itch and I have to get up into the mountains to go looking for you-know-what.

Our aim was to collect seed at altitude in the region around the El Teide volcano in the centre of Tenerife. Though spring was sweet with promise at sea level, up high there were still pockets of snow on the ground and we were hit in the face by a strong, blisteringly cold wind. I was mainly on the look-out for the Tower of Jewels, or *Echium wildpretii*, an amazingly cool borage relation which has silvery leaves and a massive, deep red towering spike. (NOTE TO READER: this is the one that can irritate the skin and be a real nuisance if you're allergic, so do be careful how you approach; they sting much worse than nettles.) I was also looking for seed from some of the Canaries' nuclear-powered thistles — big, prickly Sow-Thistle Trees in the *Sonchus* group — as well as various lavenders and catmint.

Steve meanwhile was seriously determined to see the *Pinus canariensis*, or Canary Island Pine, *in situ*; and on our daily drives to El Teide he kept demanding that we stop at El pino gordo, a tourist attraction boasting the world's biggest Canary Pine.

'Just look at the girth on that!' Steve would gasp before grasping the trunk of this monster tree. I got so fed up having to stop at El pino gordo that I started trying to find alternative routes up to El Teide.

It was while we were well off the tourist track and trying to collect high-altitude provenances of this pine that we nearly came unstuck. We had parked the hire car and trekked upwards for a good hour or so, climbing through rocky scrub, when we spotted an interesting specimen off in the distance high above us. It was growing precariously over the rim of a 200-foot-deep ravine-cum-crater, the sides of which were uncomfortably steep and strewn with boulders and loose rock. This particular tree was gnarled and ancient and seemed to be clinging to life as much as it was clinging to the edge of the crater. Though it wasn't growing in a frost pocket, it was at such a high altitude and in such an exposed spot I reckoned that any seed we might be able to collect from it would probably be hardy enough to survive well at Lullingstone. At least it was worth the effort to find out and I soon had my heart set on collecting a big fat cone we could see in its branches.

'Could be completely useless of course,' said Steve gravely. 'Might be hollow or inbred. But there's only one way to find out.'

Trying to keep my balance on the steep slope, and starting to breathe hard in the thin cold air, I began to have one of my plant-inspired tunnel-vision moments and decided to climb up to the rim to get at this baby from above.

'Tom! You sure this is a good idea?' called the voice of reason behind me as I scrambled upwards.

The climb was tough and by the time I reached the top I was knackered, my mouth dry. I remember scooping up a handful of snow for refreshment. Peering over the edge and looking down, I could no longer see Steve; and as the wind gusted stronger and colder, the thought crossed my mind that this was perhaps a bit of a hairy place to collect pine cones and maybe I should go back down. But then I saw them. A gorgeous bunch of big fat cones. They were out on the far tip of the furthest overhanging branch.

'Flaming typical!' I thought. What to do?

I sucked on the snow and reflected on the drop. It was a long way to fall if anything went wrong. But what a triumph it would be to collect some hardy seed from such a spot.

'If you want to do it, Tom . . . just do it!' I said to myself, examining the tree which I could now see was definitely dying but not yet completely rotten. Pine *is* pretty solid, I reassured myself. There was no turning back. I balanced on a rock on the lip of the crater, steadied my breathing . . . and leapt out over the void to grab hold of the overhanging branch.

Hanging on for dear life, swaying in the icy blast and with a 200-foot drop beneath my feet, the thought that what I was doing was not entirely sensible flashed through my mind. Had my frozen arms lost their grip, or had the dead branch suddenly snapped, it's unlikely I would be sitting here writing this. But to me such risks are what plant-hunting is all about: when you want something as a plant-hunter, you go for it. I didn't have too long to reflect on the matter, though. As I clung on and heaved myself towards the cones at the end of the branch, below me I heard the sudden ominous rumble of crashing rocks.

Perhaps it was my climbing up the crater's sides that had dislodged them, but somehow I seemed to have set off a rock fall. And the runaway debris was all heading in Steve's direction.

Half an hour later, with my prize safely in my pocket and Steve and I reunited down the slope, we sat on a boulder together reflecting on our lucky escapes: I was relieved the tree had held my weight and I hadn't slipped; Steve was happy to have got out of the path of the falling rocks in time.

'Sometimes, Tom, I really think you need to think things through a bit more,' he said.

Steve was not wrong. But it had been a blast, we were absolutely fine and I had the cone. Despite the lessons I had learnt in Colombia about what can happen when you don't think things through properly, my attitude was that we could have been there all day looking up at the cone and thinking things through, but there comes a time when you've just got to get the job done. Great-Great-Uncle Boyd would have known what I was talking about and so would his brother Claud — even if they did both meet untimely ends in inhospitable terrain.

In the event, our spiffing *Pinus canariensis* cone turned out to be entirely useless and an absolute git. Steve was also absolutely right about that too: it was hollow inside with no viable seed in it. But taking that leap out on to the branch was the only way to find out and, frankly, the rock fall could have happened even if we'd been sunning ourselves on the slope having a picnic. So, regrets? Not really.

It was after a much less dangerous expedition to north Wales that Steve and I had by chance met another gum nut who was also to be hugely influential in helping me get the World Garden under way. Steve and I had driven in our respective cars to the Celyn Vale Nurseries in Carrog, probably the biggest supplier of potentially hardy eucalypts in the northern hemisphere, to meet the famous Andrew McConnell, who runs it. Well, Andrew was famous to us anyway; and particularly to me, who had been drooling over his Celyn Vale brochures since at least 1992 when I planted my first eucalyptus trees at Lullingstone. I would swoon over his wonderfully descriptive catalogue and, believe it or not, I still have the 1992 edition with the stunning and magnificent *Eucalyptus coccifera*, or Tasmanian Snow Gum, on the cover which had so inspired me.

As a teenager and in my early twenties, I regularly received boxes in the post from Celyn Vale. The young trees, measuring 1–2 feet high, arrived with their root balls lovingly wrapped in black plastic and carefully supported by polystyrene blocks, and opening these boxes was an almost orgasmic experience for me, like Christmas and birthday presents rolled into one. So finally meeting the legendary Andrew, in his funny-coloured socks, was a major encounter.

234

Steve and I bought only a few bits and bobs from him on this visit, and we were just about to hit the road when we suddenly noticed lots of packets of seed on one of the tables, some of which weren't eucalyptus but seemed to be weird acacias.

'Where are these from?' I asked.

'Oh a guy in Oxfordshire,' said Andrew casually. 'An Opuntia man. Heavily into Prickly Pears. But he's a gum nut too.'

'Really?' Steve was gobsmacked and I was all ears. Another gum nut in Oxfordshire? Steve thought he was the only one. We had to track this man down.

Andrew wouldn't give us contact details for the mystery grower, but he did offer to pass on our names and numbers to him. Before the Astra was back in the garage at Lullingstone, there was already a message waiting for me on my phone. It was from a bloke called Geoff and when I telephoned him back, our first conversation lasted a good three and a half to four hours. You can imagine what we talked about.

Steve and I arranged to go to visit this fellow enthusiast and see his collection for ourselves, and we were really excited the day we drew up at his home near Witney. A neat-looking businessman-type, wearing black shoes and in his early fifties, bounded out of the front door to meet us. He was certainly a fast talker and we were soon deep in conversation. He was called Geoff Cooper; he had more or less retired, having been in bottled gas, of all things; he had a bit of land — and he had a very, very serious passion for succulents.

We're not talking a few cacti on the windowsill in the sun lounge. Oh no. Geoff had a 66-foot-long polytunnel stuffed full of thousands and thousands of stunning cacti, and they spilled out of his garage too. Geoff was an Opuntia freak of massive proportions, specialist subject: Prickly Pears. His slightly unhinged devotion made him a man after our own hearts and Steve and I were in plant heaven. Or at least I was. After Geoff had been talking cacti for what felt like a couple of weeks, I could see Steve's eyes and brain begin to glaze over.

It was clear that Geoff liked to talk about his passions — perhaps even more than Steve or I — and we had been rabbiting away for ages before he even remembered to invite us into his house. Geoff, it emerged, had apparently managed to combine his prodigious knowledge and love of succulents with an equally serious gum tree habit in a truly ground-breaking way. By now Steve and I were desperate to see his 2–3-acre plot, which was a little way away from his house. We were, in short, gagging for some serious eucalyptus action.

'Jeeze! This man has really lost it,' I thought as Geoff showed us round what was nothing less than an Australasian forest in the middle of Oxfordshire. In a mad flash of inspiration, he was growing his eucalyptus trees — some 100 feet tall: massive great things — with cacti planted at their base. This was bizarre — I'd never seen anything like it — but it was also quite brilliant and I was blown away by the audacity of his combinations. In fact I was dazed. I was almost seeing stars.

Steve was equally amazed by the way the eucalyptus trees in this Home Counties Australasia gave shelter to Geoff's understorey plants, the reasonably tender ones that need dry conditions but not full sun. There was real method to this unorthodox approach. Given the way eucalyptus trees destroy grass by sucking it dry, it was a really clever use of the gum tree canopy, and I decided to try planting some Protea relations from Australia, such as *Hakea lissosperma*, known as the Needle Bush, which likes very well-drained conditions, under my own eucalyptus trees if the frost or cold winds didn't knacker them first.

Gum Bark Geoff, as Geoff Cooper became known, turned out to be an exceptionally cool guy. A lot of his eucalyptus trees, it emerged, were from original Forestry Commission collections and the cold, hardy trials the Commission had carried out in Britain in the 1980s under Dr Julian Evans to see if there was a commercial future for eucalyptus in wood production or amenity use in Britain. In fact there is still no timber trade in eucalyptus here, where it remains an ornamental tree. Elsewhere in the world, of course, it is grown for wood pulp, telegraph poles and in reafforestation projects — the very things Dad was involved with for much of the eighteen years he spent working in Africa.

If Steve grows his gum trees as a really, really exciting hobby, I suppose Gum Bark Geoff is on more of an ego trip: growing on the edge to produce gorgeous plants that are off the dial and that people say won't or can't be grown in England. I'm somewhere between the two, though I sympathize with both ambitions.

A strong friendship has grown up with Geoff and the way he shares his expertise is wonderful. However, when he closes his eyes and starts talking, you know you are in for the long haul. He never stops. In fact, you can walk away, have a cup of tea and come back, and Geoff will still probably be talking about an Opuntia and its amazing spikes or whatever, giving the details of its original provenance down to the exact valley. So, as I said, a fellow nutter.

Through our friendship I have developed a great interest in succulents — anything with a fleshy leaf, basically — and cacti, and I've also benefited enormously from Geoff's generosity. Like Gum Nut Steve, Geoff really came into his own in the summer of 2004 when I realized that the World Garden was going to need rather more plants than Yours Truly had at his disposal.

Steve, who hadn't been sure about the project at first, was very supportive in talking things through and, when he saw how determined I was, in rolling up his sleeves to help out physically. He also donated some conifers and eucalyptus varieties which gave me a real boost. But Geoff was unrestrained in his generosity.

In early July he drove down to Lullingstone, his car stuffed with dozens and dozens of square pots, each crammed with different species of stunning and unusual succulents, including Agaves, Beschornerias, Dasylirions, Yuccas and, of course, the devilishly well-armed Opuntias, or Prickly Pears, which need armour-plated gloves to handle. These are real showstoppers as far as I'm concerned, and I happily spent morning after morning potting them on. The deal was that from each square pot I would pot on four of the best specimens for Geoff while keeping the rest back for planting on the world map. With no revenue yet from sponsorship and Dad's savings all being spent on Jim and Tony, this was a godsend.

In August, when I filled every nook and cranny of the Astra with these spiky seducers and headed to Oxfordshire to give Geoff his plants back, he was so chuffed with my handiwork and our agreement that he gave me even more square pots, massively overpopulated with exotic Opuntia cacti, their evil thorns as sharp as syringes.

Geoff explained that these Opuntias, like the first batch of succulents I'd potted on, had been collected by German plant-hunters roaming the sun-ravaged wastes of Arizona, New Mexico, Texas and Mexico. If I could only ensure that they avoided the winter wet at Lullingstone, I had a strong hunch they would be hardy enough to survive in the World Garden and look stunning in my miniature Mexico and southern United States. These plants had hardly ever been seen in cultivation and some weren't even fully botanically named yet — so thanks to Geoff and his German contacts I would be breaking new ground. This gave me a huge horticultural high.

Back on Planet Earth at Lullingstone, I was still confronted by a picturesque jungle that had to be cleared, transformed and planted in order to receive visitors in less than nine months' time. But Geoff's donations, the first big batch of plants provided by someone other than myself, were a huge result. His generosity meant that Mexico, the southern USA and South Africa could all feature their own prickly, fleshy, spiky delights.

With extensive, not to say excessive, generosity, Geoff then also gave me an amazing array of seeds — more than 1,000 packets in all, which he had painstakingly labelled and which Louisa and I now set about sowing.

The only downside to Geoff's generosity was potting on so many Prickly Pears: my hands, even in thick gloves, ended up like pincushions. But this was a small price to pay for so many cracking beauties. Geoff is such a modest guy, he doesn't want his name anywhere in the garden and I often wonder how or if I will ever be able to repay him. However, given that Jim appeared to be drawing a blank on the sponsorship front, I was grateful for as many lucky breaks as I could get in the garden. Geoff and Steve were true saviours.

# 20

## The Borrowers

Visiting Dad in hospital in the dog days of August, I tried to make what little good news there was on the home front sound like progress. In truth everything in the walled garden wasn't rosy — it was rampant.

Inside the walls, whose ancient brickwork sucked up the summer heat like a storage heater, Dad's neglected vegetable patch was looking unkempt and Crac's herb garden had gone crackers. Once-neat patches of overgrown tarragon, sage, chives, Welsh onions and a host of other herbs and veg were now becoming unruly and sticking out at odd angles like my hair after I've slept in my tea-cosy. Every time I brushed past the green stems and leaves they would send warm, herby aromas wafting up to my nose, reminding me of happy summer hours I spent in the garden with Gran as a boy. It was sad to think these aromatics would be gone in a matter of weeks, but I was really excited about what would replace them.

Along with inedible ornamentals like Gran's Himalayan Honeysuckle, everything was starting to run wild, jostling for my attention alongside the weeds that were exploding in the borders and in among the apple and quince trees. True, it was all deliciously pungent and pretty in a shambolic,

French Impressionist kind of way; and if I stood at the Moon Gate and looked in casually, the colours blurred and bled into one another in the summer haze like the surface of a Monet. It was wonderful if you happened to be a bumble bee. But for anyone who knew they had to get the whole lot cleared in the near future so that major building works could begin, the walled garden looked seriously daunting.

'Everything's under control, Dad. Really,' I said reassuringly. 'Gum Bark Geoff's been brilliant. He's given me loads of stuff and Louisa and I have been potting like crazy. We're going to have Prickly Pears coming out of our ears. Honest! And they're going to look fab.'

For me this was an exhausting, full-on time and in truth I was knackered, but Dad seemed to appreciate hearing of my efforts.

'Oh. And loads of hardy-perennial mates from Sparsholt have promised to come and help with the clearing as soon as we're ready. We're going to have a serious chainsaw session!'

Dad winced silently. The thought of the Sparsholt hardy perennials descending *en masse*, armed with sharp objects like cutting tools and petrol-driven chainsaws, was enough to worry even the most laid-back parent. But I needed all the labouring help I could get. I hadn't yet replanted half the shrubs I wanted to save from the walled garden; and once that was done I would still have to spray and burn the low-level remnants before the massive clearance of woody stuff could begin. Then there was my rickety old Venlo greenhouse to dismantle, pane by pane, and reassemble in Trevor's half of the garden where I planned to put the nursery. At the moment the Venlo was bang in the middle of where South Africa was going to be. Along with Gran, this greenhouse had been an inspiring teacher over the years and I was worried about ever being able to put it back together again properly. It would probably collapse or end up looking like a shanty-town shack. But it couldn't stay where it was.

On the other side of the Berlin Wall — a sheep fence and a couple of hedges, including the huge hornbeam one that ran down the middle of the walled garden and divided it in two — Trevor's plot was also becoming overgrown and, more seriously, still very much Trevor's. I didn't dare tackle Dad about this particular problem while he was in his pyjamas. The Trevor question would have to wait.

Nor was there much good news to report on sponsorship. So far Jim had had no big bites, bar the vague prospect of securing a couple of weeks' free stump removal and trench digging courtesy of JCB once the site had been cleared. With funding looking tight to non-existent, tensions were beginning to build between Jim on the one hand, who suggested we might have to scale back our landscaping and go for a Flat Earth, flat-garden policy with no contouring, no rocky coastlines and grass for the oceans — but what was the point of that? He had no idea! — and Adam and me on the other, who were still full-on in favour of a geological world of mountains and waterfalls — so long as we could raise the money.

Adam, who still didn't have a contract and hadn't been paid yet, had ploughed on manfully with his technical designs and landscape drawings; and Tony Russell's marketing efforts in the local press, coupled with my own Green Man gardening column, also seemed to be paying dividends by generating interest. Easily the best bit of news though came from Dad himself.

'The doctors say I'll be out next month — and about time too!'

It certainly was. The captain had been missing from the bridge for too long. I felt instantly reassured that, with Dad home, Lullingstone would return to what passed for normality and we could at least begin to resolve the cash v. creativity clash in the World Garden.

On the designated day at the end of September, Mum drove to the Darent Valley hospital for the last time. I waited at the front door of the house for their car to appear, and a surge of relief and affection ran through me when the white Daewoo finally drew up with Dad in the passenger seat. Helping him into a wheelchair felt strange. I was delighted he was home, of course; but it was sad to see such an active man rendered so vulnerable, especially since his injuries had been down to his own bravery in the face of a couple of cowardly tits.

Still, Dad wasn't moping or feeling sorry for himself, and he was soon getting around the house on his new set of wheels — though not nearly as fast as Anya and I when we used to drive him nuts skidding over the polished wooden floors in our socks. Dad's bedroom was on the ground floor so at least he didn't have to get up any stairs. But he was now most often to be found in the den, on the phone or at his typewriter. The visitor season had some weeks to run, and though he had done a heap of paperwork towards the end of his stay in hospital, he still needed to catch up. I won't say he hit the ground running; but you know what I mean. He made progress on all fronts and the wheelchair was soon ditched in favour of a kind of Zimmer-frame walking aid which allowed him to get around on foot, albeit at about the same speed as a delicate Queen Anne might have toured the estate.

Dad's long stay in hospital — he was out of action from July to September — had given him plenty of time to ponder the World Garden and how, if it pulled in the visitors, it really could help safeguard the future of our family home. He returned determined to make it happen. He wanted *action*.

'We're going to have to raise the capital ourselves, Tom,' he announced decisively one day. This was a big deal for Dad. He really had believed it when Jim said the bulk of the money for the garden would most likely come from sponsorship. But in the den, the disappointing conversations he was having with Jim had made him accept that no big business yet wanted to line us all up against the church and soak us with a money hose.

Before he was mugged, Dad had been resolutely opposed to the idea of borrowing a single penny. Perhaps the enforced lie-in had made him reflect on his own advancing years; or maybe he was encouraged by seeing Adam's plans and the interest the project was beginning to generate in the press and media; or maybe it was the increase in visitors to the castle that summer; but in the absence of Jim securing any firm financial offers, Dad decided it was time to make the call. He duly phoned his friendly bank manager in Bromley and asked for a meeting.

Like our ancestor Sir John Peche, the one who was a close chum of Henry VIII, the Hart Dykes also now needed to raise some cash. Back in 1515, before high street banks were happy to give overdrafts to pretty much anyone with a roof over their heads, Sir John's lifestyle as a royal fixer across the county meant he had to borrow £600 from the King's Treasury to tide him over. Sir John had to give 'his great collar of esses' — whatever that was — as a security; but all the nice man from Barclays wanted was for Dad to sign some bits of paper and agree to mortgage off a bit of the castle.

Dad was rightly cautions and had several meetings with the bank — the manager was a switched-on, sympathetic bloke called Nick — and I stayed well out of the way until negotiations had progressed to such a stage that a summit was called at the house. After a late burst of heat in September, summer was fading into memory when I showed the bank manager around the site of the World Garden-to-be. Given the mess I was presenting him with, I desperately hoped he had a seriously good imagination. Luckily he did, and all his questions and suggestions were positive and insightful.

Then came the big day when, in the dining room next to the Great Hall, Adam came into his own. We weren't allowed in to the dining room for an hour or so while he set up all his bits of deep blue fuzzy felt. He then proceeded to give a fabulous presentation of what the World Garden could eventually look like — right down to the kind of crushed granite he wanted for the paths. Adam had planned everything to the last micro-millimetre — even allowing enough width for two standard wheelchairs to pass each other if they ever met head on in mid-Atlantic. To my eye his drawings were spot on and exactly as I wanted the World Garden to be. But would Dad and the man from the bank buy it?

Although it must have pained him to do so, Adam boldly set out two options for the World Garden. Option A, which he and I both favoured, was the all-singing, all-dancing version and the more expensive, while Option B, the flat-garden approach, was favoured by Jim Pettipher. When Dad heard that JCB had offered to do all the work for free if we followed this basic, less expensive approach, his mind seemed made up.

'Well, Option B it is then,' he said, calculating the savings.

'Great!' chipped in Jim.

'*Dad!!!!*' I yelled, knowing in my guts that this was shortsighted madness. If we were going to create a new garden attraction, we had to do it properly. Inside I was boiling and Adam, who agreed with me, had turned redder than a red pepper.

We adjourned, and in the days that followed Mum and I, helped by insights from Nick the bank man, eventually managed to convince Dad that Jim's flat-garden idea was a no-hoper, even it was more affordable. The case for a proper contoured World Garden, and our five-year plan of eventually drawing 50,000 visitors a season to a much richer and more interesting attraction, obviously made commerical sense to Nick too. More pertinently, it also seemed feasible. After a bit more to-ing and fro-ing, the bank had no hesitation in agreeing a lending facility up to an eventual maximum of £250,000. Adam and I would get our 3D interactive plant map of the world after all!

To many people with credit-card debts and big mortgages in the south-east of England, borrowings of a quarter of a million might not sound outrageous, especially if it's being borrowed by people who live in a whacking great pile like we do and who are trying to launch a new business initiative. But believe me, to Dad, to me and to Mum it was an absolute fortune. While the bank wasn't prepared to release all of it at once, we were certainly determined not to use up anywhere near that sum if we could possibly avoid it.

Our attitude to borrowing may seem somewhat old-fashioned and quaint, but that's how the Hart Dykes are. I certainly felt the pressure that was now on Dad's shoulders, knowing the financial risk he was taking to make my pet project work. He was, after all, nearly eighty, and if it failed, basically he was screwed. Though he had had credit cards, he had always tried to stay in the black with them and he had never borrowed so much as a fiver against the house. So this was a big move for him and for all of us. As for me, I had never bought anything on the never-never and wouldn't really have known how, even if I'd wanted to.

Happily, the bank agreed to give us generous terms until the garden was up and running properly and giving what is known in the trade as an 'income stream' — i.e. visitors paying actual dosh to come and gaze in awe at our brilliant new attraction. Dad was very clear what the money we were borrowing would be spent on. It was to create the backbone of the garden and pay for its basic construction: the machinery; the drainage and irrigation pipes; the electricity ducts; the rocks; the materials and some of the contouring; and, of course, we could finally pay Adam for his brilliant drawings. The rest — the plants, the planting, the contouring of more mountain ranges like the big boys in Asia, Europe, Africa and North America, the nursery, the propagation — all that would have to be funded by me through plant sales or talks.

I knew that as an estate we were sailing close to the wind financially, but if I'm honest I suppose close to the wind is how I like to sail through everything. I definitely like to be a little on the edge, knowing that at any moment a big gust could come along and, if I'm not careful, capsize my metaphorical dinghy. I need this kind of excitement in life or I switch off. Sometimes you have to leave the safety of the bay and pull out beyond the headland and this was one of those moments.

'It's down to you now, Tom,' said Dad one day as we sat with Mum in the Great Hall discussing all that now had to be done.

Outside, day by day autumn was taking hold in the walled garden, which now resembled a mistily romantic, overgrown oasis. With the house and grounds reopening to the public the following Easter, there wasn't a day to lose. It was time the Green Man got his green buttocks into gear.

# 21

## The Lullingstone Chainsaw Massacre

I've never heard the squawk made by a constipated duck that can't go to the toilet, but I'm sure it would sound exactly like the metal detector with which I now had the garden 'swept'. Every time it hovered over a metallic object in the undergrowth, it let out a stream of frantic high-pitched squeaks and squawks that echoed hilariously within the walls.

Old coins, buttons and even a token coin issued by my great-great-grandfather were unearthed by the metaldetector man, not to mention a toy lorry and a Boeing 747 I had left lying around when playing in the garden a quarter of a century earlier. We all thought the metal detector had detected serious treasure when it went berserk at one stage and sounded like a whole family of constipated ducks. But it had found nothing more valuable than an old car exhaust. I bet Alan Titchmarsh has never found a car exhaust growing in *his* garden.

As I've said, the weeds in the walled garden were rampant, and the tenacious nature of the couch grass and the 'lovely' pink-flowered monster that is field bindweed were far too overwhelming to contemplate digging them up by hand. There weren't enough hours in the day or days in the week for that, and hand-digging would have been like painting the Forth Bridge: by the time I had lifted the last knot of roots, the little blighters would have been sprouting up again back where I started.

Poor Gran had been fighting field bindweed at Lullingstone for ever, so I decided to use a small portion of my budget on having these severely prolific weeds professionally zapped with the systemic poison Roundup. In fact I had deliberately let them run riot, climbing the walls, quince trees and even up the potting shed, to maximize the leaf surface they would expose to the deadly spray. Tim Jackson, a good friend from down the road, provided the spraying gear, and I paid £100 for the chemicals with money I had earned from a talk.

Before the spraying began, three mates from college, Sye Man, Sexy Suzie and Spud Gun Rog, generously volunteered to come over one weekend and help me dismantle my venerable old timber-framed Dutch Venlo. With the glass and wood stored and labelled for reassembly in Trevor's half of the garden, I then continued my careful clearance of Gran's old herb garden and my fertile south-facing border for the remaining green refugees I wanted to save.

There was some fairly energetic moving of shrubs like *Pileostegia viburnoides*, Granny's old roses and herbaceous plants like Viper's Bugloss, but amid all the transplanting and hacking, one particular beauty made me put down my secateurs and gasp.

There in my old border was a truly magnificent creature: a stately and towering

15-foot *Eucalyptus morrisbyi*, the world's rarest gum tree. Believe me when I say it looked sublime and took my breath away. It was still in full flower, its glowing white, fuzzy blooms exuding a delicious honey smell; and it was the first time, so far as I knew, that this species had flowered in cultivation in Britain. This was no mean feat, I reflected. I had grown it from seed I had collected in February 1999 in southern Tasmania, where it occurs on only two sites, both on farmer's pastureland. It is, frankly, King of the Eucalypts.

The *morrisbyi* is blessed with some amazing assets, including sensually pointed buds and gum nuts, large three-flowered inflorescences, delicate, smooth, creamy-grey patchwork bark and juvenile leaves that are neatly circular with crenulate edges. I love everything about these babies, including their generally shabby overall appearance. So why was I intending to consign this particular beauty to the great compost heap in the sky?

Well, like some families I know, gum trees really don't care to be uprooted once they've established themselves in a particular spot, so I felt I had no option. Luckily, the other seeds I had collected from Tasmania had survived their stay in my fridge, and the spare plants I was growing were also doing well. I consoled myself that when the world map finally opened to the public, I would at least be able to display a *morrisbyi* in my own miniature Tazzy and still have some left over to sell in the nursery.

Once the spray man, Tim, had done his stuff,

and with the 1-acre plot resembling a brownfield site, the scene was finally set for the walled garden's biggest transformation in more than fifty years. Lured by the promise of free scoff and floorspace in the gatehouse, plus some glorious chainsaw mayhem, a mega-barbecue, fireworks and a serious laugh, a posse of friends from Sparsholt agreed to help me kickstart the work over one extensive-intensive weekend.

Our mission was to clear all the remaining woody material — and there was a small forest of it. I wanted to waste as little of the garden's riches as possible, but the weekend would still require the removal of, among other things, old overgrown shrubs such as Berberis, Viburnum and Syringa (Lilac), Osmanthus, Ligustrum (Privet) and some fairly substantial Cotoneaster trees. Fruit trees like Mulberry, Fig, Medlar and Amelanchier were either to be transplanted or chainsawed.

I arranged for the plump fruit dangling deliciously from Crac's four rounded quince trees to be picked by Eynsford WI and so find its way into local jams and jellies, and the year's big crop of apples was to be sold on Gran's plant stall inside the house, along with a selection of her herbs. I also intended to make good use of the apple and yew trees themselves. The biggest logs would be kept for turning so we could one day sell artefacts from Dad's mini shop in the house, while the hollow stems would make neat nesting sites for Lullingstone's greater spotted and green woodpeckers, not to mention displays for 'air plants' like Tillandsia from Brazil.

My tree surgeon mate Laurence Dell, who works for a local gardening company called Down to Earth (which had already generously promised £1,000 worth of woody plants for the World Garden), was also donating the use of a chipper for the weekend. I intended to use this to turn the smaller apple branches into mulch, which would eventually be spread over part of the world map near the base of trees and big shrubs to retain moisture and keep down the weeds; and I had similar plans to mince up the chewier bits of the stately yews that sat in the four corners of the garden, planted in the 1940s under Grandma Zoë's reign. Their more acidic mulch would be perfect in China, home of the rhododendron, while their trunks could be planked up and turned into benches on which tired visitors could park their carcases.

The really obstinate root balls would stay in the ground awaiting the digging machines, which were scheduled to arrive at the beginning of December, and the rest of the unusable woody material we would simply pile up in four Guy Fawkes-sized bonfire heaps in the corners of the garden. When lit by way of final celebration, these giant 'torches' would illuminate the massive barbecue Louisa was promising to cook on the Sunday night once our work was finished.

I have to say all my mates were dazzlingly energetic. Sye Man, roll-up in mouth, got his head down with Sexy Suzie and started blitzing, Sye going straight for the massive Cotoneasters and the biggest yew tree before axing the hornbeam Berlin Wall. (I didn't know where

Trevor was that weekend, and to be honest I hadn't really tried to find out.)

Gum Nut Steve attacked the other yew trees, and even Tony Russell, the neatly bearded marketing man, tackled a couple of quince trees. Tom Stobbart, Laurence, Louisa and I could only gaze in awe as Richard Reeves, with his incredibly long 'Because I'm Worth It' mane, became possessed by a kind of chainsaw devil and turned into a one-man demolition derby, single-handedly flattening the orchard. The chainsaw became an extension of Rich's hand, and he wielded it to and fro as if playing crazy ping-pong in an imaginary mosh pit. While all this was going on, another close friend and former Sparsholtian, Paul Barnard, lugged and dragged our cut branches on to the fire heaps.

Luckily we managed to avoid any loss of life or serious injury over the weekend, and the only downer was that Spud Gun Rog never showed up. For the rest of us, it was great simply to catch up and enjoy one another's company again. I always love it when Laurence comes to Lullingstone because, as well as being hugely supportive and a knowledgeable tree person, he's also batty. By which I mean he's seriously into bats and spends a lot of his time running around the estate looking for them. Pipistrelles mainly, but there may be others. We call Laurence 'Bat Man' (for obvious reasons) and he often has a bat-o-meter with him. This is basically a box that helps him listen to the bats' high-pitched calls. Armed with his bat-o-meter, he always seems to have his nose up a tree or down a hole somewhere, or he can be found tuning into high-pitched noises down by the lake or river. You always know when Laurence has found a bat because he says: 'I've found a bat.'

By the time dusk fell on Sunday night our muscles ached, we were all filthy, scratched and sweaty, and a once prolific garden was now more or less stripped bare. My friends had done a brilliant job, and we were more than ready for the bonfires and the barbecue — apart from Rich, of course, who was ready for his chips fried just-so in vegetable oil. Rich again came into his own. First he hid a small but really quite dangerous arsenal of fireworks in the bottom of one of the bonfires. These fizzed and exploded in every direction, causing general mayhem and hysteria. Then he volunteered to help Louisa with the cooking.

For someone with such strict dietary require-ments, this must have been a trial for Rich, who winced at the smell of the sizzling burgers and refused point blank to try them. But it didn't stop him arguing playfully but endlessly with Louisa about how everything should be cooked. Then, as we began to stuff ourselves with the seared meat, Rich announced that he was going off into the darkness to search for something he actually could eat.

'Anyone coming to the chippie?' he asked hopefully.

'Er, no, Rich!' was the resounding response.

(Legend has it that Richard did once eat a jelly baby when he was about ten years old, since when it's been chips, chips and more chips, plus of course the Tesco Value lemonade. However, after he took me down the old Roman well with only a cycle mask for protection, for breakfast the next day he did capitulate and eat a packet of Walkers crisps. But they had to be salt and vinegar — or no deal.)

The next day, in the grey morning light after most of my friends had left and the roaring bonfires were no more than quietly smouldering piles of white ash, I stood in the middle of the garden with Dan The Man He Who Can, who had been superlative over the weekend. With the tang of smoke pricking our nostrils, we tried to absorb the scale of our slashing and burning. I suddenly felt very small.

Ever since I had been old enough to hold a trowel, this walled garden had been a lush and secret pleasure ground for me, as well as a playroom and schoolroom. Now, shorn of its trees, fruits, herbs, vegetables and exotic flowers, the evidence of so many years of hard horticultural labour by my two grandmothers wiped out in a weekend, it looked naked and about four times bigger than I remembered it.

For the first time in my life, I realized, I could now actually see out of the garden properly, and the view brought me up short. It was strange suddenly to see the place I thought I knew so well with fresh eyes, the flint walls of St Botolph's seemingly closer than ever before and the dark green cedars by the house looking bigger and more magnificent than ever. There were the gatehouse and the flint dovecote and the rolling views over the golf course that had once been Sir Thomas Dyke's deer park, with its umpteen miles of fenceposts. I felt blessed that this was the place I could call home — and acutely aware of what I had just done to our walled garden.

No doubt Sir Thomas's ancestors would have been as transfixed by the changes he brought about on the estate as Thomas himself would have been by the mass clearance I had just orchestrated. I felt somehow that a baton was passing to me and I was finally beginning to take my share of responsibility for the estate's development and survival. Having just destroyed so much that my relations had worked so hard to grow, I was making myself intimately responsible for Lullingstone's future.

These reveries were shortlived, however, when Rich and Laurence sauntered into the garden to join me and Dan The Man He Who Can, Rich being armed with a good supply of un-ignited rockets.

'Shame to waste them,' he said, before carrying out a series of dangerous launching experiments using a length of hollow pipe he had found lying around. Inserting the stick of the rockets into the pipe, he then launched them at a variety of angles around the garden and over the walls, including horizontally from his shoulder like a bazooka. The rockets fizzed, whirred and exploded around us, until just one was left.

'I think I'll put a flower pot on this one,' said Rich, driving his hollow pipe launch tube into the ground and setting the rocket up for a vertical take-off, the small plant pot sitting on top like a hat.

Laurence, who was doing something with a chainsaw elsewhere in the garden, had been oblivious to what Richard was up to. But he now stopped what he was doing and removed his ear protectors in time to witness the ignition of the last rocket and the symbolic launch of a plant pot into the skies high over Lullingstone.

Unfortunately, Rich's imagination exceeded his knowledge of aerodynamic pyrotechnics, and after he had lit the blue touchpaper he was taken aback to see his rocket scream off horizontally, flying parallel to the ground at a height of about 6 feet. It was heading for Bat Man with such determination it could have been a heat-seeking missile.

'Jesus! Look out, Laurence! Duck! Watch out!' we all shrieked.

Laurence, his senses dulled by the chainsawing, didn't have time to move. The rocket continued to screech across the garden towards him. A nanosecond before impact, it exploded massively in front of his head.

Rich was aghast. In fact we all were and sprinted across to where our friend was standing, dazed. He looked . . . well, he looked as if a rocket had just exploded in front of his head.

'I'm so, so sorry, Laurence! Are you all right, mate?' said Rich, apologizing desperately.

There was no response. Though Laurence was still vertical, he was clearly stunned. It was several hours before his hearing was restored sufficiently for him to hold a conversation, let alone to turn on his bat-o-meter and listen out for pipistrelles.

It would be another few weeks before the big digging machines would arrive to clear the roots and start creating my land masses, so for now there wasn't much more I could do outside. I retreated therefore to my computer and continued working on the World Garden's plant list. By this time I was also more in demand as a public speaker, and in November I even headed off to Ireland, where I was lucky enough to have been invited to give a couple of talks on orchids, plant-hunting and my travels in general at the Dublin Botanic Gardens and at Trinity College. It was while wandering around Dublin between talks that my mobile rang and the fall-out from the weekend of chainsaw mayhem finally caught up with me.

'WHERE'S MY HEDGE?!' screamed an angry voice at the other end. It was Trevor. 'You had NO right to cut it down! NO right at all!'

Trevor, it seemed, had also now absorbed the enormous transformation that had been brought about in the walled garden, and he wasn't happy. He was berserk.

I stammered out my apologies. I had of course *meant* to tell him I was going to chop down the hornbeam, the sheep fence and his Lawson's Cyprus hedge . . . but somehow I seemed to have forgotten to do so. Trevor had seen and admired Adam's plans of what we proposed to do, but the fact that I hadn't asked him made him see red and several other colours too.

Realizing this was going to be an awkward

conversation — and that because Ireland counted as being abroad, I was paying top whack for a portion of the call on my pay-as-you-go — I burbled out more apologies and suggested we talk about it when I returned home. Trevor continued to vent his fury and give me an earful. I hadn't been told off like this since the incident with the angry farmer in the field near Matlock. Would Trevor ever calm down long enough to let the JCBs in through his double gates?

'And no they can't come into the garden!' he snapped.

Thanks to my enthusiasm for chainsaws, bonfires and the World Garden, and my inability to think through the consequences of all my actions, it seemed I was up a gum tree. And for once I wasn't there to collect the nuts.

# 22

## Pigs in a Poke

When communicating with pigs, shouting 'Piggy-wiggies!' in a painful and unnaturally high voice usually gets their attention — especially if you happen to be carrying a bucket of highly scoffable pellets. But having their attention doesn't mean they will do what you want.

By the autumn of 2004 Woolly and Red Spider had been with us for three months and had kept their part of the bargain dutifully. They had picked Lullingstone's Queen Anne Ice House and the surrounding area clean of anything remotely green and edible, revealing for the first time in years the splendid knapped-flint walls beneath. Neither Louisa nor I could bear the thought of them going off to meet the sausage-maker in the sky just yet, so more gainful employment had to be found. Where better than in the newly cleared walled garden, where their snoutivating and turding would be a real boon in preparing the ground?

Though Woolly and Red Spider had escaped from their pen in the wooded area behind the house with tiresome regularity over the summer, showing total contempt for me and their electrified fence, they had not yet dared attack Dad's pristine lawn on any of their sorties. There was a good reason for this. In order to do so, they would have had to cross the river that flows over the lower weir out of the lake. And as I had already noticed, pigs — or my pigs anyway — couldn't stand the sight or sound of running water.

Despite grasping this vital piece of pig lore, I had yet to grasp the extent to which my pigs disliked running water. But it became all too horribly clear when Louisa, Gum Nut Steve and I tried one afternoon to carry out the simple task, or so we thought, of helping Woolly and Red Spider across the footbridge over the river to pastures new.

The walled garden had several advantages from all our points of view. For the pigs, it was an all-you-can-eat buffet that was open 24/7. For the Hart Dyke family, and Dad in particular, the high walls made it reassuringly escape proof — unless our pigs suddenly learnt to fly, dig tunnels or open Trevor's gates with their trotters. But would Woolly and Red Spider cross that footbridge? Would they bacon sandwich!

Steve, Louisa and I spent a good two and a half hours trying to get them across, using tactics that ranged from psychological warfare and subterfuge to sheer exasperated brute strength. When it came to animal cunning, however, they had us well and truly beaten.

First we tried to lure them towards the bridge with snufflesome buckets of feed.

'C'mon, piggy-wiggies! Lovely pellets!' we drooled.

Each time they got anywhere near the bridge,

they pulled back at the last moment and snorted at us derisively.

We then tried laying a trail of food over the ground leading tantalizingly on to the bridge itself. But both porkers knew exactly what we were up to and wouldn't be fooled. We even tied ropes around their necks and tried to drag them over the bridge physically. They simply dug in their trotters and refused to budge.

Desperate, I turned to Louisa. 'Flamed if I know what to do. Any ideas?'

Louisa shrugged. She was at the end of her tether too. Then inspiration struck.

'How about the car?' said Louisa. 'We could drive them round!'

'*In the Astra!*' Steve and I chorused. I thought it was a mad, brilliant idea, but Steve seemed less than convinced. We were due at our friend Tim Jackson's eighteenth-birthday party that evening — a black-tie job, unusually — and Steve was itching to get home to de-pigify himself and get ready.

Thus it was that I crossed the bridge by myself and hurried to fetch the car from the garage. Short of hiring a crane and cradle, it seemed our only hope; but as I drove out of the lower entrance, along Lullingstone Lane and through the village, I was secretly praying that some miracle might be occurring and that Red Spider and Woolly were even now trotting gaily across the bridge of their own accord. I was having second thoughts.

Coming in through the top entrance and down through the woods along the front drive (at the back of the house, remember), I found the pigs, along with Louisa and Steve, exactly where I had left them.

I parked and opened the boot. Thank God it was an estate car, I thought, and a not terribly clean one. Louisa, bless her, climbed in the back seat and started trying to entice the pigs inside with yet more food. Red Spider, the greedy so-and-so, jumped straight in and we slammed the boot shut. This was going to be a doddle.

With one little piggy in the car, we now set about trying to cajole Woolly. But she was a lot less woolly than her name suggested and far less gullible than Red Spider. We decided to throw caution to the wind and open both doors to the rear passenger seats. Gum Nut Steve and I took up sentry positions on either side, waiting to slam the doors shut once Louisa had lured her in and Woolly had taken the bait.

Wary at first, Woolly put her front trotters up on the seat, leaned in towards Louisa and duly started munching. Unfortunately, she refused to climb into the car properly and obstinately kept her rear trotters on terra firma. Tired of waiting, I decided it was time for action. I put my hands on her bum — always a risky manoeuvre with a frisky pig — and shoved her into the car with all the strength I could muster. Woolly let out an ear-piercing squeal — but I at least managed to bundle her on to the back seat. Job done — or not.

Unfortunately Woolly wasn't the only one caught unawares by my shock manoeuvre. It caught Gum Nut Steve by surprise too, and he could only watch open-mouthed as Woolly then bounded across the car seat towards him and jumped out of the Astra through the open door. She then scampered off to some grass, snuffling and whingeing as she went.

'Sorry, Tom,' said a defeated Steve.

For Round Two we put even more food on the back seat, and, learning from our mistake, this time left only one door open. A simple ruse, I thought, and quite brilliant. But Steve wasn't convinced.

'It's never going to work, Tom. You're going to need a horse box, not a flipping Vauxhall.'

Maybe he had a point. In any case, afternoon was rapidly becoming evening and Steve had had his dose. He wished us luck and headed off home. Did I care that my friend was deserting me? No. I was beginning to have one of my tunnel-vision moments — I'd become obsessed with getting this bloody pig into the car before nightfall when we were due at Kevington Hall for Tim Jackson's birthday — and Louisa, loyal Louisa, was still there to help. Everything would be fine.

Louisa climbed gamely into the front passenger seat and laid out yet more food. Woolly, once again, put her front trotters on the seat and started munching. As she did so, I sneaked up on her from behind. Once again I grabbed her flanks, but this time I pulled her to my groin and thrust her into the back of the car as if I really meant it. God knows what an onlooker or RSPCA inspector would have made of it — but Woolly was in. I slammed the door shut behind her, ran round the car and jumped into the driver's seat. We'd done it!

If you've ever driven a Vauxhall Astra estate with two angry pigs in the back, you may have some idea of the pandemonium that now ensued. It started with squealing — 'Are we there yet?'; that sort of thing — which was fair enough, I suppose. But the protests quickly grew louder and louder as I put the Astra into gear and accelerated up the drive through the woods. Woolly immediately leapt over the back seat and crammed herself into the boot to join forces with Red Spider.

Perhaps it was the excitement of being reunited, but what followed wasn't pleasant for any of us. No doubt it didn't help that both pigs had been pigging themselves stupid all afternoon on the titbits with which we had been trying to lure them across the bridge, but both now launched a serious dirty protest, farting loudly and defecating violently as I drove like a nutter towards Eynsford.

'Oh God, what have we done, Louisa!' I said, as one or possibly both pigs sprayed a powerful arc of liquid shit all over the windows and upholstery. 'Good job we didn't borrow Dad's car,' I added, as we approached the pub. The smell in the Astra was now almost unbearable.

'Or mine!' shrieked Louisa, half in hysterics, another arc of liquid shit spraying across the interior of the car.

As we passed the pub, the pigs seemed to go ballistic with their grunting and squealing. A solitary drinker stood outside, enjoying the country evening quiet; but out of the corner of my eye I definitely saw him pause while lifting his glass and stare at us in disbelief as the two angry pigs continued to redecorate the back window with gallons of liquid crap. He must have wondered what he'd been drinking.

By the time we reached the gatehouse, Woolly and Red Spider were butting their heads against the boot in unison. They were trying to break out. Two minutes longer and they would have done so. The lock was ruined, the upholstery was in tatters and the car stank even worse than those public toilets in Matlock. But we had made it. Just.

It took a while for the pigs to forgive me and settle in to their new home, but the culinary delights of the walled garden were rich compensation. They were soon feasting in my proposed Australasia region, with a huge metal greenhouse bench for a shelter, and quickly discovered that they actually preferred ground elder, roots and all, to proper pig feed. (I must admit I tried the ground elder myself and found it rather minty.) Best of all, however, was gorging on hundreds of apples from our bumper autumn crop. Once they fermented, this resulted in two definitely pissed piggy-wiggies, complete with the bloodshot eyes of an outdoor cider drinker.

Woolly and Red Spider then picked clean all the crazy-paving slabs from the section of path that was enclosed in their pen. In the days that followed, they greeted me with affectionate snorts as I worked elsewhere in the garden. The first frosts would be coming soon, and I had to get the Dutch Venlo greenhouse rebuilt in my nursery area to shelter the world map's more sensitive treasures. It was nice to have their company.

As I pottered and transplanted, Woolly and Red Spider just fed and fed and fed, clearing and fertilizing as they went. The pigs also pruned better than a pair of Wilkinson Sword secateurs. Cannily, I was even able to harness their insatiable desire to eat and rootle to help me shift some of the bigger shrubs whose rootballs were too deeply established for me to dig them up comfortably. By laying out a circle of sticky oats and bran around a big plant that I wanted to move, the pigs literally ate round it in a circle, snoutavating downwards as they went. By putting food down in the same spot for a fortnight, my rootballs were soon neatly exposed.

By the time December arrived and the JCBs were due, thanks to Woolly and Red Spider the garden already looked as if it had been given a good going-over by a bull-dozer. In fact, the only downside to the whole pig-moving episode had been the state of my car.

On the evening of the party, me wearing Dad's dinner jacket and with Louisa dressed to the nines, before we could drive to Kevington Hall we had had to line all the seats with newspaper. Louisa and I must have smelled absolutely rotten, but no-one seemed to bat an eyelid. Once the stinking mess had set hard, caking the interior of the car in dried slurry, I then had to scrape down the windows and upholstery with sandpaper and a putty knife. But it was a valuable lesson on my gardening odyssey: never put angry pigs in the back of a Vauxhall Astra unless you really have to.

# 23

## An Inspector Calls

As the fourth anniversary of my release approached, my former captors Whispering Death, Trouble Ahead and Space Cadet, not to mention the girl guerrilla Paul and I had nicknamed Loose Teenager, continued to cast sinister shadows over my psyche.

The Darién was never far from my thoughts even during the day, but labouring outside in the garden or sitting at my desk in the gatehouse late into the night, I was always too absorbed by work to feel panicky and the memories, always containable, were usually gone in an instant.

Once in bed, however, when physical exhaustion made me flop and fall asleep, a slim crack would sometimes open in the rockface of my defences. One by one, these shadowy characters would then squeeze through the gap and climb out from the dark corners of my subconscious to populate my dreams. Once there were enough of them and I was heavily outnumbered, the nightmares could begin.

The scenario was always slightly different and sometimes there was no particular memory of jungle at all. Generally my faceless tormentors would round up Mum, Dad, Anya and the cat, and latterly Gran too, by the church, where they would all get their respective heads hacked off with a machete. The images were horrifically graphic: the machete slicing into Granny's skull and getting stuck while one of the guerrillas tried to sever it completely. Then the cat that had been dead for years got diced up like a pepper or sliced like a cucumber you might put in a salad. There were exploding grenades too: Dad got well and truly splattered across the church. And all this was my fault.

Sometimes in the nightmares Paul and I, various bits of our bodies weeping pus from agonizing infections, would be spirited back to the jungle proper and subjected to mock or even actual execution. What was common to all the dreams, whether set in Kent or Colombia or some terrifying no-man's land, was that the sense of dread was so intense it eventually woke me and left me in a white chill of fear. It always took a while to come to my senses and remind myself where I was and that actually I had quite a good day ahead of me.

Compared with the nightmares, coping with the physical day-to-day challenge of creating a garden that would open to the public in a matter of months was, I suppose, a doddle. Nevertheless, the workload was now becoming intense and each day threw up some hefty new obstacle.

Trevor, who had been so furious after his hedge was whacked by the chainsaw, was still not a happy bunny. I have to admit I could understand why he was so angry. Not for the first time, I had been carried away and done something I shouldn't have. In the circumstances I still thought it best to keep my head down and leave negotiations with him to Dad and the smooth-talking Tony Russell.

Dad told Trevor we needed to buy back his half of the walled garden; but they couldn't agree a price and my actions had done little to create a tension-free atmosphere of goodwill. This was unfortunate, because the JCBs were booked for the beginning of December, and the only way the machines could get in was via the rickety green wooden gates in Trevor's half of the garden. In the absence of an agreement, the disgruntled Trevor now started to dig in his heels, hinting again that access through his gates might be barred. If so, the only way in would have been by smashing down the ancient walls to enlarge the circular Moon Gate. But that would have been illegal as the walls were listed (though not yet listing) and there was no way that was going to happen.

I reckoned five grand should have been a more than handsome payment for Trevor's bit of the garden, which he no longer seemed to use. But when Tony, acting as middleman, returned from a meeting and told me Trevor was hoping for twice that, I threw my hands up in horror. Given the amount of stuff that still had to be paid for in the garden, there was no way Dad could afford another £10,000.

We were committed to bringing Adam's technical designs to life exactly as he'd drawn them and to do so there was a long list of Things To Do And Buy. This included at least 110 tonnes of acid soil for mainland Asia — China mainly, and Japan — not to mention 340 tonnes of exotic-sounding rock for our different continental coastlines. These included red granite around England, Scotland and Wales; purple schist in New Zealand; firebird gneiss on the coast of Asia; and something called harlequin quartzite in Japan. We also needed enough silver aggregate to gravel 1,650 square metres of pathway — so an extra ten grand on the bill wasn't what we wanted. Dad and Tony kept negotiating with Trevor. Luckily, they placated him sufficiently that there was no actual unpleasantness when two diggers and two dumper trucks arrived at the gates on low-loaders on the morning of Monday 6 December.

It was barely light when the JCBs chugged up at 7.30am, but by 8.30am the contractors from Star Plant were hard at it. Adam's intricate 3D map made use of every last millimetre of the World Garden's single acre, and there was a great deal of earth-moving and precision landscaping to be done before we were ready for our rocks. The massive task of shifting tree stumps and levelling the site before digging trenches for all the new irrigation and drainage pipes, and electricity ducts, was soon under way.

The diggers also began to pile up tonnes of Lullingstone's rich black topsoil where Australasia was going to be; and seeing all this physical activity gave me a rush of exhilaration. *At last!* After all the doubts and prevarications, those red biro squiggles I had made in the jungle were finally coming to life before my eyes. It's hard to describe how significant this was for me. Even though we were still at an early stage, I felt that building the World Garden was the single most important reason for my being on this great green planet of ours.

While the diggers and dumpers did their stuff, with Granny's permission I carefully moved her tiny greenhouse up to my proposed nursery area and designated it my new Orchid House. If you could see how small and rickety it is, you'd realize that, despite the big loan from the bank, we were still a shoestring operation. I also badgered one of the contractors to show me how to drive the mini dump-truck so I could shift barrows full of pots, benches and transplanted plants out of harm's way. In the busy days that followed, the only setback was when someone created a waterfall where the Sahara was going to be by hitting an old Victorian cast-iron waterpipe which was not nearly as disconnected as we thought it was.

'You couldn't hit a water main nearer China, could you?' I joked. 'That's where I'd really like a waterfall.'

Given the gallons of water that were now gushing over Africa, Paul the cool foreman was in no mood for jokes.

'Tom! Plumber! Now!' he yelled.

Yes, sir.

There was also an impressive fountain just north of Niagara Falls in North America when another old pipe got whacked with a spade. Despite these little local difficulties, it was deeply satisfying to see the outlines of my dream garden slowly taking shape. For the first time I even allowed myself to believe that everything was going to work out just fine. But, as I've said before, when you think things are going (relatively) smoothly, real life has a habit of coming up and giving you a good hard kick in the tadgers. And this happened one day shortly before Christmas.

The excavators were already beginning to shape my continents, but the heavy machinery was momentarily silent as we showed officials from Sevenoaks District Council around the site. The visit, I presumed, was no more than a formality, and at first everything was friendly and positive. Then one of the council chaps began studying the detailed plans the contractors were working to. He started to look pensive in that disturbing way members of officialdom can.

'So . . . you're not doing anything with the existing walls?' said the nice listed-buildings man.

'Oh no,' I replied. 'Nothing at all.'

I took a deep breath and wondered what he was going to ask next. But that was it. Finished. He seemed happy.

The planning officer, however, was also studying the contractors' plans and had a look on his face that said: 'I think I've just sat on a Prickly Pear.' Something was up.

'There's nothing about rocks in these plans,' he said straightforwardly, studying what appeared to be two sets of diagrams. *Oh balls!* He was comparing an early draft we had sent the council with the more up-to-date plans the contractors were now using. And he was right. The early draft had been drawn up *before* we had decided to build mountain ranges and place rocks around our continental coastlines, partly for visual impact but more importantly to keep those tonnes and tonnes of alkaline-rich soil in one place.

Our jaws hit the floor collectively. We stood open-mouthed waiting for him to speak.

'And you need consent for them,' he informed us quite matter-of-factly, referring to the rocks we hadn't told him about.

It was a bombshell all right and I didn't know what to say. Consent? Was that another word for planning permission? Not for a second had I thought we would need planning permission to turn an old garden into a new garden. I mean, why would you? I realized we had to be careful not to damage the existing walls in any way . . . but *consent*? It hadn't entered my mind nor, it seemed, anyone else's.

'Why do we need consent?' I asked anxiously.

The atmosphere was now decidedly frosty.

'It's the height of some of your contours. And the bigger rocks around the outside. They need consent too.'

I was pole-axed. My mind struggled to absorb the significance of his message. Could we chip a bit off the rocks to make them smaller, perhaps? The contractors had been working their socks off since the start of the month and the garden was really taking shape now. We had less than three months until we opened. I started to panic.

'So what does that involve exactly? Consent?' I stammered.

The planning officer explained that he thought we should stop work immediately and submit the plans via the normal planning procedures.

'Because if you continue building the garden and we refuse consent, by law you will have to demolish everything you've built.'

*Demolish the garden?* He had to be joking. I lost all ability to think or speak and the lump in my throat was throbbing. I wanted to weep. All I could picture was dismantling the world map bit by bit. Dismantling my dream. Destroying the garden that had kept me going through nine months of hell; the garden for which I had spent years trying to raise money; the garden for which Dad had borrowed a small fortune against our family home; the garden I had spent every day of the last six months preparing for. Gone. Poof! And all because a pile of rocks were slightly too big in places. Unbelievable.

The planning officer was adamant, however, that we would have to apply for planning permission. I knew my lips were moving, but it was someone else's voice that asked the question.

'And how long will that take?'

'Normally three months,' he said.

Three months? We were due to open to the public in three months. We couldn't down tools and wait three months — not unless we were going to issue visitors with hard hats and day-glo waistcoats and invite them to inspect the abandoned building site of the World Garden That Might Have Been.

'Right, OK, well thank you for that,' I said, feeling like a choked and humiliated five-year-old. I was totally demoralized. The rollockings I had received from Trevor and from that angry farmer near the Duchess of Devonshire's place were nothing to this nuclear bomb. With Christmas looming, it was time to get together with Dad and talk turkey.

# 24

## Pork Stuffing

'Bloody ridiculous,' said Dad as the two of us walked dejectedly back through the dusk towards the house, the glow from Trevor's unshuttered windows sending fingers of light out across the darkening lawn.

I imagined Trevor sitting in front of a fire in one of his funny hats, his large frame rocking with mirth at our predicament — and I couldn't really have blamed him if he had been laughing at us. If you weren't directly involved, our planning cock-up had been hugely shambolic.

I wanted to kick myself for not having been better organized and for not ensuring that the most up-to-date version of Adam's plans had been sent to the council. Even so, neither Dad nor I could fathom why a garden needed planning permission to remain a garden. It hadn't crossed either of our minds nor anybody else's. But it was a cock-up all right.

The planning officer's bureaucratic bombshell meant we were between a rock (that was something over 500mm high) and the proverbial hard place. Should we stop work, tell the contractors to go home and delay the opening of the World Garden while waiting to see if we ever got planning permission? Or should we crack on and hope for the best?

You can imagine which option I fancied. No contest. But Dad, being rather more sensible, said he wanted to think things through over the Christmas holidays when work would in any case come to a halt. As it was his neck that was on the financial block, this was reasonable.

Anya was due home soon on leave from Belgrade and her presence in the house was sure to lift the mood. Even though Anya didn't really see her future as being resident on the estate, it was always great to have her home and to hear of her adventures. As it was our turn to have the relations over for Christmas itself, I also hoped that Bristles' arrival and preparations for the big family get-together would distract us from the dilemma we faced outside in the muddy building site that was supposed to be a visitor attraction in less than three months.

Two characters who were oblivious to our predicament were, of course, Woolly and Red Spider, both of whom were now really fat. Before the arrival of the diggers, the walled garden had become a kind of pig heaven for them, elder roots being their equivalent of chocolate mousse. They had gorged themselves and defecated merrily. Oddly, they both had such happy dispositions that they didn't even seem to mind when we moved them (on foot this time, not by Vauxhall Astra) out of the way of the JCBs. Penned in behind an electric fence down by the back ditch, these ingenious escape artists even seemed to relish the fresh challenge of trying to find some new way back into the walled garden to truffle hunt for more tasty roots.

Now that both pigs were so big and bolshy, they no longer even bothered with the bucket that they used to stick on their heads in order to ram the electric fence when they wanted to break out. Now they just barged straight into it and trampled it under foot, to hell with the shock. Their sorties were an almost daily occurrence and Dad, who had enough on his mind for one Christmas, was becoming irritated.

On Christmas Day itself Bristles and I reckoned that Woolly and Red Spider deserved a treat of their own. But what can you give a pig who has everything? This was something I pondered as I sat through the Christmas morning service in St Botolph's, the Hart Dykes in our seats near the altar and Trevor seated a distance away, tinkling festively on the keys of the organ. After the service we trooped back across the lawn to the house, where a 12-foot Christmas tree was twinkling next to the massive fire that crackled in the grate. Mum's brother David and Aunt D were up from Portsmouth with my cousins Miranda and Alice, and we hovered around the grate in the Great Hall trying to get warm, all looking forward to Mum's massive blow-out.

After lunch, but before tea and presents, Anya and I decided it was time to give Woolly and Red Spider their treat. We rummaged through Dad's drinks cupboard and Anya poured out a bucket of beer for them. Armed with some crackers, we then went to their pen by the back ditch.

'Here, piggy-wiggies!' we cried in that high-pitched scream they seemed to love. 'Happy

Christmas, piggy-wiggies!'

By now everyone had come out to watch as Bristles and I pulled crackers for Woolly and Red Spider and read out the jokes before giving them both their coloured paper hats. They certainly seemed pleased to be part of the fun, but were even happier with their 'present' and slurped greedily at the beer.

Back in front of the fire, with the ancestors looking down on us from the walls, we were all gagging for our tea when the atmosphere was shattered by the one thing none of us wanted to hear.

'*The pigs are out! The pigs are out!*' someone cried.

Sure enough, there on Dad's pristine grass in the falling dusk were two very merry pigs, their ears flapping, trotting their way towards the churchyard, snoutivating as they went.

'For God's sake don't let them get in there,' said Dad, his pig-patience now sorely tested. 'And get them back in their pen before they dig the bloody lawn up!'

It was battle stations all right. At Dad's command Bristles and I leapt into action. Leaving the warmth of the fireside, we hurried out into the dusk and set off across the grass. Our main objective was to stop Woolly and Red Spider getting into the churchyard. Pigs love bones and the smell of ash, and the remains of several generations of Harts, Dykes and Hart Dykes were lying under the turf crying out to be snoutivated. Dad would have had a seizure if any of his forebears had turned up for Christmas in

284

this way, and none of us really wanted to see Colonel Meates again, whose mortal remains were also in the churchyard.

Happily, we managed to shoo Woolly and Red Spider away from the ancestors with only very minor snoutivating damage. But our surviving relations — and Dad in particular — were not at all impressed by the damage the pigs were now causing to his lawn. Cajoling them back into their pen, it was a Christmas Day none of us would forget in a hurry, least of all the pigs.

Bristles and I were quite upset, but not too surprised, when Dad made his grave announcement on Boxing Day.

'It's no good, Tom. The pigs will have to go. You'll just have to . . . make arrangements.'

As soon as the world went back to work in the New Year, I did precisely that. I hope Woolly and Red Spider enjoyed their stay at Lullingstone as much as I enjoyed having them before they went to join their sausage-breeding programme.

# 25

## Look, No Plants

Dad emerged from the Christmas holidays with a firm sense of what we had to do. 'Tom, we must carry on. No choice, really. Just have to keep our fingers crossed about the planners.'

Of course we *did* have a choice, but we both knew it was a rotten one. The idea of stopping now, with a huge bank loan in place, the garden half-dug and a new open season looming, seemed even more bonkers than the possibility that the planners might pull the plug on us because some of the rocks on our contoured continents were too big. So as 2005 dawned and our planning application began to grind its way through the system, we told Paul the foreman, Mick and Dave, the boys from Star Plant, to get on with the job.

The short grey days of January, often a time of torpor and post-Christmas melancholy, were actually buzzing in the walled garden as the heavy machines chugged back to life, their sudden exertions shifting mounds of soil or tricky roots causing them to cough up big clouds of grey-black diesel exhaust. The contractors, who also rustled up great bacon sandwiches every morning, made cracking progress — so much so that, despite the nagging doubt over planning permission, the fact that Trevor was

286

now said to be talking to his lawyers about taking out an injunction against us, and the small matter of my still having virtually no plants to stick in the World Map of Mud come March, I managed to convince myself that everything was going really well.

In our darker moments in the Darién, Paul and I had always tried to laugh in the face of adversity, relentlessly singing Monty Python's 'Always Look On The Bright Side of Life'. But it really was becoming easier to look on the bright side as the days began to lengthen and I clocked some of the amazing changes taking place within the higgledy-piggledy walls.

Creation-wise, I remember from my Bible that it took the Man Upstairs six days to create Heaven and Earth. By February 2005, in my own one-acre universe I was still only about halfway through Day Three. We still had dry land that needed to be separated from sea, and I certainly didn't yet have a healthy horticultural environment that would 'bring forth grass, herbs yielding seed and fruit trees yielding fruit', etc., etc. But we were definitely getting there.

The World Garden's one-acre patch was completely cleared of vegetation, and the water and electric pipes for the site had been dug into place and covered up before any serious rainfall could cause Noah-style floods in the trenches. At the foot of the walls, meanwhile, pine planks had been laid to contain the rectangular flowerbeds that would one day be home to the cultivars and hybrids I wanted to display in my Man's Influence Borders. On the map itself, the coastlines of my continents were beginning to be drawn properly with the early deliveries of boulders.

With the boys from Star Plant, I started to map out the rocky coastlines of North and South America, with silvergrey and green granites respectively, and it gave me a huge rush to see the massive rocks gently levered and lowered into position. I really did feel I was playing God in a sense. I had the most enormous toy box in the world and it was a blast.

Once the coastal boundaries were in place, we started to pour the rich black topsoil into the continent-shaped spaces. Over in China and Japan, of course, once I had scalped out the ordinary soil (it was destined for the mountains of Africa), the Camellias, Rhododendrons and Pieris would require tonnes of acidic topsoil if they were to flourish on our naturally alkaline, slightly chalky, flinty base. But all that would come later.

With Dad now using our borrowing facility to shell out serious sums, his mood wasn't helped when Adam's first order of granite arrived. It looked very impressive as the boulders were lowered to the ground and shunted into place, but it soon emerged that a lot of granite doesn't go a very long way. Adam's order was 10 tonnes short. Or to put it another way, Dad needed to stump up another £700 if we wanted to avoid a bad case of continental drift.

Despite some atrocious late weather — frequent snowfalls and hard frosts that even dipped down to −9°C — as soon as the ground was soft enough I began my own frantic digging regime. It sounds crazy, but I really did have to hand-dig every emerging land mass, forking the topsoil to break it up where it had been compacted and squished down by the machines. Almost unbelievably, I still had to remove yet more bothersome bindweed roots, along with Granny's old daffodil bulbs, both of which had been liberally spread around the developing garden by the earthmoving. The only bone of contention with the contractors was that I kept leaving muddy boot marks on the light-grey crushed granite they were laying as my ocean pathways.

While I took enormous satisfaction in finally being able to roll up my sleeves to do some serious digging, not everyone shared my enthusiasm for how things were developing. Adam, for example, became quite glum when he learnt how many plants I intended to have in the ground by Easter Saturday, the day the house and grounds were due to open for the new season. With March fast approaching, the short answer was that I didn't intend to have many plants in the ground at all.

Adam was aghast.

'But, Tom! You've got to have *something* in the ground surely . . . I mean . . . or you're going to look a bit stupid, aren't you?'

Adam had a point. Thanks to Tony Russell's efforts on the marketing front and my own gardening column in the *Kentish Times*, there was a lot of interest brewing locally and people were bound to want to see what all the fuss was about. Though I didn't intend to open the World

Garden officially until July, by which time I hoped the sun would have brought about some decent growth, and though I had always seen full planting as a long-term project, a World Garden of plants with no actual plants in it at all would indeed look a bit silly.

But there were good reasons why the ground would be relatively bare come Easter, which was early in 2005. First, winter wouldn't be done yet at Lullingstone, where frost can still strike as late as May; and there was no way I wanted to risk putting out what few tender plants I did have, even in pots, just to see them massacred by the cold.

The main reason, though, was that I simply didn't have that many full-on plants yet to go in the ground. Given our lack of sponsorship, after paying for the heavy earthmoving equipment, the lumps of granite, and all the pipes and drains, Dad and I simply didn't have the dosh to go out and buy a big load of mature plants with which to create an 'instant' garden. My plant shopping had to be parsimonious. Besides, I told Adam, I didn't really want to create an 'instant' garden anyway. As far as possible I wanted the garden to contain plants I had germinated and grown on myself from seed. So on Easter Saturday there would be what there would be in the ground. If any visitors bothered to turn up and poke their heads through the Moon Gate, I would tell them what I was doing and planning — and pray that my infectious enthusiasm would persuade them to return, again and again, to see how my garden grew.

Another reason the garden was going to be pretty sparse to begin with was that I had deliberately decided to jump in the deep end. I wanted to try to grow the most difficult plants first, starting in the southern hemisphere, where most of the plants I wanted were frost tender, expensive and hard to find.

Adam wasn't at all convinced by my reasoning and looked a bit sulky. Gazing at the big patch of mud before me, I began to feel ever so slightly foolish and realized he was right. We did need more plants.

Luckily, Tony Russell took a leaf from Grandma Zoë's book and wrote a begging letter to nurseries across the UK and Ireland appealing for donations. The response was literally staggering. My email inbox practically exploded with replies — from some 250 individual nurseries, in fact — and these eventually yielded more than £3,000-worth of donations. Just as Zoë received bundles of fresh mulberry for her silkworms through the post, most of my donations arrived at Lullingstone via the Royal Mail too and I was ridiculously grateful.

Some larger specimens had to be picked up, and Louisa and I decided to spend a couple of days speeding around southern England and cramming the Vauxhall pig-mobile with a jungle of goodies. How can you tell that you have a wonderful, patient, understanding girlfriend? Well, see how she responds to a 750-mile road trip in a car that's carrying a 7-foot-long North American Sweet Gum (*Liquidambar styraciflua*), its rootball resting on the passenger seat beside her. What a star! Changing gear and seeing out of the rearview mirror was a nightmare, but that was thanks to a dazzlingly spreading Dicksonia Tree Fern that filled the entire car, the fronds even finding their way up Louisa's nostrils. She was cool about that too.

Back at Lullingstone, with the Easter opening bearing down on me like the bow of an ocean liner (or was it me who was on the *Titanic*?), I was as far away from being ahead of schedule as it was possible for any rational person to be. The Canary Islands, Britain and Ireland were finished. Bar having any plants, that is. And North and South America were completed — though they also needed plants and to have their respective mountain ranges built and contoured.

Contouring was really vital, and not just to make the garden look as geographically interesting as possible. The smaller plants needed a raised stage on which to be seen and, most crucial of all, the flowing, stepped layering would allow for good drainage of the rain and cold air that would hit the garden from November to March. If the garden were flat, half the plants wouldn't stand a chance.

'Right, boys, it's the Rockies!' I announced to general disbelief from Paul, Mick and Dave one day.

'Really?' they chorused.

Armed with a copy of the *Oxford World Atlas*, I set about the God-like task of creating the Andes too, using 7 tonnes of rocks and umpteen more tonnes of soil. I must have looked slightly odd clambering over all this stuff with the atlas open in my hand, but I needed to keep referring to the topographical features so I could create my own version of the Andes as accurately as possible.

Undeterred that we were still waiting to hear whether we would get planning permission, I placed rocks and small amounts of soil around Britain for the Grampians, Lake District, Snowdonia and Exmoor; and I got on with planting Ireland with some Shamrock seed I'd bought dirt cheap on the ferry back from Dublin. I also put in a rather more exotic *Arbutus unedo*, or Strawberry Tree, which was going to make my Irish land mass look the business. Technically, the Strawberry Tree should have been in south-western Ireland, as that is where it originates; but given the acute problems of scale I had in a World Garden of just one acre, *Arbutus unedo* would have to be the main feature in central Ireland. I didn't think anyone would sue me for such artistic licence.

Though the days were lengthening appreciably now, I was still working outside long after it was dark. The contouring certainly kept me busy, but there was yet more of that pernicious bindweed and couch grass to be removed, plus the occasional bit of rose or apple tree root that had been missed. We had also laid thick sheets of black plastic at the edges of the continents to stop the soil tumbling through the rocky coastlines and to force rainwater down to the drainage system rather than all over the oceans. These all had to be trimmed by hand too.

With just three weeks to go before the house and grounds were due to open, Dad and I were then summoned to an important evening meeting of Eynsford Parish Council. We were there to make our case formally for the World Garden and did our best to explain our ambitions — and to reassure councillors that the hundreds (or maybe thousands) of extra visitors the World Garden might eventually attract wouldn't bring Eynsford to a standstill. In fact, we hoped they might even bring extra trade to the village's pubs and shops.

Then, with just days to go before Easter, Sevenoaks District Council faxed through the letter we had been on tenterhooks for. I was sitting at my desk in the gatehouse with Tony, and we both watched impatiently as the paper crawled tantalizingly slowly out of the machine. The council had decided that the World Garden at Lullingstone should be granted unconditional planning permission. *Unconditional planning permission!* We were in business. The only proviso was: no coaches, please, along Lullingstone Lane. We could live with that.

# 26

## The Moon Gate Opens

The opening of the house on Easter Saturday, 26 March 2005, wasn't the only significant date that was looming. Ten days before that, on 16 March, I had an important anniversary to mark. It would be five years to the day since Paul Winder and I had been sharing lollipops in the sun with Carlos and Francisco, our Colombian guides in Central America, when armed men burst out of the bushes at us and we experienced the numbing fear of believing that we were about to be shot.

There were many occasions during our nine months in captivity when we believed the guerrillas were going to shoot us, either deliberately or by mistake. The garden that was now taking shape before me in cosy Kent was my response to those dark days, when we were route-marched from one crappy jungle camp to another, never knowing if we would leave the fetid, tropical forests of Panama and Colombia alive. The garden was slowly demonstrating that something positive and life-affirming could come out of an ordeal that should have broken me physically and mentally.

As I've told many people since, it's amazing how creative you can be when you have a loaded AK-47 pointed at your temple and you're told you only have a couple of hours to live. In more 'informal' moments, guerrillas like Lost Cause, Scarface and Perty (we called him that because of his enormously prominent nipples!) would have a laugh by aiming their loaded guns at Paul and me and simply *pretending* to be about to shoot us. For them it was a hilarious way to deal with the excruciating boredom of their lives. But it was never a laugh for us. We lived with the constant fear that if we weren't executed formally, we would still end up taking a bullet when one of these idiots pulled the trigger by accident.

If writing a diary in secret in the jungle was my way of blocking out thoughts of impending death, turning the red biro sketches into something tangible and earthy, and talking publicly in lectures about my plant-hunting adventures and about my capture, were my attempt at 'therapy'. I needed to flush the horror of these experiences from my system. Friends often asked why I didn't just see a proper shrink or counsellor; but the thought of sitting down with someone like that never occurred to me. I would have driven any therapist nuts with my rambling, and in any case I wanted to resolve matters in my own way.

I hoped that one day I would feel sufficiently confident to return to Latin America to renew my acquaintance with its amazing flora. Perhaps the plants that I hoped I would now make flourish and flower in the World Garden would encourage my own return to health. But I still had a way to go.

As I stood in the middle of my crushed granite

Atlantic and flicked mentally through the snapshots in my photographic memory bank of 16 March 2000, random thoughts kept popping up. For example, I found myself wondering why the number 16 seemed so significant in my life. I was captured on 16 March (which is also my sister Anya's birthday); I was told on 16 June that I was going to be executed; and poor old Dad was mugged at the gatehouse on 16 July.

I also thought about the nightmares that still haunted me from time to time and wondered when their power to chill might begin to wane. I was sure the hard, muscle-aching graft of stripping the old garden bare, burning the memory of it, heaving out the tree stumps, humping rocks around and driving my fork into the soil again and again was a help. If nothing else, night after night it left me physically spent. More than ever I felt the garden was what I was put on this Earth to create and I needed Paul to see it.

'Hey, Paul, it's Tom. What you up to on the sixteenth?' I asked down the phone when the urge to see him again became irresistible. 'Thought we might take a stroll through the Darién in north-west Kent. What d'you reckon?'

'Er . . . sounds good, Tom. Though let's not get lost this time, eh?'

We exploded in laughter as we had so often on bleaker occasions and arranged that Paul would come to Lullingstone for the two of us to mark the fifth anniversary of our capture with some suitably defiant gesture. I had just the thing in mind. Through a local plant wholesaler called

Coblands I had managed to snaffle a really huge *Agave americana* — an absolute snip at £50. It was so massive we had needed a forklift truck to get it into the back of the Astra. It would go perfectly in my north Mexican Copper Canyon section, which was where I had met Paul for the first time. It would be the first significant plant to go into the ground in the World Garden and there was only one man on the planet with whom I wanted to plant it.

Paul and I hugged like lost brothers when he turned up, and seeing his slight, wiry frame again I couldn't help thinking how he looked even less like a CIA spy or drugrunner than I had. What had the guerrillas been thinking? Paul was still wearing specs — and the sight of them instantly brought back more snapshots of the day of our capture. I could see Paul and me being marched at gunpoint deeper into the forest. I remembered how Paul was walking in front of me, his hands bound tightly behind his back. For some reason the guerrillas had tied my hands in front, which meant that when Paul's specs were knocked off, I could pick them off the jungle floor and with shaking hands put them back on his face. They were smeared with mud. Despite the heat on that day, Paul's face was sheet white, as if every single drop of blood had drained from his head.

Happily, Paul's complexion had now improved and his frame had filled out too since our misadventure. He had also stopped suppurating from the interesting assortment of flesh wounds he had collected. Being in his presence again was an intense reminder of the unique bond we had forged — quite different from anything I felt with any of my other friends.

'Come and have a look at the garden, Paul. No orchids yet, you'll be pleased to know — but it has got its very own Darién Gap.'

We huffed and puffed getting that *Agave* into position, Paul cutting the pot away with a knife and me helping him peel away the plastic. We then managed to roll the massive rootball into position in the pre-dug hole which was lined with gravel for drainage. Once it was in the ground, we fell quiet for a moment. There was no need to speak and each of us knew where the other's thoughts were.

'One down ... only nine thousand nine hundred and ninety-nine plants to go!' said Paul with a teasing smile as he broke the silence. 'And thank you for choosing the prickliest and spikiest plant available!' he added, examining the fresh cuts and scratches on his arms. With the wounds, it was almost like old times.

'But you are going to get some more plants, aren't you, Tom?'

In the days after our 'ceremony', much as I enjoy life on the edge, I found my work schedule was becoming slightly bonkers. The contractors finally left a week before Easter; and though the site was more or less completed physically, it still needed some extra 3D contouring and — ah yes! — some more of those actual worldly plants. Luckily, Laurence Bat Man Dell had given me a headlamp to wear on top of my tea-cosies so I could go on working late into the night, even if gardening by torchlight isn't always ideal.

After all the obsessive plant madness and horticultural tunnel vision I had inflicted on poor old Louisa — easily the most serious girlfriend I had ever had — I was lucky she was still speaking to me. But even after the pigs-in-the-Astra incident and our recent crazy road trip, we were still speaking. With Bat Man and Gum Nut Steve she agreed to help the Green Man with some manic last-minute planting. All three volunteered to give up their Good Friday to help me get as much in the ground as possible before the house and grounds opened officially to the public for the 2005 season on the Saturday. Even I realized I was cutting things very fine, but there was no way I could put a sign on the Moon Gate saying: 'Sorry. Closed Due to Owner's Poor Organizational Skills'.

Good Friday was fraught even by Planet Tom standards. Steve had donated bananas, Japanese Red Cedar and one of the rarest firs in the world, which he had planted by nightfall; and Louisa focused on the sunny lower slopes of the Andes. The three of us worked through until it was pitch black. By dawn on Easter Saturday the World Garden had a grand total of . . . 200 exhibits. Well, it was a start.

After a couple of hours' sleep I legged it back to the garden, where I was now operating on just adrenaline, chlorophyll and cans of sweet fizzy drinks. Four hundred visitors turned up that first weekend, which was a bit of a record; and I tried to explain to every single one of them how the sparse garden they saw before them would eventually develop. Most people were sympathetic, though some got confused as to which muddy continent they were supposed to be examining.

'That's Australasia! Er . . . and that's Africa! No, no . . . you're in Western Europe, madam! And that's going to be the Canaries!' I sounded like an international tour guide who'd lost his party. I hoped no one noticed what a wreck I looked, having had so little sleep, and that they all accepted my explanation that the World Garden was still a work in progress.

'Of course it'll take two or three years to be up to full strength,' I stressed. 'And there's not much in the ground at the moment because of the frost.'

I didn't mention my lack of funds for plant-buying and implored people to return in a couple of months' time. 'You'll see a huge difference then! Really!'

I hoped my unbridled enthusiasm was enough to make up for the lack of plant action and to enable people to make giant leaps of imagination. The visitors certainly seemed interested in what I had to say. Or maybe they just thought I was that nutter who had been kidnapped and that I was still having some kind of post-traumatic stress reaction. In any event, no one actually asked for their money back.

One punter summed up the mood by writing in my visitors' book: 'It'll be great when you get some plants.' How true!

# 27

## The War on Weeds

Back in the mid-1670s in the days of Sir Percyval Hart Mk III, the walled garden was home to a formal orchard. On the old engravings and paintings I've seen, it looks so neat and sparse it could have been planted with those little plastic toy trees you use to decorate a child's model railway. But the fertile reality in this old river valley would of course have been far fruitier and messier than the artists' idealized visions.

Later, a series of herb, vegetable and kitchen gardens erupted within the walls, Lady Zoë's herb garden being featured in *Country Life* in 1947 and Granny Crac's featuring massively in my own career as a gardener. Hundreds of years of fruitful cultivation meant, however, that when I sent in the JCBs at the end of 2004, I was actually ploughing up an incredibly rich, biodiverse one-acre seed bank.

The consequences of this were felt as soon as spring had sprung in 2005 and the ground began to rouse itself after its long winter sleep. As the temperatures rose, the garden also received buckets of rain — on one occasion, so much that it washed away the crushed granite oceans. The flood literally turned my pathways into seas, especially around the Canaries where the

302

Atlantic flooded persistently. This combination of warmer temperatures and rain lashing down on a buried treasure store of hidden seeds that had recently been dug up and redistributed could have only one outcome. Plants that hadn't been seen for donkeys' years began to sprout up all over.

Although they came up in entirely the wrong continents, it was a true delight to see some of them: Tree Peonies, for example, that had originally been planted in the 1950s. Lilac, quince and *Acanthus spinosus* reappeared too, and the World Garden of Plants suddenly seemed to be reliving its glorious past lives. But these delights weren't the only things demanding a place in the sun. Pernicious perennials like couch grass and ground elder had been successfully snoutavated by Woolly and Red Spider, but the pigs had been unable to uproot completely the dreaded field bindweed, its re-rootable stems going down a full 19 feet in places, and it returned with a vengeance like the Undead.

Whereas before the weeds had been restricted to a few trouble spots in the garden, thanks to the efficiency of Paul, Mick, Dave and their diggers, weeds were now spread liberally over the entire world, from the southern Andes to Outer Mongolia. Annual horrors like groundsel and prickly sow thistle were rampant once more and carpeted my pristine Man's Influence Borders with unwanted greenery. Without trying, I had created a World Garden of Weeds, featuring what was rapidly becoming a collection of national importance of utterly rampant speedwell.

Nick, the nice man from the bank in Bromley, wasn't at all impressed when he came to check on my progress and his investment. In fact, he was appalled by the weeds and so worried by the psychological effect they would have on visitors that he offered to send over a team of volunteers from his branch to help clear them. I had heard about free pens and calculators, but free weeding was not a service I had ever associated with a high street bank.

While the bank manager's offer was certainly generous, at this stage in the garden's development it was not one I could accept, much as I needed the help. I knew the soil upheaval would throw up many really interesting plants; and though I was tempted just to let them all grow big to see what wonders emerged, it was only Granny and I who could spot the treasures at an early stage and transplant them.

Realizing that Nick had a point, however — visitors might really resent paying good money to see a garden that was even messier than their garden at home — I got my head down and started to double-dig the entire site single-handedly as if my life depended on it. This was backbreaking and I was often still at work, headlamp on tea-cosy, long after Lullingstone's owls had started to-whit to-whooing. With the official opening looming, I didn't have a choice.

Come May, and despite my enormous efforts, the weeds were really winning. I tried to remain defiant and draw inspiration from the amazing Japanese Banana Plant (*Musa basjoo*) I had bedded down (while crossing my fingers) in the miniature Japan. For the third time in as many weeks, it responded to a late frosty night by raising two fingers to the cold and producing an almost instant display of rapidly unfurling tropical leaves.

'That's the spirit!' I thought.

I had planted a couple of these stunners, and every time frost attacked the tender leaves, the sappy trunk would fight back by producing a spiralling jet of new ones that positively oozed tropical electricity. Not only did this gee me up: it told me that this particular Banana might prove surprisingly winter hardy at Lullingstone.

As the heat increased and my one-man war against the weeds became more futile by the day, I had another small triumph in Australasia with the completion of Ayers Rock. When the JCB machines first arrived, I had intended Ayers Rock to be a 25-tonne monster lump of the actual hard stuff. But health and safety issues intervened, along with a sudden burst of common sense, and I realized we would never have got such a big stone into the garden through Trevor's gates.

We did consider using a crane; and at one point somebody suggested trying to catapult it over the walls. This last idea really did appeal until I thought it through. Even if it had been possible to construct a catapult big enough to get Ayers Rock over the walls, it would probably have landed in the middle of the Atlantic or whacked the Norman church. Even I would have had a job explaining to the parish how I had knocked down St Botolph's.

The solution was to ask a local sculptor, Guy Portelli, to *make* an Ayers Rock *in situ*. This he duly did, saving the day in just forty-eight hours. Once Guy had taken some measurements, he and his helper, 'Mr K', knocked up a brilliant miniature around a wooden frame in the shape of a big, rounded hump. They covered it in chicken wire and hessian, then smothered it with plaster and cement and a bit of straw to give it bulk.

Somehow it was obvious that Guy had once been a set designer on TV science-fiction dramas. A couple of visitors thought as much when they saw the rock's straw and dark cement finish before it was painted.

'It looks like a giant dinosaur turd,' one observed.

I suppose it did. But not for long. After a final smoothing to contour the rock as accurately as possible, we took extra care with our colour mix. Being 4 feet high, 4 feet wide and a good 8 feet long, it really stood out from the surrounding land mass like the real Ayers Rock. Better still, we achieved a cracking finish to ensure that this spiritual symbol of Australasia appeared to have a classically rich, red-coloured permanent sunset on it, even on days when Lullingstone was sunless, and all for £60.70. Although slightly gimmicky — Adam was not a fan — I felt that kids might like this Ayers Rock and I wanted to do anything I could to stimulate children's interest in gardens and gardening generally.

The whole Asian region was by now rich with

the acid soil I had bought in for plants like my rhododendrons. But alpines such as the moisture-loving gentians, like *Gentiana sino-ornata*, and the orchid *Primula vialii*, not to mention trees and herbaceous perennials such as gingers, also love acid soil and seemed to be settling in well.

As the day of the official opening approached — I had settled on another significant '16': Saturday 16 July — the long hours and non-stop seven-day weeks of digging, building, planting and weeding, interrupted only by intense conversations with inquisitive visitors on opening days, had left me knackered. The Green Man was at the limit of his physical capacities; and it was a real godsend that I was now visited by two horticultural angels who volunteered their services.

It was thanks to Aunt D, wife of Uncle David, that I met the legendary Jim Buttress, a Royal Horticultural Society judge and chairman of Britain in Bloom, no less. Jim is extremely knowledgeable (he worked for the Royal Parks and before he retired was superintendent of Greenwich Park) and he had recently been in Bahrain for the RHS to judge a flower show that Aunt D's mother had founded. I think the two of them were standing in a massive, flower-filled marquee in the desert when Aunt D told Jim about her nutty nephew's project, and Jim was keen to have a butcher's. He came to the castle in May and I'll never forget our first encounter.

'Well, Tom, I can tell you one thing,' he said, smiling mischievously. 'You've got a lot of weeds.

I think you need some help.'

Like a gift from the pool of fortune, Jim volunteered his services there and then. Looking back, I simply don't know how I could have coped without him . . . or without another angel who also now volunteered to help get me out of the mess I was in: Sylvia Halls.

Sylvia was also incredibly knowledgeable, and I first met her when a group came over from Crockenhill WI, just up the road near Swanley. Like Jim, Sylvia is a far more experienced gardener than I am and working with them both has been a joy and an eye-opener. It's true, we have had the odd clash — but only over some of my more maverick ways with the rarer plants which I have seen in the wild but which Jim and Sylvia may have not. At times they have been particularly alarmed by my gung-ho approach to pruning.

Take my Queensland Flame Tree, or *Brachychiton acerifolius*, for example. I had grown it from scratch in 1995, Mum having brought some seeds back from the Bulawayo municipal baths in Zimbabwe. I had already slashed back the roots of this tender, frost-sensitive soul and as a result had had to remove every one of its leaves and reduce some of the new growth points too to reduce the transpiration and keep it alive. Jim was appalled.

'It looks like a bloody hatstand!' he said when he saw how enthusiastically I had slashed it. 'You can't prune like that! You must be crackers!'

'You wait and see, Jimmus! You wait and see.'

Jimmus wasn't convinced.

'I'll give you a fiver if it survives,' he said.

'Deal!'

There are no formal pruning tips for the Flame Tree, and my approach was based on what I had observed with my own eyes. In Launceston, north-east Tasmania, I had once seen one at close quarters growing as a cultivated street tree. It had been roughly treated, to say the least: its roots had been tarmacked over and also appeared to have been slashed at with some kind of cutting machine, while local vandals had carved their initials and other dedications in its bark and trunk. Despite the extensive damage, I could see that this toughie was still thriving. So I was pretty sure that in cultivation in the greenhouse at Lullingstone I could move it back and forth safely and even drastically reduce its roots and leaves without danger. Allowing for the earthworm I once ate for a dare in the Camellia bed at Stanbridge Earls, I reckoned Jim's fiver might be the second easiest bet I'd ever won. Time would tell.

Where Jim and Sylvia were always absolutely spot on, I have to admit, was over their treatment of gardening tools. Being 'proper' gardeners, they always cared for theirs meticulously. Jim even cleans his *spade* after use and puts it away in the shed, which to me seems pretty weird. But even weirder is that he also cleans out his wheelbarrow. I empty my barrow, for sure; but I've never cleaned one in my life unless it's had lots of alkaline soil in and I'm about to use it for acid soil.

My approach to tidying up is also very

different. I often don't put my gardening tools away after I've used them and tend just to put them down in the place I was last working. To my mind this saves time when I resume work the next day, picking them up and just carrying on where I left off. True, occasionally they get a bit of rust on them, but they seem to last just as long as the cared-for variety. Jim thought this was potty.

Working alongside Jim and Sylvia, I might ask, 'Where have my tools gone?' only to find them not on the ground where I had left them, but carefully tidied away in the shed because Jim had been clearing up and doing things properly. He also stacks his empty plant pots by size and arranges them in neat rows. I leave mine in a heap. I know he is right and I am wrong, but that's the way I am.

Thanks to Jimmus and Sylvia, and a chap called Mr Adrian, the weeds were gradually brought under control. (Mr Adrian, who had appeared in May, is a seriously hardy-perennial helper who lives in a caravan and comes to earn a few bob from Dad each week.) The thought of showing off the garden to all our friends and supporters at the official opening now seemed a lot less daunting than it had a month or so earlier. With just forty-eight hours to go before the ribbon cutting, I was excited, therefore, but quietly confident. I wasn't even too upset by the news that Trevor and his lawyers were apparently still arguing with Dad over access . . . and now wanted £7,500 for his bit of the garden.

# 28

## Sneak Preview

Summer 2005 was doing what summer should, slowly coaxing the World Garden to lushness; and as a 'visitor attraction' it was growing more credible by the week. It was nowhere near fully planted yet and I had made no start on my Man's Influence Borders; but there was more than enough of interest in the ground to justify a full-on tour.

At this stage any sneak preview of the top exhibits would probably have started in North America, where I would direct visitors straight to *Fremontodendron californicum*, often called California Glory, a small shrub that to my mind has everything. You couldn't call Californian Glory a rarity and nor is it gardening on the edge — I got mine from Homebase in Sevenoaks, for heaven's sake! — but it is still a great looker and performer, most interesting for its wonderful, glistening, golden rich, yellow-coloured waxy flowers and its added-value leaves. Sure, the leaves are nice to look at; but if you flick them in summer they also release a weird cloud of dust. As I said, an amazing performer — though less amazing if you suffer from asthma and breathe in the dust.

*Fremontodendron* Californian Glory isn't massively hardy, and I still had the added thrill of wondering if mine would survive the winter. Generally the plants are susceptible to wind-rock, so they need to be pruned and they like their stability. My advice to anyone trying to grow one in Great Britain would be to train it against a sheltered wall so that it's stable and has the sun, though in southern England it should be fine away from walls, stability allowing.

Leading the visitor down to Mexico, I would definitely stop at Crac's Delight, the penstemon I discovered in Copper Canyon. Naturally this is one of my favourite plants in the garden — but for personal as much as horticultural reasons. My discovery had been checked out by the RHS at Wisley and registered with a plant professor at Nebraska University in the US (where all penstemons are registered); and they confirmed it was a naturally occurring hybrid that was sufficiently different from any other recorded penstemon in cultivation that I could choose a name for it. Hence my naming it after Granny. I had been trying to keep this news under wraps for months, along with another Crac's Delight plant that I intended to present to Gran in a pot at the garden's official opening. But would that one come into flower in time? I was doing my best.

Also in Mexico I would want to shout a little about my Tree Dahlia — or *Dahlia imperialis*, the tallest dahlia in the world — while pointing out that, thanks to my chum in Oxfordshire, Gum Bark Geoff, we were now also officially standing in Opuntia Heaven.

Tearing ourselves away down to South

America (no dawdling in the Darién Gap, please!), we would then pause at the statuesque Monkey Puzzle, a genuine classic from Chile. Indigenous people eat the nuts, but when this giant was reintroduced and cleverly marketed in Britain by William Lobb, it became famous instead for its staggering ornamental credentials. The Monkey Puzzle is now almost critically endangered in the wild, so I also reckoned I was doing a little bit for conservation by growing it on another continent.

Equally eye-popping in South America are the Puya pineapple relations. These terrestrial bromeliads are lovely, spiny plants which produce a rosette of leaves and are horribly well armed against intruders, gardeners included. They have sharp spines that point inwards and strong gloves are a must if you want to reach in to take out a bit of dead leaf. Even so, you will still end up well and truly spiked.

In the highland areas of South America, where there are around 170 true species, Puya are often covered with the hair and fur of wild creatures that have been too nosy. I had dozens in the greenhouse from Peru, Argentina and Chile, and was looking forward to wowing visitors with their exotic architectural leaf design and the fantastic blues of their flowers — a rich, dazzling, jewel-blue that only God himself could have painted. Hardiness-wise, however, there was a question mark over their survival. I seemed to be doing well with *Puya castellanosii* and *Puya alpestris*, which are supposed to be among the toughest; but I would just have to wait and see.

Sadly I didn't yet have the one Puya that I really, really wanted — *Puya raimondii*. Over a period of 80–150 years, these can produce the biggest inflorescence or flower spike on the planet and grow to more than 30 feet high, just the rosette at the base being about 5 feet across. Merely thinking about this Puya gave me goosebumps and I was determined to see it on the plant list at Lullingstone one day.

Skipping across the Atlantic to Africa, I had high hopes for the magnificent King Protea, or *Protea cynaroides*, the floral emblem of South Africa. This beauty has massive, cone-shaped flowers with spikes from the bracts wrapping around it like a turret. It also has amazingly long furry stamens and is, quite simply, mesmerizing. Or it is when it's mature: I was growing mine from seed, so visitors would have to exercise a little imagination for a while yet.

Elsewhere on the continent I would point out the altitude plants like *Impatiens tinctoria* from East Africa, with its wonderful busy lizzie-like flowers; and from the Atlas Mountains *Cedrus atlantica* 'Glauca', the Blue Atlas Cedar, an emblem of Algeria and Morocco and a tree with bluey foliage that looks brilliant when young. With only an acre to work with in the World Garden, I really had to be careful about scale and all my plants had to be capable of doing their show-stopping stuff before they grew too large. The Blue Atlas Cedar has a tendency to develop middle-aged spread after about twenty years; but as mine was a nipper from a garden centre down the road, this wasn't going to be a problem for a while. When it got too big, I told myself, I'd simply cut it down, dig out the root and start again with a new one.

In North Africa my real star attraction was probably the Pineapple Broom from Morocco, *Cytisus battandieri*. It has yellow flowers that smell amazingly similar to a pineapple and are held magnificently above silvery, velvety leaves. Absolutely gorgeous.

Whizzing up to Ireland, the Strawberry Tree, or *Arbutus unedo*, is a genuine stunner. They have fruits that are like big red pimples which you can eat (though too many might give you the jiggers). But the main interest is that this tree is so very unusual. You find it only in south-west Ireland or southern Europe, suggesting the existence long ago of a land link. Traces of it have been found in the fossil record, so it has certainly been in Ireland for a long, long time. The other point about this unusual evergreen, with its attractive peeling bark and glossy leaves, not to mention its lovely fruits and flowers, is that it is one member of the Ericaceae, a Rhododendron relation, which actually tolerates alkaline soil. In fact, it positively thrives on chalk — which was handy here at Lullingstone.

My Ireland wouldn't have been complete without the Shamrock I had bought on the Dublin ferry; but to be honest this trefoil, *Trifolium repens*, is really just a creeping weed and we've stacks of it on the front lawn. Horticulturally it's a terrible plant, but I wanted to include it because of all the wonderful stories associated with it since pagan times.

On the UK mainland, I was proud of my Greater Knapweed, or *Centaurea scabiosa*, an indigenous plant I grew up with on the Lullingstone Park golf course. This daisy relation from the massive Compositae family forms satisfyingly substantial clumps, with leaves on stems and flowers that explode at the ends, growing in all directions like a starburst of pinks and light purples. Nor would I want UK visitors to miss the deep purplish spotted flowers and spotted leaves of *Dactylorhiza × grandis*, the hybrid Common Spotted Orchid from the south of England. This had been my first-ever hardy orchid, acquired from Sissinghurst all those years ago under Crac's influence.

Mainland Europe naturally featured Edelweiss in the mini contoured Alps, but it was in Spain and Portugal that I was hoping to turn heads — especially with the glorious Blue Borage, *Anchusa azurea* 'Dropmore', and with *Salvia discolor*. The latter really is special with its extremely unusual black flowers and sticky, sweet-smelling stems. Admittedly they do tend to droop and when you pick up the flowers the extraordinary exudation of oils makes them very tacky to the touch. But I was sure these black beauties would knock my visitors' socks off.

Still in southern Europe, I had planted what I hoped would be another crowd-pleaser, and especially one for children: a squirting cucumber, no less, from Greece. *Ecballium elaterium* is basically a squash relation that grows along the ground and is quite hardy (not like a pumpkin, which can be done in by a single frost), and the greenish-white, oblong-shaped fruits eventually become slightly bristly. When they are about 2–3 inches long and have a tint of yellow, if you squeeze them lightly in a certain way the seeds come shooting out of the end at a hell of a pace. This is a very clever way of reproducing; for when the fruit is ripe the numerous seeds launch themselves energetically into the air, complete with gooey liquid, to get as far away from the parent plant as possible. Of course, you can always give the squirting cucumber a helping hand and I hoped that, towards the end of the season when they were ripe, kids would do precisely that. Free goggles, anyone?

Over in the Middle East, meanwhile, I was featuring oleanders, a classic plant from Lebanon, Iran and Israel, and cyclamen. Oleanders are famously recognizable worldwide for their cultivation uses and often appear as a hedging plant. But I also wanted visitors to see the really wonderful *Fritillaria imperialis*, or Imperial Fritillary Lilies, from the mountainous areas of northern Iran. These grow from a bulb and produce a huge stem about a metre or more high (or should anyway!) with a big tuft of leaves, underneath which is a circular mass of gorgeous flowers in yellows and, my personal favourite, rich orange.

Up in the Tradescants' old stamping ground of Siberia, I was also looking forward to showing off *Bergenia cordifolia*, with their wonderful pink flowers and big elephant leaves — hence the common name Elephant's Ears. Apart from their looks, what is wonderful about these is that they can tolerate baking sun or the deepest shade, not to mention dry or wet conditions. You can virtually pee on them and they will still thank you. They are often used in planting schemes and people think they come from France or western Europe. In fact, they hail from areas where temperatures drop through the floor. They are not only interesting horticultural survivors but they make brilliant ground cover too.

Down in the Antipodes, the plants in Australia and my enlarged Tasmania broadly speaking fell under three genera: Eucalypts and Callistemon, that is bottlebrushes, both from the Myrtaceae family; and Acacia from the Leguminosae family, commonly known as mimosas or wattles. I decided to treat Tasmania separately, even though strictly speaking it is Australia, because it is such a horticulturally different place and it allowed me to display stacks of mint bushes (*Prostanthera*), banksias, hakeas and other plants I had seen in the wild there.

In mainland Australia it was the smells that really appealed: citronella, for example, which is used in mosquito repellent. I hoped visitors would take one sniff of *Eucalyptus citriodora* and be knocked over by the Lemonscented Gum.

In New Zealand I would draw attention to the *Brachyglottis repanda*, otherwise known as the Bushman's Toilet Paper Plant, which was a feature in my South Island. It's not Andrex exactly, but the delightful soft white velvet leaves, with extra hairs on the underside, are very useful in an emergency (apparently). Although North

Island is full of wonderful fuchsias, including the only one that flowers pointing upwards, *Fuchsia procumbens*, back in South Island I would direct visitors to marvel at another rarity: the Dead Stick Tree, or *Chordospartium stevensonii*. This wisteria relation produces flowers from weird-looking, stick-like leaves, not in chains like a wisteria but in bunches. Pure plant magic. The only problem with this weirdo is that I knew I would have to put a sign up saying: 'Please Do Not Pull Me Up. I'm Not Dead. Honest.'

Out east in Japan, I would want visitors to see the wonderful cone-like leaves of the Japanese Cycad, and in tropical India to savour the peanut-butter-smelling leaves of *Cassia didymobotrya*. Last, but absolutely not least, any tour would linger at my expanded Canaries. For me, these islands were home to plants that look simply sodding stunning.

Overall, I couldn't pick a better example than the unbelievable black-leaved *Aeonium arboreum* 'Schwarzkopf'. It reacts to sunlight, and the stronger the sunlight, the blacker it becomes. It really is quite extraordinary. It's fleshy; but then if you touch it to break the end of the leaf, it feels almost like plastic. Elsewhere in the Canaries I would also point out the Canary Island Pine that Gum Nut Steve and I eventually collected following our abortive, hair-raising climb in the El Teide region, and the Canary Island Foxgloves (*Isoplexis canariensis*) with their stunning orange flowers, not to mention some massive Tree Thistles.

So yes, as high summer approached, after all

the sweat and uncertainty and frustration, and despite the time needed for plants to mature and the hardiness of many to be assessed, I felt confident that my one-acre version of our gloriously green globe finally deserved to be officially named the World Garden of Plants at Lullingstone.

# 29

Crac's Delight

It was barely light when I opened the curtains and looked out on the morning of Saturday 16 July 2005. Summer had been a scorcher until now, and Lullingstone was uncharacteristically burnt out and brown. With the wood pigeons still in their roosts and the dark tops of the cedars motionless against the lightening sky, it was a picture of summer-morning stillness. But inside my guts were already beginning to churn and I hadn't even had my customary can of ginger beer to make me zing. Today was the Big Day.

It was the day the Green Man would really stick his neck out, the day he would finally stand up in front of his family, his friends and the scores of people who had given him support, moral and material, and announce that the garden he had promised would be the horticulturally wackiest of visitor attractions was finally officially open. It was still several growing seasons away from being finished (or as finished as a garden ever can be) and if anyone was disappointed there was only one person to blame. No wonder I was jittery.

Today was also a big day for my parents, my grandmother and my sister, who had come back from Serbia for the opening — but especially for

Mum and Dad, who had invested so much in their not always reliable or sensible son. I had put them through some seriously hard times over the years and had occasionally been a terrible worry to them. Yet they never bawled me out; and in their patient, steady way they still believed in me and loved me. This was a gift beyond words and I didn't want to let them down.

I also hoped today might mark a turning point in the fortunes of the estate and the Hart Dykes, and help to ensure our continued presence here. If a world map of plants could put Lullingstone Castle back on the visitors' map as it had been in the time of Zoë and her silkworms, all the aggro, back-breaking toil and gnawing anxiety about money and where it was going to come from would have been worth it.

On a more personal level, it was a big day for me for two other reasons. Most obviously, it marked the coming to fruition of my crazy dream. I really hoped today would be another milestone, perhaps the final milestone, on my road to recovery as I freed myself from the dread grip of the Darién. Most important of all, however, it was the day I wanted to say an enormous public thank you to the most important person in my life, my grandmother Crac. She above all others had given me my reason for being, when all those years ago she had revealed to me the magic and mystery of being a gardener.

This jumble of thoughts and feelings jogged back and forth between my head and my guts as I pulled on a fleece and tea-cosy, gulped down a can of fizz and hurried out into the garden on a sugar high to start the last-minute titivating, weeding, planting and dead-heading.

Adorable Louisa had been a tower of strength as we prepared for this day, showing patience with my one-track horticultural mind way beyond the call of duty. Another superstar friend from the village, Vikki Rimmer, a PR wizard, had also been a godsend, helping Mum and Dad organize what we hoped would be the biggest party in Lullingstone's history — or in our tenure of it anyway.

Vikki, who's tenacious and persuasive and charming and funny all at the same time, had managed to drum up massive quantities of free food and drink from a variety of local businesses, including the Shepherd Neame brewery, not to mention a marquee from the local Scouts, plus various tents, a killer cake, exploding balloons, flags and even lollipops that we intended to string around the marquee in a nod to the last moments of freedom Paul and I had enjoyed before our captors had leapt out of the undergrowth pointing guns at us.

Even dear old Trevor was contributing in the most positive way he could. He and Dad had managed to put their differences over payment and garden access to one side for the day, Dad promising Trevor we would fix him up with an alternative bit of garden down by my eucalyptus plantation. Maestro Edwards, as I would have to call him today, had generously agreed to put on his best bib and tucker and conduct his brass band on the lawn. Would he mention the hedge or what he perceives as my family's feudal approach to some of our neighbours? I didn't think so. Well, I hoped not anyway.

Thanks to Louisa, Laurence and Steve, Mr Adrian, and Jimmus and Sylvia, the world map itself was displaying around 3,500 plant species and in places looked really quite lush. It was a bit bare in other places, agreed; but it was certainly respectable and full of promise. We had concentrated on planting the areas I had either visited personally or loved to bits: Mexico, parts of North America, Australia, North and South Island New Zealand, the Canaries and of course dear old Tazzy. I told anyone who'd listen it was a 'work in progress', but the garden still deserved a party.

Despite all that still had to be done before the evening celebration, my biggest concern as I hurried out of the gatehouse that morning was the condition of one single pot plant. It was the most important plant in the whole garden: the one I intended to present to Granny before she cut the purple ribbon at the Moon Gate.

I had been fretting about this plant one way or another for a year, and intensely so over the preceding weeks as I tried to ensure that it came into flower bang on schedule. Today was the moment of truth. Happily the Green Man's old 'Flower Boy' skills hadn't deserted him: this gorgeous Penstemon was looking just grand as I carried it into the greenhouse to examine it more closely. The whole plant was now about 18 inches — 2 feet high, with broad, tapering leaves that clasped the stem. And the flowers that had appeared two days earlier, like a blessed omen? Mmmm. Granny would be well chuffed. They were stunning.

Penstemon 'Crac's Delight', as my cultivar was officially called, had wonderful purple flowers with a rich, creamy white, slightly fuzzy throat. The flowers were a bit like those of the Snapdragon, tubular bell-like in shape and slightly drooping; but the main thing was that they were so *big*. It was the size that had particularly impressed the people at Wisley when they had seen plants I had grown previously from cuttings of this baby.

During the year I had been preparing it for Gran, I had had to take great care it didn't dry out and even more care to keep it hidden. The day the letter arrived from Nebraska University with official confirmation that it was a new cultivar, my head had almost exploded with excitement. Naturally Gran was the first person with whom I wanted to share the news, but luckily I managed to keep my gob shut.

Throughout the spring I had kept the plant under cover to give it a good start and then put its massive pot outside the greenhouse in the sun. Granny may have spotted it there, but she would have had no idea how special it was because it had only come into flower in the last forty-eight hours. I really, really hoped she liked it.

The hours leading up to the opening passed in a whirl. I was far too excited and busy to eat. In a stunning burst of neighbourly co-operation, Trevor, his dog Jo, Laurence Bat Man Dell and

I, with the help of various friends and local Scouts, had managed to put up the marquee. With the guy ropes tightened and the drinks delivered, along with the food and the glasses and the cake and the chairs and the balloons — these last, in the shape of animals particular to the continents, would float above my land masses in the warm summer air — suddenly it was late afternoon and time for me to get changed.

Wearing black trousers and an orange T-shirt neatly ironed for me by Mum, I joined a hundred or so well-dressed guests, plus Richard Reeves in his trademark combats and army boots, outside the Moon Gate. Everyone was looking at me, waiting for me to say something sensible . . .

*Wow!*

This was nothing like giving a talk or showing slides at the Women's Institute. This speech was going to be so seriously from the heart that I wondered if I would get through it without cracking up. I suddenly felt very nervous as I stood in front of the wrought-iron gate that Red Indian Reg had carefully tied up with an enormous purple ribbon, the colour chosen to match the blooms of Gran's Penstemon.

Given the interest the World Garden had provoked locally, we could have invited a 'celebrity' to cut the ribbon. But there was no contest. At Lullingstone the only star was Gran, and seeing her smiling at me as I began to stammer out my speech, thanking everyone I could remember, gave a sharp tweak to my tear ducts.

Dear old Granny, so shy and so quiet. She was genuinely touched and delighted when Reg and I took the penstemon out of its hiding place behind the wall and she saw its enormous purple flowers and heard that it was her nutty grandson who had discovered it, cultivated it and named it after her.

Tears certainly welled in my eyes when, in front of what felt like the whole wide world, I told her how grateful I was for all she had taught me and given me over the years. There was an aching great lump in my throat when I finally invited her to cut the ribbon at the gate through which I had run to her so many times when I was little. Then, at 6.45pm precisely, when Gran finally declared the garden officially open, there was only one thing to do: give her an enormous hug and peck on the cheek and announce that the party could begin. An enormous cheer went up, balloons exploded and Trevor's band struck up 'Congratulations'.

As the party began to hum and the band played on, to hear 'In An English Country Garden' ring out across an actual English country garden — albeit an exotic, global one that only a few months earlier had been a picturesque jungle — was for me pure, unimaginable joy. The jitters and churning in my stomach stopped and a feeling of calm descended. Deep, satisfying calm and contentment. Through salty eyes the world suddenly looked pretty wonderful. As I gazed at the amazing seven-tier World Cake with a marzipan model of me on top, sitting astride a small globe,

I even allowed myself a small pat on the back as I ate part of my own leg and Paul Winder tucked into my marzipan head.

Looking around us, it was strange but profoundly gratifying to realize that something so positive could come out of an episode that had been so painful. For without our experiences in Colombia, in particular the events of 16 June 2000 when we were told we had only hours to live and I sought sanctuary in the pages of my diary and an imaginary garden, this real garden would never have happened.

Seeing so many people laughing and smiling and chatting animatedly as they now wandered between the semiverdant continents I had worked day and night to build, mostly with my bare hands and those of my devoted friends, was certainly the highlight of my career as a gardener. But seeing Granny cut the ribbon to the garden where we had spent so many wonderful, brilliant hours together, all inspired by that first tiny packet of carrot seeds? Well, that was the highlight of my life full stop.

# 30

## Notes From the Gatehouse

It's November 2006 and autumn is finally beginning to take hold outside after the toastiest September and October ever. I am sitting in the gatehouse at Lullingstone with a definite case of the jitters. Why so jittery? Because in front of me on my desk is an airline ticket with my name on it. In a few days' time it will take me back to South America. Just looking at it and thinking about what might happen over the month I shall be there fills me with excitement and trepidation in equal measure.

I'm flying to Caracas in Venezuela. The last time I was there I was with Paul Winder, on my way home from Bogotá, barely able to believe that I was about to be reunited with my family and that I was a free man once more.

My confidence took a huge knock in Colombia, so returning to South America even now, six years on, still feels like a big test. It will be a chance to get my gremlins out into the open and see if I can face them down once and for all. I'm confident ... but cautious. The really graphic, chilling nightmares — the ones about the decapitation and murder of my family in the castle grounds — seem to have abated, thank goodness. But not a day goes by when I don't think about the Darién in some way. They may only be fleeting thoughts — about one of the crafty guerrillas or about eating iguana and the taste of armadillo, or about a particularly stunning orchid — but anything can trigger them.

Nowhere in South America is totally safe for the backpacking traveller, I realize. But where I intend to go — high in the foothills of the Andes in the shadow of Pico Bolivar, Venezuela's highest peak and a long bus ride and climb from Caracas — I will still be a lot safer than in the Darién Gap. However, I shall be on my own this time. There will be no Paul to lift my spirits when things go wrong; and I shall be plant-hunting in remote areas. Camped not a million miles from the Colombian border, I wonder what dreams I shall have at night when I'm alone in my tent.

Am I crackers? I don't think so. What I do think is that after the crazy hard work of the last couple of years, I desperately need to get away. Despite my nervousness, I can't wait to get on that plane. My mission? To find the UK's first hardy plant from Venezuela and grow it successfully in the World Garden of Plants here at Lullingstone.

I will be leaving a very different Lullingstone from the one I returned to from captivity. For a start, I believe the estate and the Hart Dykes now have a rather more secure future together. Without wanting to sound too proud or boastful, I'm chuffed to bits to report that the World Garden's first summer was a rip-roaring success. All the efforts made by Tony Russell, inspirational Vikki Rimmer and Yours Truly to spread the word about the garden paid off. The number of visitors nearly hit the 10,000 mark in 2005, which was a massive improvement on the 3,211 who had come the year before. Mum and Dad hadn't seen that many people at Lullingstone for donkey's years; and I hope Grandma Zoë, no doubt running a silk farm in the sky somewhere, smiled at our achievement.

Of course our 10,000 visitors fell some way short of the 680,000 or so they get at big places like Chatsworth. But it was a good start for us and reassuring — not least for Nick, the nice man from the bank in Bromley, because it meant Dad could start paying back our loan.

The Man Upstairs, however, made sure that the autumn that followed our successful opening was one of mixed blessings, reminding us that we couldn't sit on our laurels or our backsides.

September 2005, for example, saw a truly torrential downpour of rain and hail which caused major flooding across the district. The World Garden's oceans were washed away, and I suffered severe coastal erosion in West Africa, southern Brazil and the south of the Canary Islands. I spent days shovelling what felt like tonnes of displaced Cornish grit back into the Atlantic and then knackered myself trying to roll it all smooth again.

Perhaps to make amends, God then gave us a barmily balmy October. The heat confused the birds, who kept on singing, and confused me too: I was still wearing shorts in the garden come Guy Fawkes Night, despite having the luscious yellows, oranges and browns of autumn all around me.

November also saw me having to pinch Dad's dinner jacket once more (accessorized this time with a nifty golden-brown corduroy tea-cosy lent by Steve Godber) to attend a function at the Savoy Hotel in London. Knock me down with a fistful of field bindweed, but the World Garden of Plants won a UK Tourism Award from the British Guild of Travel Writers, no less!

When things are going swimmingly, of course, you know it won't be long before life comes and kicks you hard in the whatsits again. Right on cue, on the night of the award ceremony, 13 November, Jack Frost came a-calling . . . and this time he was angry. After the late heat, the 13th turned out to be the first night of a viciously sudden two-week frost attack, the worst hot-then-freezing cold snap in our bit of Kent for thirty-three years. After gaily basking in heat of 19°C, the plants had no time to adjust and didn't know what had hit them. In the World Garden frost pocket, temperatures dived to −13°C at ground level and −8°C at chest height; and much of Australasia and parts of New Zealand, the Canaries and South America were walloped.

Luckily I had already put all the really tender plants safely under glass; but many of the supposedly 'hardier' ones that I hoped would survive outdoors got nailed. When the extent of the damage eventually became clear, the carnage was far worse than I had expected. I wasn't back to Square One exactly, but I was certainly back to Square Three from about Square Twelve. It meant I would have to resume my search for newer strains or higher-altitude, hardier forms to cope with future winters. As the World Garden is an exercise in on-the-edge horticulture, I couldn't complain that some elements of my experiment had gone tits-up. But it was still a knock.

Over the winter of 2005, the garden then changed shape radically. Every Saturday from November to March, Mr Adrian (who is hardy to about −30°C!) and I started work at 7am and toiled through till dusk trying to make mountains by recycling car tyres. These ran from the south-eastern tip of Scandinavia to parts of Turkey, Iran, Mongolia, Russia and Afghanistan, and they ate up a staggering 2,000 old tyres, including some phenomenally heavy ones from tractors and combine harvesters. Adrian and I filled in the hollows with rubble, not to mention Gran's old radiators and whatever else we could find, covered them in a membrane called Teram, which is used to line roads, then dumped thousands of barrow loads of topsoil on them, from 6 inches in depth to a couple of feet. I was inspired to do this by what Bob Flowerdew once achieved on *Gardener's World* while growing strawberries and potatoes. Now you would never know the tyres are there and the drainage is superb.

The legendary Jimmus and Sylvia have really come into their own, working like beavers to transform the nursery area and, by sheer dint of their personalities, adding to my general joy at being able to work outside in the garden with them. Despite the fact that Jim is a hardcore Crystal Palace fan (fitting for a greenhouse man, I know, but he looks so glum when they lose) and that I know next to nothing about footie, working with him and Sylvia was, and is, a pure delight.

All our respective (and very different) gardening skills were put under the spotlight when we agreed to have our every move recorded for posterity by a camera crew from KEO Films. After a six-part television series called *Save Lullingstone Castle* was then broadcast on BBC2 in the spring of 2006, my email inbox went bananas and the telephone virtually melted. Like the flooded oceans, I was swamped by hundreds and hundreds of questions, comments, suggestions and offers of plant donations, all of them blissfully welcome but totally knackering to reply to single-handedly while I was also trying to get the garden ready for the new season.

The public's interest in what I have been trying to achieve is genuinely touching, and this interest translated into yet more visitors traipsing over the footbridge or tripping through the gatehouse arch under my sitting room throughout the World Garden's second summer. By the time October was drawing to a close, Dad — who by now was *gagging* for a holiday — reckoned we had had nearly 20,000 visitors.

For all of us, and for Lullingstone itself, this was unbelievably positive. It bodes so well for the future too, when I hope one day to extend my themed planting by continent across other parts of the estate. First, though, there are much more pressing priorities.

I really must find the time to do something about the signage and labelling in the garden, which even I find embarrassingly naff! And what else is on my list of Things To Do? Well, I also have to crash on with the planting; keep developing the nursery; build a working waterfall in Asia; construct a metal Baobab tree in Africa; generate some more mountain ranges in central Africa and North America; dig out and create a cracking, insectivorous bog garden down in the south-eastern United States; and — most important of all for the visitors — find somewhere to give them a cup of tea and a biscuit.

The World Garden of Plants, which we now see as central to the estate's survival, has created many new responsibilities for all of us. The phone rarely stops ringing now with parties wanting to book group visits months ahead, or, in the case of my talks, sometimes as much as two years in advance. Indeed, the whole experience of creating the garden and seeing it succeed against so many odds has brought Mum, Dad, Granny and me much closer together as a team. It's also helped me learn more about the sort of niggling responsibilities I will face one day when it is eventually my turn to take over. I'm still daunted by the prospect, but slowly, I hope, I'm becoming more qualified not to make a complete pig's ear of it.

Despite the joy of seeing the World Garden

succeed, the chance to close the shutters in the house and put the garden to sleep for the winter in order for us all to have a break didn't come a moment too soon for us in 2006.

How will the garden cope while I'm away? Well, Jim and Sylvia will be on hand, so it'll do just fine. Outside, thanks to Gum Bark Geoff, who gave me an entire polytunnel frame, and thanks to the very generous donation of 1 acre of tough plastic from the local David Lloyd Leisure Club, I have now dramatically increased my greenhouse capacity and reduced the chances of too much winter carnage. With the tender parts of Mexico enclosed under their very own polythene awning over a 53-foot-long, 12-foot-high and 43-foot-wide scaffold cage, all I can say is: Jack Frost . . . *bring it on!*

This last stroke of genius — putting up scaffolding poles and then draping a temporary shelter over them to protect dear old Mexico — was a major joint initiative. The scaffolding was Sylvia's idea, the plastic mine (with the help of Peter Ripley at the sports centre) and the scaffolding itself was kindly organized by the brilliant Mr Dave Chitty. The idea all stemmed initially from a problem I had dealing with an excessively generous plant donation from Gum Bark Geoff: that of a truly massive, humdinging *Opuntia gregoriana*. This baby was so very, very big that I could only lay it out on the floor of the greenhouse and gaze at in awe. It had dozens of pads on it — you simply can't buy them like that anywhere — and though I desperately wanted to put it on show in Mexico, it was so huge I wasn't sure that moving it indoors again for the winter would be a good idea.

'No problem,' said Geoff, thinking laterally. 'Leave it where it is. Just shift the greenhouse.' And that in essence is what the team has done. It explains why, as well as a spanking-new polytunnel alongside the old Venlo, I also now have what is a giant plastic tent suspended over Mexico in my mini North American section.

In the soil itself there have been several small but very significant triumphs in 2006. With lots of help I managed to sink around 6,000 species in the map and also find room to bring on another 2,000 in the greenhouse. However, easily the biggest coup, and one that sparked interest as far away as Australia, was the magical moment in May when my stunning Silver Princess flowered. This was the first time a *Eucalyptus caesia*, as she is known, has *ever* been recorded as flowering in Britain. Not at Kew. Not at Wisley. But here at Lullingstone! Boy, was this a result for the Green Man. It even prompted an article in *The Plantsman*, which, take it from me, is a *seriously* hardcore publication.

The Princess's six buds produced some hugely wonderful big reddy-pink fuzzy flowers; and Jeff Irons, the president of the Australian Plant Society, nearly dropped the phone when I rang him to tell him the news. What was the success down to? Well, perhaps my intuitive gardening techniques aren't quite so 'gonzo' after all. I grew this baby from seed that I had collected from a mate's front garden in Melbourne, and it proceeded to take over my greenhouse while stubbornly refusing to flower. It was taking up so much space, I decided that if it didn't flower it would simply have to go; and I decided to give it one last chance by slashing its taproot with a spade!

'Yikes!' it must have thought. 'I'm going to die! Perhaps I had better try to reproduce before I end up on the celestial compost heap.'

Hey presto, the Silver Princess then started to recover and produce my long-awaited flower buds. She now has at least thirty of them. With her lovely weeping habit and white powdery stems, she's an absolute stunner and I simply can't wait to see what she does next year.

This year has been memorable in the garden for other reasons too. On one particularly baking hot day I was persuaded to take off all my clothes and, with a lovely lady called June by my side (fittingly it was in the month of June), pose naked on Ayers Rock. We were both starkers bar some strategically placed Fatsia leaves and a breadfruit loincloth I made while orchid-hunting with the rat boys in Indonesia. Like us, the leaves soon began to wilt alarmingly in the hot sun, but it was all in a brilliant cause: a calendar to raise money for the Demelza Hospice Care for Children charity, organized by the Downe Dames.

Also in early summer Red Indian Reg in full regalia, armed with Californian White Sage, blessed our three newly acquired decorative totem poles, which Sylvia had erected in Canada, though it turned out they had been made in Bali, not Canada. They came from an antique shop in Tunbridge Wells and I certainly turned some heads on the M25 with them strapped to the roof of the Astra. Boy, has that car seen some action!

I really threw the versatile old Astra a challenge at the end of September, when Mr Adrian and I had a rendezvous with a particularly troublesome 21-foot-high *Trachycarpus fortunei*, otherwise known as the Chusan Fan Palm. This fantastic specimen had been donated by an ace chap called Derek; but its rootball was deeply embedded in his back garden in Yapton, near Bognor Regis, and the palm needed to be carefully dug up and transported back to Lullingstone. As I didn't want to fork out for a removal van, the Astra's roof would have to suffice.

Mr Adrian and I left Eynsford early, armed with spades, forks, an axe and pick-axe; and by 9am were already hard at work. After about an hour of digging, however, I noticed that the normally hardy Mr Adrian, a tough old boot originally from Moldova, was beginning to grimace. Soon I was gagging too as a truly foul stench began to emanate from under Derek's back garden.

Readers of a sensitive nature should look away now. For it turned out that Mr Adrian and I had uncovered two thick black plastic bags, the contents of which would turn the stomach of even the hardiest plant nut.

One of the bags had what looked like a slightly furry root dangling out of one end. Undaunted, but barely able to breathe, I decided to pull on the 'root' and have a closer look. By doing so, I disturbed the other contents of the bag and released an odour that was so rank and so overwhelming it sent Adrian rushing to the flowerbed to throw up.

Through my own watering eyes, I could see that this furry root was in fact the tail of a cat. When a small skull then popped out of the other bag, it became all too revoltingly clear that we had exhumed two dead moggies that had been buried more than a decade previously. A solemn reburial was held once we had safely lifted the *Trachycarpus*.

With the palm lying across the ground, the next challenge was to strip away its gorgeous fan leaves with a pruning saw, leaving just the leaves at the apex. These we protected by wrapping them in an old pink duvet cover, before standing back and wondering how on earth we were going to get this 21-foot pink-headed beast, which was far too heavy to carry, down the side alley of Derek's house and on to the roof of the Astra.

Mr Adrian had an ingenious solution. We attached a length of climbing rope to the palm's rootball, ran it from the back garden round the house and along the alley, and tied the other end to the back of the car. With Derek's neighbours now watching intently, we were able to drive the car forward and slowly drag the *Trachycarpus* inch by inch to the front of the house.

Using a similar manoeuvre, with the help of Derek's family we were then able to get the monster palm into the upright position — its pink duvet cover headscarf was almost as high as the house — and lower the beast gingerly on to the roof rack of the Astra, which we had augmented with a roof rack Sylvia had lent us. The car groaned in protest under the weight and the bars of the roof rack bent beyond recognition, but we at least had our Chinese monster in position. With the rootball overhanging the boot and the pink-duvet-covered leaves touching tarmac over the bonnet, we then wrapped the rootball in a blanket and Adrian created a rope labyrinth of knots and loops to ensure the palm never moved again.

'Adrian! Why's the palm on the left side of the roof and not in the middle?' I asked, baffled by the lack of symmetry.

'Want to put aerial back so we can listen Kiss FM!' he said in his intense Moldovan accent.

Adrian and I certainly turned plenty of heads as we drove at a breezy 60mph along the A264 past Horsham, and then on the M23 and M25 as we headed back to Lullingstone. It was dark when we finally nudged the Astra into the World Garden and parked between the rocky coastlines of Japan and China. Then, with head torches attached, at 9pm we set about digging a massive pit into which we struggled to slide our enormous prize. I subsequently learnt that the palm was worth at least £4,000 and I had Derek to thank for one of the garden's most significant (and certainly its largest) donations. But the Astra and Sylvia's roof rack would never be the same again.

The plants in the garden themselves also saw

some action as summer 2006 drew to a close. September and October were so very, very warm that growth was simply spectacular: we saw more in those two months than in all of the year put together. To see the lush southern hemisphere ablaze with colour and almost fully planted was a huge boost for all of us after the floods and frosts.

On the downside, Lullingstone's rabbits have been an absolute pain in the proverbial, digging under the doors and gates and even chewing their way through our chicken-wire defences to feast on a gourmet's array of world cuisine. Specials of the Day have included Dead Stick plants from South Island New Zealand (which look even deader than usual thanks to the rabbits' precision pruning), exotic, sea-blue green grasses from northern France and deliciously succulent Prickly Pears from the eastern seaboard of the USA, like *Opuntia humifusca*, in which the rabbits have left cheesy moon-shaped bites, before digging up the roots and scoffing those too. The Prickly Pears in Mexico have survived because of their prickles, but the *Opuntia humifusca* is the only Prickly Pear in the garden with no spines and the rabbits soon spotted this. They're not stupid, rabbits.

Sylvia energetically put down concrete where we thought they were getting in, and Red Indian Reg has despatched a brace of bunnies. But I am still convinced we have at least one rabbit if not two trapped somewhere within our 2 walled acres.

Hard to believe, but the rabbits could even

turn out to be more bothersome than dear old Trevor Edwards, our neighbour, who has not been an entirely happy bunny in the ongoing negotiations with Dad over the garden, while trying at the same time to sell the lease on his magnificent south wing and emigrate. Though no injunction ever materialized from his lawyers denying me access to the walled garden, and although I dutifully fixed up a new garden for him behind the house (I needed this extra responsibility like I needed the rabbits), somewhere in the negotiations over garden swaps and leases, explosive Trevor suddenly went off pop one day when I wasn't around.

It was a Thursday night in June, and on a rare moment away from Lullingstone I was going over to Bromley to see Louisa for the evening. As I left, I noticed that Trevor was pushing a wheelbarrow across the drive in the direction of the garden. I had an inkling of what he was up to, but it wasn't until I went into the garden at 7.30 the next morning that I was met by one of the most bizarre sights I will probably ever see at Lullingstone.

The new hornbeam hedge which I had dutifully planted 10 feet or so to the west of the old one which my mates from Sparsholt and I had felled, had been partly ripped up and its dozens of plants strewn across the Atlantic. The benches in the garden had also been uprooted; and, most bizarrely of all, the garden was now festooned with black-and-yellow accident tape delineating Trevor's original garden boundary. The whole place looked like a crime scene.

Negotiations had obviously turned slightly sour — to be honest, I had lost track ages ago of the process — and he had clearly wanted to make a point, though what the point was I was never entirely clear. There was nothing I could do except try to save as many of the uprooted hornbeams as possible by dunking their roots in water. Unfortunately, most of them croaked. Then, even more bizarrely, Trevor trundled back into the garden at midday and removed all the black-and-yellow accident tape before the visitors arrived.

He was also pretty strident about my splendid new polytunnel, which had taken three days to erect but was, technically speaking, still in his half of the garden.

'It's got to come down!' he barked. 'It's got to come down!'

'But I've only just put it up!' I complained.

Suffice to say, the polytunnel is still there, and dear old Trevor is now rumoured to be moving to Italy. I wish him well and will miss him; as I'm sure Dad will too.

Despite everything, I still have an affection for Trevor and will never forget the genuinely warm way he embraced me when I walked so shakily down the stairs into the Great Hall for that first Christmas following my return from Colombia. I must make sure I say goodbye to him properly before I leave for Venezuela.

'It's all right,' I reassured Mum when I told her I was going to South America again. 'I've bought a return ticket this time . . . and I'll definitely be back for Crimbo.'

We do hope that you have enjoyed reading this large print book.

Did you know that all of our titles are available for purchase?

We publish a wide range of high quality large print books including:
**Romances, Mysteries, Classics**
**General Fiction**
**Non Fiction and Westerns**

Special interest titles available in large print are:
**The Little Oxford Dictionary**
**Music Book**
**Song Book**
**Hymn Book**
**Service Book**

Also available from us courtesy of Oxford University Press:
**Young Readers' Dictionary**
**(large print edition)**
**Young Readers' Thesaurus**
**(large print edition)**

For further information or a free brochure, please contact us at:
**Ulverscroft Large Print Books Ltd.,**
**The Green, Bradgate Road, Anstey,**
**Leicester, LE7 7FU, England.**
**Tel:** (00 44) 0116 236 4325
**Fax:** (00 44) 0116 234 0205

*Other titles published by*
*The House of Ulverscroft:*

## THE CLOUD GARDEN

### Tom Hart Dyke & Paul Winder

A place of legend, the Darien Gap is an almost impregnable strip of swamp, jungle and cloud forest between North and South America. Stories of abduction and murder there are rife. In 2000, young botanist Tom Hart Dyke set off to Central America to search for rare orchids. Pure chance brought him together with another young explorer, Paul Winder, in northern Mexico. Ignoring a warning from the *Lonely Planet* guide — 'Don't even think about it!' — Tom and Paul set off into the Darien. For six days they made good progress. Then, near Colombia, they were ambushed by FARC guerrillas, who were to hold them hostage for the next nine months. Their survival was a matter of extraordinary endurance, incredible ingenuity and not a little good luck . . .

# A FRIEND LIKE HENRY

## Nuala Gardner

When Jamie and Nuala Gardner chose a puppy for their son Dale, they weren't an ordinary family choosing an ordinary pet. Dale's autism meant that deviations from his routine could provoke a terrifying tantrum. Family life was almost destroyed by his condition: most of his parents' lives involved attempting to break into their son's autistic world and give him the help he so desperately needed. But after years of effort and slow progress, the Gardners' lives were transformed when Henry, a golden retriever puppy, became a member of the family. The bond between Dale and his dog helped Dale's parents produce the near miraculous breakthrough in their son they had long sought and set him on the road to leading a full and happy life.

# FOSTER KID

## Paul Barber

Paul Barber, the actor best known for his roles as Denzil in *Only Fools And Horses* and Horse in *The Full Monty*, grew up in 1950s Liverpool. After the death of his mother, Paul and his brothers and sister spent the rest of their childhood in a succession of children's and foster homes. Paul left care at the age of sixteen, and three years later landed his first acting role, by accident, in the musical *Hair* which put him on the path to London and a successful career in show business. *Foster Kid* is a frank, sometimes funny, account of a young boy's life spent in care, his troubled youth and how one lucky break got him to where he is today.